I0754977

A Veteran Specie Clerk.

THE BANKS OF NEW-YORK,

THEIR DEALERS,

THE CLEARING HOUSE,

AND

THE PANIC OF 1857.

WITH A FINANCIAL CHART.

BY J. S. GIBBONS.

THIRTY ILLUSTRATIONS, BY HERRICK.

NEW YORK:
PUBLISHED BY D. APPLETON & CO.
1864.

TO

GEORGE H. ELLERY,

OF NEW YORK,

THE AUTHOR DEDICATES THIS VOLUME, AS A MARK OF ESTEEM FOR HIS PERSONAL CHARACTER, HIS UPRIGHTNESS AS A MERCHANT, AND HIS CONSTANCY AS A FRIEND.

PREFACE.

It is not possible to introduce into a single volume all that is curious or interesting about banks; and scarcely less difficult to avoid some things that may appear trifling or impertinent.

The author has endeavored to give a picture of the banks of New York as they are; to describe the duties of the officers and clerks, and their daily experience in transacting business with the dealers; also to describe the conduct of dealers in their intercourse with banks. Some of the scenes presented may seem extravagant, and perhaps would be accepted as caricature, if not vouched for as literally true. The errors of the book are not, at least, in *that* direction. The real exaggerations of fact and manner, if rendered with the exactness of a daguerreotype, could hardly fail to excite a suspicion of designed caricature.

A considerable part of the author's purpose has been to give a general knowledge of the method of bank book-keeping. It would be impossible to do this thoroughly, without running into the dullest of details. Any person of intelligence and vivacity will supply the omissions or oversights under this head.

If the volume fails to show that there is nothing in

the business of banking to entitle it to more respect than any honest mercantile employment, and that therefore, the banker and the dealer meet on equal terms, it is deficient in a very important respect. A dealer commits no greater mistake, than to begin treating with a bank as if it were a superior power; and its officers do not need such a stimulus to their self-conceit.

The description of the Clearing House, and the sketch of the panic, have made the volume one third larger than was originally intended.

With respect to the panic, the author owes every thing to the invaluable records of the Clearing House, an institution which has brought about a new era in our city banking, and the full usefulness of which is hardly yet imagined even by a majority of those who share in its direction. In a few months, it has done more real service to the interests of trade in New York, than the Chamber of Commerce in the century of its existence; though that has done as much as it could, without the organization of an effective financial bureau, such as the Clearing House must become, as an auxiliary to its labors.

CONTENTS.

CHAPTER XIX.

ILLUSTRATIONS.

☞ A number of the Illustrations in this Volume were executed, under the instructions of Mr. HERRICK, at the New York School of Design for Women.

THE NEW YORK BANKS.

CHAPTER 1.

INTRODUCTION.

There are fifty-three banks in the City of New York, with an aggregate capital of about sixty-six millions of dollars. The number of persons immediately connected with them, as directors, officers, and clerks, is nearly two thousand. The number of those who transact business with them as stockholders, depositors, borrowers, or in some other capacity, is several hundred thousand. In addition, a still larger number reap from them a sensible convenience in less direct methods; and as to the influence which they exert over the affairs of the community generally, there is no way of forming even a proximate estimate of it. Not an individual inhabitant of New York can say that he is not, at every moment, either the better or the worse for the existence of banks; or both better and worse. There are some, probably, who never touch a bank-note, who never cross the threshhold of a bank, who use gold and silver only in their business, and who think that they are therefore free from all the influences of banks; but this is a mere fancy. They can no more escape from them, than they can from the influence of our common schools, or than they can avoid breathing the common air. If they are day-laborers, and get their wages in silver, those wages are greater or less, because of the existence of banks; and so with the price of every thing they eat or wear.

Banks represent the capital, labor, and commerce of the country. The fact that they exert such influence over the people, and that there is no escaping from it, is of itself enough to set jealousy to work, and to create parties in opposition to them. Even if they had always been sources of unmixed public benefit, there could be no guarantee for the future. But they have rarely been conducted without sufficient abuse of powers, to keep alive perpetual hostility towards them, on one ground or another. The right to issue "paper money" (to the public their most interesting function) has not always been so guarded as to prevent fraud, which has fallen chiefly on the poor and working classes, and has therefore readily been made the foundation of popular excitement; and this kind of fraud, more than any other, has escaped the just penalties of the law. Politicians have eagerly seized on these facts to win the support of "the outraged million." It has not suited them to speak of the advantages which have resulted from the organization of capital; but they have kept before the eyes of the multitude an exaggerated picture of the evils which flow from the existence of banks, even charging upon them the consequences of individual extravagance and dishonesty. It is surprising to what an extent they have succeeded in imposing these errors and falsehoods on the public mind. Not only the ignorant, but many who are well informed on general subjects, have been made to accept the teachings of the demagogue, that banks are, in their very nature, opposed to honest industry, and oppressive to the poor; that they favor a monopoly of rights and privileges by the few; that they promote the extremes of wealth and poverty in a country; and finally, that they are dangerous to popular freedom. For the last thirty years, opposition to banks has been a lever in the hands of politicians, with ignorance as its chief fulcrum, to keep parties in office. The growing intelligence of the people has gradually corrected this state of things; while better laws and methods of business have removed much of the old ground of opposition to banks.

The purpose of this volume is, to present a literal history of the New York City banks in their present organization and action; to show how they are connected with the interest and the convenience of all classes of people; to explain the manner in which they transact business; and to place them in their true position as correlative with commerce, and not above it. This will include a description of the duties of the officers and clerks, and the daily incidents of the business, with the frauds and abuses to which it is liable; and also of the Clearing House, which introduced a new era in American Banking.

Some data, bearing on the causes of the panic of 1857, have enlarged the volume beyond its original design.

A bank is simply a plan of organizing capital, by which the full benefits of it are secured. The separate means of individuals are united together, and a large sum thus constituted, which is hired out on interest to those who need it. This combination, and the manner of its use, may be compared to a dam across a valley, and the accumulation in one body of the water of the separate springs, which otherwise would be of little service; but being united, they form a propelling power for extensive machinery.

Without the organization of capital in some form, a community must remain in comparative barbarism. The few who possess wealth above their wants must either send it away for investment where it would enrich other places, or it would for the most part lie dead, while the poor would continue in ignorance and drudgery. A public school, a library, or a church, would be impossible without combination. It is therefore a social necessity to organize capital, and communities thrive in proportion as this organization is effected. They prosper, not only in material substance, but in education and morals.

Any one who has travelled among our country villages, out of the immediate influence of cities, has occasionally been struck by the neglect of natural advantages, the lack of energy, the rudeness of life and character, and the almost savage features of the common people. But on visiting the same place after an interval of a few years, he has seen a total change: a larger population, a better class of buildings, an air of thrifty growth, and a manifest increase of comfort. The old lethargy has disappeared; a new life has been infused into everything; even the countenances of the people are softened; a less brutal and more intelligent spirit beams from their eyes. A *bank* has been the starting point of this new career; the mill-dam has been built across the little streams of capital, and the social machinery is brought into play.

After it is organized, a bank gathers other capital by *saving*. It presents the first practical idea of economy and increase to thousands of people. It brings out the old stockings, and pours their contents into the common dam, which rises higher and drives more wheels.

The objection to banks, that they foster credit, is a complete solecism. Credit is at the same time the co-efficient and the supplement of capital. The business of banks is, *to prevent abuse while making the most of it.* And so well have they succeeded in this, that they have mostly retained popular favor and confidence, in spite of their own errors, and of the denunciations of their enemies.

The present system of banking in the State of New York, is the result of much experience, and of many failures in financial legislation. The plan of creating banks by special charter was abolished in 1838, by the enactment of a general law, under which any person, or a number of persons, with the required capital, may organize a bank. The law has since undergone many alterations, and it continues to be "amended" at every session of the Legislature. New restrictions are constantly suggested by newspaper editors, or by politicians who cannot in any other way so easily make themselves talked about as by threatening to disturb the organized capital of the State. The owners of one hundred and eight millions of bank stock have cause for alarm, when Mr. Smashemup brings in a bill for their "better protection." He is waited upon by committees from New York, receives letters from distinguished bankers, and for a time is the focus of an immense circle. No name is so much in other people's mouths, as Mr. Smashemup's! It is Mr. Smashemup's bill in the Assembly, and Mr. Smashemup's bill in the Senate. Then come the amendments to Smashemup's bill in both Houses, and Mr. Smashemup is called on to explain, which he does, by a great speech on banks, economy, corruption, and the public debt. Mr. Smashemup's name is in all the newspapers, and even if his bill with all the amendments is indefinitely postponed, he returns to his constituents in "a blaze of glory," with good chances of nomination to Congress.

The general banking law of the State of New York, with its amendments, and all statutes relating to it, consist of more than three hundred octavo pages. The system is hampered with superfluous provisions, but with the voluntary guards thrown around it, and especially that of the Clearing House in the City of New York, it is probably the best now existing in any part of the world. The principal features of it are as follows:

1. The deposit in the Bank Department at Albany of ample securities for the redemption of all bills issued for circulation. The original law admitted as security, stocks of the United States, and stocks of

the several States which should be satisfactory to the Comptroller,* to the amount of one half at least of the bills called for by any person or association, the same to be equal to a stock producing five per cent per annum. The security for the other half of the bills might consist of bonds and mortgages on unincumbered, improved, and productive real estate, within the State of New York, worth by appraisement double the amount of their face, independently of any buildings thereon. This latitude of security proved unsafe. The stocks of several of the Western States especially, fell much below par, and the real estate in many cases was accepted at a fictitious valuation. The consequence was, the bills of banks which were forced into liquidation, were not redeemed in full. The amendments of the law, suggested by its longer operation, have corrected this ground of insecurity, and the bank-bills of the State of New York may now be considered "as good as gold," with the advantage of more convenience for many of the practical uses of trade. The basis of their issue is restricted to stocks of the State of New York, and of the United States, with a proportion of mortgages on real estate, not exceeding two-fifths of its appraised value. The kind of security is always expressed on the face of the bill. Those which are based on real estate, are therefore distinguishable by the public, and are treated with little favor. The Bank Superintendent has recommended to the Legislature to admit only stock-securities hereafter.

* Now called "the Bank Superintendent."

The plates, from which the bills are printed, are not allowed at any time to be in the keeping of the bank. On satisfactory securities being deposited in the Banking Department at Albany, the Superintendent issues an order to the engraver to prepare a plate under the direction of the bank requiring it, and to print therefrom as many bills as are covered by them. The bills are sent to the Department to be numbered, registered, and countersigned, and they are then forwarded to the bank. The plate is deposited with an agent of the Superintendent in the same city with the engraver, from whom the latter obtains it by order, for any future printing. The following print shows the state of the bill when it reaches the bank.

Secured by deposit of public stocks, countersigned and registered in the banking department. A. Pruyn, Regr.	A No. 350. **The Bank of the Republic** *Will pay* ONE HUNDRED DOLLARS *on demand to the bearer.* *New York, Jan.* 4, 1856. *Cashier.* *President.*

When the blanks are filled by the signatures of the President and Cashier, the bills are ready to be paid out as money.

The over-issue of bills by the Superintendent, or the surrender of securities before the circulation based on them is returned to the department, is punishable with a fine of five thousand dollars, or with five years imprisonment, or both.

2. The law requires a quarterly statement of the condition of each bank, under the oath of the officers, and the publication thereof in one of the newspapers of the same locality as the bank. The original sworn statement is placed on file in the Department; and a summary of the quarterly statements of all the banks in the State is published by the Superintendent, who also compiles from them an annual report to the Legislature.

The banks of the City of New York (which have nearly two-thirds of the banking capital of the State) are required also to publish in one of the daily newspapers, on every Tuesday, a sworn statement of their average of loans, specie, circulation, and deposits, for the week ending on the previous Saturday.

All banks under the general law are required to place on file, twice a year, in the office of the clerk of the county where they are situated, a list of their stockholders, as they stand on the first of January, and the first of July, and to send a duplicate thereof to the Department.

3. Under the old charters, the stockholder was responsible for the debts of the bank, only to the amount of his corporate interest. He might lose his stock, or such proportion of it as would suffice to pay the debts, but no more. There were instances of managers using bank funds for speculations, which enriched themselves while ruining the institution, and then retiring to live in luxury, leaving the depositors and bill-holders without redress. Under the present law, the circulation is provided for by the securities; and to pay the depositors, the stockholder

is legally bound for the par amount of his stock over again, if that should be necessary. In the worst cases of bank insolvency, this extent of loss has never been incurred; and with such a system of revision and publicity as we now have, the condition of a bank must be discovered long before it can reach that extremity of misfortune.

The banks in the City of New York are further subject to the regulations of the Clearing House, of which a full account is given in its proper place.

The plan of organizing a bank under the general law is very simple. Articles of association are drawn up, in which the title, capital stock, and other particulars are recited; the names of the first directors are generally inserted, the act of subscription covering their election. The subscriber places opposite to his name the number of shares which he is willing to take, and pays for them in convenient instalments, as may be agreed upon. When the amount of capital is fully subscribed, a certificate of organization must be filed in the office of the Secretary of State, and another in the local office of County Clerk. The final act of organization is the deposit of not less than one hundred thousand dollars of securities with the Superintendent of the Banking Department. An individual banker is allowed to begin business with a deposit of fifty thousand. It is not imperative that circulating bills should be taken out for this deposit, though there is but one case among the city banks in which it has not been done. The high premium on stocks, and the labor and expense of maintaining the circulation, are poorly compensated by its profits.

A bank is authorized to transact business immediately after depositing its securities with the Superintendent. Until its own bills are prepared for use, it pays out those of other city banks, retaining them from the deposits of the dealers. It is usual for any city bank that has a deficient circulation, to adopt that of other banks as far as may serve its convenience.

The business of the first day brings upon a new bank the necessity of coming into harmonious relations with every other city bank. It receives in deposit checks on them, and also their circulating bills; and checks on itself are received by them in like manner. The only avenue to exchange is through the Clearing House, to which it is admitted by a vote of the Association, after its affairs have been examined by a committee of that body, and reported "sound." The matters inquired into by the committee are, whether the capital has been actually paid in, and whether the general organization of the institution is such as to merit public confidence. If they find any cause of suspicion on these points, they report adversely to the admission of the candidate; and such is the influence of the Clearing House with the public, that this would be a serious, if not a fatal blow to its credit. On the other hand, a favorable report would give it at once an honorable standing.

The executive management of a bank is vested in a Board of Directors, who select one of their number to act as President. The directors are elected annually by the stockholders. The articles of association generally require a director to hold not less than a certain number of shares in his own right, on the presumption that his personal interest will induce him to look diligently after that of the institution. Nevertheless, it is common for half the members of a bank board to become irregular in their attendance at the meetings for discounting paper, either from engrossment with their own affairs, or because they have confidence in other managers; the tendency of which is to throw the general administration of the bank into the hands of a few persons. If the officers are very efficient, the few are apt to become less diligent, seeing that the routine goes on, whether they are present or not. This concentration of power takes place more or less in all our city banks. The average number of directors to each is about thirteen, of whom, in ordinary times, six or seven attend the semi-weekly meetings. In a dull season, the number is often reduced to three or four. Most of the banks have in the Board several retired elderly gentlemen, who, having nothing else to do, make a hobby of their office, and call in almost daily to look over the Discount Register, and to discuss the merits of every commercial name for the fortieth time. To tell the truth, they are capable of little else, and they often destroy sound character by mischievous gossip.

It will be seen in the statement of the duties of the officers how naturally they acquire exclusive control, when they are competent and trustworthy; and it is a frequent observation, that the business of a bank is more successful when that is the case, than when the directors are very tenacious of their executive functions. The latter give their attention for a single hour, on two days of the week, while a list of discount offerings is read over; whereas the officers devote their whole time to obtaining and sifting the information by which their judgment is swayed.

Bank directors are chosen for their wealth, commercial experience, and influence in attracting to the institution a good class of dealers. If they fail in business, they either resign, or are left off the ticket at the subsequent election. If they continue in prosperous circumstances, and act harmoniously together, the same set are annually re-elected for a long series of years. They own, in the aggregate, a considerable portion of the stock, and they hold the proxies of personal friends who take no direct part in the elections. The officers generally hold the proxies of distant stockholders—the president, especially.

The government of our city banks is remarkable for unanimity in council. It is seldom that the harmony of a Board of Directors is disturbed by dissension. Parties and cliques are uniformly fatal to the business. They drive away depositors, and injure the public standing of a bank. The stockholders sell their shares, and re-invest their money in other institutions.

Most of the technical expressions employed by bankers are sufficiently explained by their connection; but some have various applications, and some are duplicates.

The terms " dealer," " depositor," and " customer,"

are synonymous, and are used, as to frequency, in the order named. "Dealer" is the most common.

The word "line" applies to deposits, and loans or discounts, either in the bank total, or on the individual ledger. The officers say: "Our deposit line is low," or "our discount line is full," in reference to the aggregate of deposits and discounts. "Our specie line," refers to the average of specie. The dealer also says: "My discount line has run off," &c.

There are a number of slang terms and phrases in general use, which would fall harshly on polite ears, if left entirely without apology. The words "tight," "easy," "blue," "short," "tough," "nervous," and their synonyms, contain the pith and significancy of whole sentences of ordinary description, and are common among all classes of people—the most refined, as well as the most uncultivated.

The author has no other apology to offer for conversations that may appear trifling or rambling, than that they are literally true. The history of negotiation would be imperfect without them.

CHAPTER II.

THE PRESIDENT

THE PRESIDENT is the chief executive officer of the bank. He presides at the meetings of the Board of Directors, and to a great extent exerts the authority of the Board in its recess.

In some of the larger banks, there is a stated Vice-President to aid him in his duties, and to assume them, entire, during his absence; but generally a President *pro tem.* is chosen in the latter case.

In all legal relations, the President is *the bank*, though still subject to the Board of Directors. The title of any real estate that it may own is vested in him, and his official signature gives title by conveyance.

He is plaintiff or defendant in suits at law.

He is made the assignee of property as security for debts due to the bank.

He signs, with the Cashier, all certificates of stock issued to shareholders, and the notes or bills which are paid out as money.

He is generally a large stockholder, and is the only officer connected with the bank who does not give bonds for his integrity in the management of his trust. His identity of interest, with a public character for uprightness, and the circumstantial guards which are thrown around him, are held to be a better assurance for his fidelity.

The salary of the President varies, according to the time and labor which he gives to the business, from two or three to ten thousand dollars a year. In some institutions, he is a diligent and laborious officer, entering with spirit into details, and making himself acquainted with every important transaction. In others, he is satisfied to leave details to the Cashier and the subordinate clerks, holding himself rather at a distance, and cultivating his official dignity.

It is considered desirable that the President should possess an independent income, and be free from the entanglements of trade. Engagement in other business would distract his attention from the bank, and might give rise to a conflict of interest. Under the pressure of personal embarrassment, with the means of relief in his official hands, even a rigid sense of duty might be overcome. The highest tone of sentiment on this point is, therefore, adverse to his connection with the hazards of commerce. Yet several of our most prosperous city banks have always been presided over by active, enterprising merchants.

There are other reasons why a bank president should hold himself aloof from mercantile business. With large capital invested in a particular branch of trade, his views might insensibly become narrow and partial. An engrossing special interest would divert his mind from the close study of credits generally, and make his judgment less clear, as the condition of commerce becomes more critical. In a season of growing stringency in the money-market, self-interest compels bank directors, in common with others, to withdraw their attention from all affairs but their own, and thus additional responsibility is thrown on the officers — particularly on the President. The discounting of paper is then less strictly confined to the sessions of the Board. It is spread through every hour of the day, with specialities and importunities which can be dealt with, only individually and privately.

A bank president should be a man of education and general knowledge. The accidents of the office bring him into contact with every variety of disposition, and with all the different pursuits that are followed in a great city. He ought, therefore, to be sagacious in observing character, and to have a practical acquaintance with modes of business. He should also be familiar with the principles and practice of bookkeeping; otherwise, he may be blinded to any extent by the vast accumulation of figures, and the changes which they perpetually undergo in bank accounts. It is impossible for the executive officers to follow all these changes in detail from day to day. A summary of the condition of the bank is, therefore, made up by one of the clerks, showing all its assets and liabilities, and enabling them to judge of the extent to which bills may be discounted. This is called the *Bank Statement.* It is generally prepared twice a week, for use at the meetings of the Board of Directors; but in some of the larger banks, the footings of the several accounts composing it undergo such material changes as require it to be made up every day. These footings have a mutual relation which must be preserved; they are correlative also with the general aggregates of the market, as will be apparent in a description of the Clearing House settlements.

The Directors of the bank depend on the President to explain to them the particular bearings of this Statement. They are occupied during the recess of the Board, each with his private affairs, and their views of the market are influenced by the condition and accidents of trade in their respective circles; but the President observes the whole field of commerce, taking cognizance of the general causes of ebb and flow in the financial tides. He examines, not only the immediate capacity of the bank, but also its contingent resources and liabilities. He watches the course of the exchanges in the Clearing House, and the wider currents of trade beyond, endeavoring to weigh the probabilities for the future in the vast speculations which rise before him. He observes the shipment of coin to foreign countries, compares the imports and exports of successive years, and so works his figures into the great sum of the combined markets of the world. To a man unskilled in accounts, the figures of this prodigious sum are as unintelligible as characters in an unknown tongue.

THE PRESIDENT, AND THE BOARD OF DIRECTORS.

The regular meetings of the Board of Directors are held twice a week. Generally, the principal business transacted is the discounting of promissory notes, and the loaning of money on securities; but this often involves a good deal of discussion. The circumstances of merchants, their standing in the community, the character of the trade in which they are engaged, the credit of persons whose notes they offer for discount, the state of the market, the value of securities, and whatever concerns the safety of the bank dealings, are subjects of conversation and scrutiny in these semi-weekly meetings.

The President is seated at the head of a table, and the Cashier opposite, or by his side, as may be most convenient. The Directors are seated around it, as at a dining-table. In some banks, considerable formality is observed in this arrangement, members having particular chairs. A place next to the President may be accorded to the oldest or most influential. In other banks, the arrangement is determined by accident or habit.

The Cashier reads the minutes of the previous meeting of the Board, and they are approved in the usual form. He records the name of each director in attendance, that questions of disputed responsibility, as to particular measures, may not arise in the future.

The business transacted, during the recess of the Board, is submitted at each meeting. Some bank officers are very particular to have all discounts and negotiations which are made by their personal discretion, sanctioned by a vote of the Directors—a wise precaution for themselves, and a good guarantee for the stockholders. The practice is irregular with respect to this revision. It is apt to be passed over rather lightly, especially if the officers stand very high in the esteem of their associates; but it ought to be remembered, that greater aggregate loss has resulted to banks from unwise or dishonest conduct on the part of the superior officers, than from dereliction in any other quarter. Numerous instances are on record, of institutions, with large capital and thriving business, being crippled for years, or forced upon insolvency, by trusting too much in the hands of the President or Cashier. It should, therefore, be an absolute rule of the Directors to revise the business transacted between the Board meetings, with the same rigid scrutiny that they give to that which comes up at the regular sessions.

The Discount Register, which is the book of original entry for all paper discounted, is commonly placed on the table, and if not specially referred to by the President, is open to any director for inspection. Likewise, the Loan Book, if this is kept separately from the Register.

The Statement, or such portions of it as are necessary to show the extent to which paper may be discounted, is read by either officer. The aggregate of loans, deposits, and specie, are enough for this purpose. The reading of other items is generally dispensed with, as they do not materially affect the state of the funds. The book is left within reach of directors who may wish to examine it more critically.

The President announces his judgment :

"Gentlemen, the condition of the bank is favorable. Our liquidations have been prompt since the last meeting of the Board. We have no protests, and the market is quiet. The amount of notes offered to-day is about four hundred thousand dollars; and I am happy to say that we can discount the whole, if they are satisfactory."

The Offering-Book, with an alphabetical record of the notes, lies open on the table before the President. The Cashier has the package of notes in corresponding order, prepared to open each envelop, and to state particulars:

"The first offering, Mr. President, is by Adams, Jones & Co. Their notes are: one of James Wilson, having seventy days to run, of sixteen hundred dollars; and one of Thompson & Moore, forty-five days to run, of twenty-five hundred dollars."

James Wilson is a well-known merchant, of capital and integrity. Several of the Directors express their judgment in favor of discounting his note. No objection is made, and the President scores opposite to it, on the Offering Book, the letter A—which means, *accepted.*

Thompson & Moore are not known, or but slightly. The indorsers, Adams, Jones & Co., are entirely responsible, and would, doubtless, pay the note promptly, if the drawers should fail; but it is an established rule of the bank, that no paper shall be discounted without at least one good name besides that of the indorser.

"Gentlemen, who knows Thompson & Moore?" The Directors enter into a free conversation, which, if the parties are merchants of long standing, is likely to elicit enough information to cause the note to be accepted, or rejected. Or, it may be referred to the officers, with discretion to act as their judgment may dictate on further inquiry.

The Cashier reads offering number two, by Bailey & Rush. This firm are in high credit with the bank, and their paper is of the first class. "Note of Sears & Co., three months to run, eighteen hundred dollars; and one of C. Jackson, sixty days to run, for four thousand five hundred dollars."

"Gentlemen," says the President, "if no objection is made, I will mark the notes of Bailey & Rush, accepted. It is done. Let us have the next in order, Mr. Cashier."

"Joseph Chambers offers a draft of Green & Davis, of San Francisco, on Thrush & Co., of New York, and accepted—at seventy-five days, for five thousand dollars."

It is, perhaps, the first time that the paper of Thrush & Co. has been offered for discount in the bank. The President is entirely unacquainted with it. He asks for information.

Mr. Breckenridge knows something about them: "They began business, a year ago, with thirty thousand dollars capital—are said to have done a profitable trade in the produce line—had shipped heavily to California. The Co. was a young man who come out of Bacon's—the big packers on West street. Guess he hadn't much money—say, five thousand dollars; but very smart. Thrush was the capitalist. Put in twenty-five thousand dollars, hard cash—about all he had."

"What age is he?"

"Thirty-five to forty."

"Man of family?"

"Oh yes! I've known him these twelve years. Got

"Come, gentlemen, don't wander too far from the subject before the Board. The question is, whether Mr. Thrush's

half a dozen children. You must know him, Mr. Groull! He married Stubbles's daughter, wine merchant, there at your corner. Guess he run away with her, and made the old man mad. But they're all reconciled long ago, and now he's Stubbles's principal adviser in them new stores he's building in Murray street."

"Is that the man?"

"That's the man, sir."

"Well, who married Stubbles's other daughter?"

The President warns gentlemen that they had better not wander too far from the subject. The matter before the Board is, whether Mr. Thrush's note is good enough to be discounted.

"You said he was in the California business, Mr. Breckenridge?"

"Yes, sir. Made some very successful shipments there last Spring."

"I've got mighty little confidence in California!" says Mr. Groull, "mighty little!"

"It's a good way off, that's a fact," adds Mr. Breckenridge. "I'd rather do business with people that trade near by."

Mr. Groull speaks again. "Wouldn't touch it with a ten-foot pole. Bad line. Let it slide, Mr. President. We can do better with our money."

Some of the Directors may have been listening indifferently to this rambling conversation; but the majority are otherwise engaged. One has seized on a morning paper, and all his thoughts are engrossed by the latest news from Europe. Another has just taken a fit to examine the Statement Book, and several are talking on their real estate prospects. Messrs. Breckenridge and Groull make themselves heard above the suppressed confusion of other voices. The President has tapped on the table with his pencil, but failed to restore order. To a person outside of the door, it would seem as if the members were engaged in a general wrangle. Meanwhile, Mr. Marks, with a lively perception of the ludicrous, and skill enough to prove that he is not now practicing for the first time, has sketched sundry odd figures on the blank page of a "tickler," and finishes by a caricature of the two gentlemen above named, which he shows to his neighbor, and he to the next; and then follows an explosion of laughter, which breaks up all other distractions of the Board, and finally gives the President a chance to be heard.

"Come, gentlemen, come, come! we shall never get through our work at this rate."

But the President must have his laugh too; after which, the members fall into comparative order and silence.

Such a scene as this is neither extravagant nor unusual. The directors of a bank, like boys at school, gradually get rid of personal restraints, when they come together, and join heartily in a "little fun." And why not? To be always grave and dignified is next door to being reserved and dull—which would make their meetings irksome, and lead to their being shunned as "a bore." It does not follow, that the real interests of the institution are treated with less serious consideration than they deserve.

The Cashier now informs the Board, that Mr. Chambers had called on him, and stated the capital of Thrush & Co. to be unimpaired. They were prudent men, and stood in deservedly high estimation; had but little paper out; could buy any amount of merchandise on credit, and so forth. He adds, also, that the dealings of Mr. Chambers with the bank had always been liberal and honorable. Owned considerable real estate; was known to have a large capital, and to be prudent in his credits. Had nothing under discount; and his average balance of deposit was seldom less than six or eight thousand dollars. "We ought not," he concludes, "to reject his offering without good reason."

"Mr. Cashier, would you discount California paper?"

"Yes, sir, if it is good."

"If! You may well say that! But California is

not good. Not to be trusted, sir! Too far off! T'other side of the world!"

"What's the matter, Mr. President? What's the business before the Board?" asks Mr. Marks, suddenly, with an air of breaking loose from some engrossing abstractions. "What are you talking about, Mr. Cashier?"

"Mr. Marks," answers the President, "we've been discussing the standing of Mr. Joseph Chambers, and of Thrush & Co., and their sons-in-law and family relations generally. If you had been attending to your duty, sir, you need not have asked the question."

"Didn't hear a word of it."

"No, sir; so it seems. What have you got to say?"

"Joseph Chambers is first-rate. I know all about him, from his toes up to his hat. Good as wheat. Worth over a hundred thousand dollars. It'll never do to reject his paper!"

Several other directors express themselves favorably to the discount of it. There is also some confirmation of the good reports of Thrush & Co.

Mr. Starr insists that a man must not be repudiated as unworthy of credit, because he deals with California, any more than if he were trading with Mexico or South America. "If there is any specific cause of discredit, let's have it out."

The President announces, that objection being withdrawn, the note of Thrush & Co. is marked with the letter A. The formality of a vote is not common in determining the discount of paper; the usual practice being to decline it in the face of serious opposition, even by a small minority. In other words, the general and harmonious sense of the Board is preferred to the mere majority rule in disputed cases. No prudent director will urge particular claims against the prevailing judgment of his associates.

The several next offerings in succession may be by dealers of established credit with the bank, whose paper is well known. They are marked by the President with the letter A, nearly as fast as the Cashier reads them off, if no objection is interposed.

The next is one of a less usual class. The large dry-goods house of Merrimack & Slater wants a discount of twenty-five thousand dollars. They offer notes, which the Cashier reads off as follows:

White & Marshall, thirty-five days to run	$2,576.15
Robert Hancock, forty days . . .	5,250.00
Wellington, Fairfax & Co., forty days,	8,976.40
Osborn & Wells, two months . .	15,75.00
Conrad & Co., three months . .	4,150.25
Oakford & Smith, four months . .	2,960.00

The President waits a moment for some indication of opinion from the directors, although he may have a decided judgment in the case.

Mr. Cassimer, a leading merchant in the dry-goods line, suggests that there can hardly be any doubt as to the disposition of that paper. "Nothing better in the market, and no better customer in the bank. I s'pose you'll have to pass the whole, Mr. President."

"Too big," says Mr. Groull. "Twenty-five thousand dollars! I'd rather divide it among twenty-five different persons, than give it all to one. Bad policy —these big licks!"

Another director proposes to discount the half, rejecting the long paper. "Some of it," says he, "has four months to run. All good, no doubt; but twenty-five thousand dollars is a large sum."

A pause in the conversation.

Director Kent, also in the dry-goods business, admits the sum to be large; but reminds the Board, that "the *men* are large. Don't they keep nearly that amount on deposit in the bank, Mr. President? They are literally asking us to loan them their own money. They can take the paper to any bank in the city, and get it passed at a word; and they will be likely to do so, if you reject or change their offering. You don't want to lose their custom, do you?"

"No, sir," answers the President. "It is the policy of the bank to treat this class of accounts in the most liberal manner. They have nothing under discount at present. We ought to pass the paper at once, to their credit. I hope objections will be withdrawn. Do I so understand it? The Board acquiesces, and I will mark it, accepted. The next in order, Mr. Cashier!"

"Shultz & Cooper offer three notes—Jacob Liston, forty-five days, six hundred dollars; and two notes of Cobb & Walker, each one hundred and fifty, at two and three months."

Director Groull wants to know "where's the use of taking up time with that class of customers? They apply every offering-day, and keep no balance of account. Let 'em slide."

"Has their account improved any of late, Mr. Cashier?"

"Not much, sir. They keep a balance of one or two hundred dollars, and have a thousand under discount."

"Letter R. Let's have the next."

"Hold on, Mr. President! Not too fast. These small men are of use to us. They ought not to be discarded too abruptly. They really want the money. Give 'em that little note of six hundred dollars. It will do them more good than twenty-five thousand does to Merrimack & Slater."

An agreeable personal acquaintance between the dealer and the director is the ground of this favor. The note is discounted at the request of Mr. Miller; none of his associates deeming it worth while to press an opposition in such a trifling case. But this class of applicants receive no consideration when there is a pressure of more deserving customers.

Among the offerings, is one by John Tillotson & Co., who "respectfully propose" the note of Phineas Crowfoot, three months to run, six hundred dollars; and one of Thomas Noble, sixty days, three hundred and fifty. The offerers have no personal friend at the Board, to speak promptly and to say: "I know them. They are good, and ought to be accommodated." But Director Buttonwood, who attends the meetings once a month by convenient accident, asks:

"Who are Tillotson & Co.? Aint they the concern that broke a year or two since, and compromised with their creditors at twenty cents on the dollar? I wouldn't discount any paper for a broken-down dry-goods retailer."

"They are not in that business," answers the Cashier. "They are crockery-dealers, and have kept a fair balance of account in the bank for several years, asking no more than reasonable accommodations. Their capital was originally ten thousand dollars, and they have probably doubled it in trade."

"How much have they under discount?"

"Twenty-five hundred dollars."

"And what's their average balance?"

"From eight hundred to a thousand."

Mr. Buttonwood thinks he has a right to talk more than any other member, to ask more questions, and to suggest more doubts of the solvency of dealers, because he doesn't trouble the Board often with his presence. "He wants to be thoroughly posted up. You don't expect him to give his voice, as a director of this bank, in favor of discounting people's notes, without knowing what they are, do you? He has a higher sense of his duty to the stockholders than that!"

Mr. Buttonwood's sense of duty revolves about a very small point within himself. He looks after the interests of the stockholders, perhaps on twelve several occasions of an hour each, during as many months. He cannot afford to withdraw his attention for a longer time from his private affairs. Consequently, when he comes to the bank, he is ignorant of the state of its business and of the standing of its dealers. But his sense of duty will not allow him to countenance, by his bare presence, the discounting of paper with which he is unacquainted. He has adopted the notion that all the losses of banks come from the officers and directors being unable to say, "no." They are either too easy, or they have "got their hand in the lion's mouth, and dare not draw it out." He concentrates on the few occasions on which he is present, the churlishness and the caprice that might be less intolerable if spread over a longer period. He obliges the officers to explain, for the twentieth time, the circumstances of individual dealers, their capital, extent of business, and so forth. His associates in the Board submit, out of politeness, whilst inwardly wishing that he would absent himself entirely from their meetings.

Every Board of Directors has one or more of this narrow-minded and self-conceited class in its composition. They do not get rid of them at the annual election because of the fear of giving personal offence, and making outside gossip injurious to the interests of the bank. Or there may be less creditable grounds of conciliation connected with the management of its affairs, which might be exaggerated or perverted for a malicious purpose by a disaffected man. It is hardly possible to constitute a Board of Managers, representing, the different interests of trade, without a mixture of the Buttonwood mould; and this is often the source of injury to the more obscure, but still deserving credits that enter into the business.

It is one of the duties of the President to protect the dealer when he is unjustly assailed; and it is directly for the advantage of the bank. Besides the general results of the fair treatment of credit, there is this particular result; that the best class of customers that a bank can have, consists of those whom it has nurtured from moderate to larger success, and whose experience has been all along linked in agreeable intercourse with its officers and directors. These are not easily seduced to open accounts with other banks; but they are faithful to their old friends, and they introduce other dealers.

If Mr. Buttonwood persists in opposing the discount of Tillotson & Co.'s paper, the President adds his testimony to that of the Cashier, and calls on the directors for any information they are able to give.

Director Platt knows Crowfoot.—"He is perfectly good, keeps a retail store on Canal street. I would sell him two or three thousand dollars of merchandise on credit, without hesitation."

"What's his capital? What do you know about that?" asks Director Buttonwood again.

"Nothing very specific. Only the man has kept store there many years, and is in fair credit."

"Then let his paper go. What do we want with the notes of people that have no capital?"

"What do you call capital, Mr. Buttonwood? Isn't stock, established business, ability, and good credit, very substantial capital? What Crowfoot has, is invested in these. Has he not frequently paid notes at our counter, Mr. Cashier?"

"Yes, many a time."

"Has the bank ever discounted any of them for Mr. Tillotson, or other dealers?"

The Cashier turns to the Discount Bill Book, where

he finds a record of all the paper passed to the credit of Tillotson & Co. for two years, and the notes of Phineas Crowfoot recurring at intervals during that time. He adds:

"We have had as high as seventeen hundred dollars of these notes under discount at once, and now have none."

Director Potts is half impatient with this protracted discussion. "Mr. President," he says, "I know both Tillotson and Crowfoot. I would as soon trust either of them three thousand dollars in trade as I would any member of this Board. Where's the use of consuming so much time about so small a matter? Mr. Buttonwood knows more about the price of sugar than about crockery credits. Pass the paper, and let's go on with the business."

This being manifestly the general sentiment of the Board, the President marks it accepted, and requests the Cashier to go on.

"Robert Thompson offers a note of Samuel Price for three thousand dollars, sixty days to run."

Price is known to be a retired merchant of large wealth. Thompson gives his name as security instead of his country business paper. Director Breckenridge objects to it, on the ground that it is "accommodation paper."

Then for the hundredth time, perhaps, comes up a discussion as to what constitutes accommodation paper, and the impropriety of banks discounting it on any terms. Without reaching a decision on this contested point, the directors are satisfied that the note of Mr. Price is "fire-proof," and Thompson keeping a good account, is entitled to the credit The President announces that he has marked it, accepted.

Thornton & Whitaker, iron dealers and manufacturers, inclose twelve thousand dollars of their business paper as collateral to their own note for ten thousand dollars at ninety days. The house is so favorably known as to preclude discussion; but on the suggestion of one of the directors, the term of the discount is changed from ninety to sixty days.

White & Co. offer several notes for discount. Director Crotchitt has an indistinct notion that "those fellows have been dealing pretty largely in railroad stock. Can't say with certainty, but if the Board will let that stand over, he'll get the information, and report to the officers."

John Wilson offers his note at sixty days for five thousand dollars, with one hundred and ten shares of the Salamander Fire Insurance Co. as collateral.

"Good security, Mr. President. That stock is at a premium of ten or twelve per cent. Wilson is a fair man, and I guess his account deserves it.

No objection is made, and the President marks it with the letter A.

Young, Sterling & Co., heavy sugar-dealers, offer several New Orleans drafts for discount. They are accepted by parties residing in New York.

Cranston & Thomas,	on Charles Bancroft, .	$10,000
William English,	" Russell & Co. . .	7,500
Do.	" Perry & Co. . .	15,000
T. Robinson	" Smith & Wheeler .	10,000

The firm has already under discount twenty-five thousand dollars, and their average balance of account is forty thousand.

The President informs the Board, that Mr. Young had called on him, personally, to say that the object of so large an offering is to provide for their payments through the coming month, and that the proceeds will be drawn out gradually.

"You don't mean to discount the whole forty thousand at once, do you, Mr. President?"

"That is for the Board to determine. Young, Sterling & Co., are among our wealthiest dealers. They have a capital of one million of dollars, independent of the private property of the partners, which would sell for as much more. The proportion of their current balance with their discount-line, entitles them to the highest consideration."

While the President is speaking, the drafts are passed from hand to hand, and examined by the directors. The general tenor of remark is favorable to the offering, as a whole. The principal peculiarities of the sugar-business are recited—how the prospects of the growing crop are speculated upon—how the market is sometimes controlled by a few operators in concert with the great sugar-houses of New Orleans or Cuba, and prices kept up or allowed to decline, until the moment comes for combined action, and so forth. It is suggested that all the sugar-men must have incurred prodigious losses by the recent fall of thirty per cent; and that even at present prices, there is room for a decline of nearly as much more.

Mr. Buttonwood, who deals largely in sugars, says,

that no matter what the decline is, Young, Sterling & Co., are above all casualty. His objection to discounting large amounts of paper, so freely expressed when dry-goods houses are in question, vanishes when the sugar-trade calls. The dry-goods directors are less likely to be influenced by prejudice against particular branches of business than any other class of merchants. Their habit of longer and larger credits, if more dangerous, is also more liberalizing than dealing in the shorter credits of the grocer. They are seldom found in the opposition to such offerings as that of Young, Sterling & Co., when the condition of the bank will admit of their discount.

Mr. Cassimer is in favor of passing all the drafts to the credit of the offerers.

The President wants a general expression by the Board for such large operations. "The house is rich, gentlemen, beyond a doubt. But you must remember, that no house is exempt from great losses on a falling market. The transactions in sugar have been excessively inflated within the last few weeks. I called on a friend in that line of business yesterday, and he related to me some facts that you ought to be made aware of. Four or five houses bought up sugar to the amount of one hundred and forty thousand dollars, giving their notes at six months in payment. They held it a week, and sold at a cent a pound advance, taking the notes of the purchasers for the same time. These second purchasers sold at an additional advance of a cent a pound, for notes at six months. The first set of notes have not yet matured, so that there is now afloat nearly half a million of paper on that single lot of sugar—to say nothing of the subsequent sales, of which we are ignorant. I do not state these facts to prejudice the account of Young, Sterling & Co., but on general grounds of caution. Before passing their offering, I want the unanimous approval of the Board."

Mr. Buttonwood wants to know if the bank has any of the paper of "our old friend Dennis, in Reade street?"

The Cashier answers in the negative.

"Because," resumes Mr. Buttonwood, "I suspect he had something to do with the last purchase of that sugar. He has lost a hundred thousand dollars in his business within the last year, and his credit is now at a pretty low notch."

"What do you say, gentlemen? Bring the matter to a close. Shall the paper of Young, Sterling & Co. be passed?"

The directors respond unanimously, "Aye;" and it is marked to be discounted.

The Cashier announces that all the notes offered have been discounted, and that there is no further business.

"Move we adjourn."

Before the President can put the question to vote, Director Breckenridge requests the Board to "hold on a minute." He has "a little lot of coffee to pay for, and wants some paper discounted to the extent of six or eight thousand dollars." Two or three voices say: "Send it to the President." Two or three more repeat: "Move we adjourn;" and all second the motion by a general pushing back of chairs, and putting on of hats. Mr. Breckenridge understands his paper to be discounted, and informs the President that he will send it to the bank as soon as he goes to his office. Half the members are already out of the door, pairing off together to consult on their individual speculations, and to forget that the bank is in existence until the next discount day comes round. It is as likely as not, that the President and Cashier may congratulate each other that they are happily out of the way.

Mr. Miller having disappeared for several minutes in company with others, now returns alone:

"Mr. President, havn't I a note with collaterals coming due to day—ten thousand dollars?"

"Yes. You didn't offer at the Board, and I expected of course you intended to pay it."

"Pay it, indeed!" says Director Miller. "Here. Let's look at it?"

The two go inside of the counter to the teller's desk. The President gets the note, looks over the collaterals, and finds them to consist of about twenty business notes, the drawers of which live any where between Halifax and the Gulf of Mexico, not one of which he can know anything about, and the half of which are payable at Mr. Miller's store.

"When are these coming due?" he asks.

"Not this six months," answers Director Miller. "But they're all as good as wheat. I'll tell you what I'll do. I'll make a new note at ninety days. Just pass it to my credit, and I'll send a check to take up the old one."

"Go ahead," says the President.

The times are easy. He knows Mr. Miller to be a responsible man, or thinks he knows it, and marks the note for discount. His slackness of authority and his sense of strict propriety are at variance. The result is, a weak protest or expostulation, which does not even "lock the door after the steed is stolen."

"This is all right Mr. Miller, I dare say; but I'd rather you'd offer these matters regularly at the Board meetings. You know how I'd be censured, if they should turn out wrong? I'm entirely willing to pass such things occasionally for you or any other director. We understand each other—but there's Buttonwood! He don't come to the Board often; but when he does, you see how he pitches in! And there's old Crotchitt, the biggest stockholder in the concern. He shuffles in at odd times, and will have the discount register carried into the private room; and there he reads it as regularly as the newspaper. It's well enough not to give these fellows a chance to find too much fault? Don't you think so?"

"Oh yes, I understand all that! It's a good rule, if it was only generally observed. I'll try and remember it next time."

The next time, Mr. Miller remembers it in the same way. Or, instead of coming back after the adjournment of the directors, he steps in before the hour, and has the transaction accomplished in advance.

This irregular and careless manner of discounting bills for directors has not unfrequently led to the most serious results. Tacit consent to the practice might easily grow up from the direct personal confidence established between them, which makes it difficult to express dissent without indicating censure. It was also found more agreeable to obtain their accommodations privately, than to submit their offerings in open session of the Board, where they would be competed with by the claims of dealers generally. The practice led to anticipating the means of the bank as these were liberated by maturing investments; so that, in a stringent market, there was often but little left to divide among the dealers on regular discount days. This undue absorption of bank facilities by a few privileged persons became matter of common complaint; and it was not difficult to induce the State Legislature to require a specification, in the quarterly returns, of "all sums due by the directors of each bank," separately from the entire amount of loans. The abuse has been measurably checked by this statement, though there are various methods by which the law may be evaded.

The authority of the President is entirely competent to correct this abuse; but it may be as much of a convenience to him, as to any of the directors. His private speculations would be narrowed, if he could not get ten or twenty thousand dollars without submitting his wants at a regular session of the Board.

Mr. King is another sort of president. He is a stern disciplinarian; never borrows a cent of the bank; thinks borrowing discreditable in a bank officer. It is a stretch of propriety, in his opinion, for a director to borrow from his own institution; but usage tolerates it. The by-laws of the bank require the directors to meet twice a week, to discount the paper offered by its dealers. That is the time and place to lend the funds. The dealers send in their offerings on the stated days, with the understanding that they are to share equitably in the facilities of the bank; and it is unjust to them to dispense those facilities at irregular times. Moreover, this is a fruitful source of bank losses. If all the paper is investigated at the Board sessions, we shall probably discover any that is weak. He positively declines to exercise the discretion of discounting notes without the concurrence of the directors. He will not have his mind burthened with such a responsibility. That must be borne by the directors. If they can get their paper discounted by the officers in the recess of the Board, they absent themselves from its meetings, and gradually come to consider the bank as a mere personal convenience to themselves, forgetting that they owe any duties to the stockholders, and to the general commercial interest.

The habits of private life are often freely scanned at the Bank Board.

"Yes! Mr. Black is clever and smart. He has capital, too. But he had no business to buy a house on Fifth Avenue at sixty thousand dollars, and spend forty more to furnish it. There's a hundred thousand dollars gone clean out of his business; and what's the consequence? Why, he comes here and wants to run a discount line right along for the whole amount! Gentlemen, banks were not got up to enable a few people to live like lords, while the rest of the world are sweating to keep body and soul together! It's just as sure to come to an end, as a man's notes are to come due."

"That may be, Mr. Fairfax; but let me tell you that Black is rich beyond a contingency. He owns half the upper end of Brooklyn, and the city's stretching out in that direction like a young race-horse. Why, in the course of another year, Black will have a Fifth Avenue there, all to himself. I wish I had only the quarter of that piece of property, and you wouldn't catch me dickering dry-goods."

"Well—I'd rather see the tenth part of it realized, than hear what it's going to bring a year hence. Mr. Black may be in his grave before the month's out, for what I know; and what then? How are his notes to be paid? If his estate's worth five millions, the bank would have to wait, perhaps, as many years. Mr. President, my notion is, that we have no right to discount any thing at this Board but a *bona fide* commercial note that will be paid when due. And on top of that, the indorser must be able to take it up himself, if the drawer should fail or die. Don't you see that we are discounting this paper to pay for Mr. Black's house and furniture, just for his single enjoyment? This isn't commercial paper, sir! It's accommodation paper, in the true sense. Mr. Black has invested his commercial means in a house and furniture; and now he wants us to ride him through! No, sir; I'll never give my voice to any such thing while I'm a member of this Board. Besides that, such an establishment necessitates enormous expenses of living. There's to be two or three grand parties and balls every year. And a carriage, and a footman, and one of these fellows with breeches and white stockings, to scrape and bow at the door, and not less than a dozen servants, to keep the great house up. Mr. President, when you add Stewart's bill for silks, and Weller's bill for ice-creams, and all that Frenchified sugar-work, with the foreign wines and hot-house grapes, I can only say that it is fearful! No business in the world can support it, sir."

Mr. Joseph Exeter speaks only on extraordinary occasions.

"There are certain principles, Mr. President, on which sound trade is built up; and one of them is economy. I agree with my friend, Mr. Fairfax, in what he has said about carrying a heavy discount line for the personal accommodation of Mr. Black. That is not commerce, sir. It is personal expenditure, personal extravagance, personal luxury, and, in the end, personal ruin. I don't want to see this institution involved when the end comes."

Mr. Exeter points out the bad influence of such examples on young men who are beginning business, and concludes by a strong protest against Mr. Black's offering. He is most likely to be set down as "behind the age." He is unequal to the emergencies of modern enterprise!

The President listens deferentially to the discussion of the directors. Mr. Black is probably known to him as a bold and "lucky" operator in whatever chances the market may present—to-day in real estate, to-morrow in steamships, and next day in a guano expedition, or a government contract. He has important connections in trade, and his name may be seen in half a dozen insurance, railroad, and mining companies. It is not so easy to reject entirely the offering of such a man. He must be conciliated.

"Gentlemen, if you will refer Mr. Black's offering to me, I will endeavor to put him off with as little as possible. It will be to the interest of the bank to do something for him."

It is so referred; and that gentleman is satisfied with the one-half or one-third of the amount which he asks for.

The duties of the President, in personal intercourse with dealers, are regarded as limited to the treatment of credit from a strictly commercial point of view. He takes no direct cognizance of their moral habits—though these, in fact, often turn the scale against an account.

Mr. Crafft has been a customer in good standing with the bank. He has kept an average balance of six or eight thousand dollars, and obtained a discount line of twenty thousand—one of the most satisfactory class of accounts.

It is whispered one day, that Mr. Crafft is a gambler, and his offering is rejected. His credit sinks, and in the course of a few months, his line of discount is reduced more than one-half. The paper that he offers is the same that has heretofore been esteemed satisfactory by the bank; but it is frequently refused. Personal solicitation of the President is equally unsuccessful.

Mr. Brewer drinks brandy to excess. As with Mr. Crafft, his accommodations are gradually reduced. He keeps up his balance of deposits with more than common assiduity, to strengthen his claim. Note after note of his discount line is paid off, and he seldom obtains "a favor." In endeavoring to maintain his affairs with the bank, he frequently comes in contact with the President.

"No, sir. We cannot do it. I am very sorry."

"But, Mr. President, my line is reduced from twenty thousand dollars down to five. My balances are even better than ever, and I offer you unexceptionable paper, that is always paid at maturity."

"I am aware of that, sir; but it is out of our power to discount for you at present. We are obliged to decline a large proportion of our offerings."

"Will you discount for me next week?"

"Can't tell, sir. If you offer at the Board, and your paper is satisfactory, it may be done."

This is an example of the common dissimulation practiced by bank officers to get rid of undesirable customers. How much better would it be:

"Your paper is rejected, Mr. Brewer, because you are destroying yourself by habits of intoxication. You are on the highroad to insolvency. Your account entitles you to liberal accommodation, and it would give us pleasure to render it. But your credit is rapidly on the decline, and will soon be gone altogether. Every bank in the city will hasten to get your name off its books before it becomes positively unsafe."

Such a warning would be more authoritative from a bank president than from any other person. It might be lost on the man who has gone so far as to be already discredited; but the example would not be without influence on those who are following at some distance in the rear. A merchant values few things so much as his good name in the market; and he ought to know that every bad habit which affects his character, is scored down opposite to it in the Reference Book of the bank officer. If Mr. Crafft and Mr. Brewer could have seen records like the following, they would have hardly thought it worth while to make any appeal to the President:

"Richard Crafft, flour-merchant, No. – Pearl street. Began business in 1840 with $25,000 capital. Managing, economical, and conscientious. Very successful. Standing good. 1842, continues to prosper. Built large house on Madison square, cost $30,000. Said to have cleared fifty in the previous two years. Capital now $40,000, besides real estate. 1843–44–45, affairs well conducted, credit unquestioned, makes money fast. 1846 to 50, worth now $150,000, besides real estate. 1851, living high, and takes 'flyers' in the stock market. Caution. 1852, credit still good, large business, but has been seen at gambling-houses. Keep a sharp eye on him. 1853, operates extensively in stocks. Is now often seen at the gambling-table. June 1854, Crafft is reported to have lost $40,000 at play, and in Erie, within the last six months. October 1854, no better. Credit on the decline. January 1855, continues in a bad way. Think it advisable to reduce his account."

"Esau Brewer, dry-goods jobber, Broadway. Began in 1846 with capital of $40,000. Up to 1852, successful, and highly esteemed. Capital at later date increased to $125,000. April 1853, bought country-seat. Expensive family, but enjoys good credit. Paper to his own order sells at the best rates. 1854, is getting rather free with brandy. Business continues thriving, and credit unimpaired. October

1855, Brewer called in to press for discounts. Looks like a confirmed toper. Running down hill at a gallop. January 1856, poor Brewer in again—past saving."

Information comes to the bank officers without their seeking, and is generally brought the more promptly in proportion to its evil character. Dealers who wish to gain favor with the President, whisper rumors in his ear, confidentially, that another dealer has met with serious losses, or has fallen into bad company. Each director contributes his share of gossip; and the "Commercial Agency" is bound to give immediate notice to its subscribers of whatever may affect their interest.

A bank president may be regarded, in some degree, as a sponsor for the integrity of commerce. He is perpetually in contact with the mind of trade, and why should he not instruct it? Where, if not by him, shall a beginning be made? Is he clothed with the greatest power in society, merely to put a motion, or to announce a vote in a Board of Directors, at a salary of ten thousand dollars a year? Are his hourly opportunities for giving wise counsel and timely remonstrance to be turned off by a trick of dissimulation?

Another question might be asked:

Are our Bank Presidents qualified by knowledge, cultivation, and general weight of character, to exert a good influence over their commercial pupils?

They are not chosen for that purpose. The possession of wealth, and the power to control deposits, take precedence of all questions relating to conscience, intellectual accomplishments, and financial ability.

If a man is rich, he has many friends, and a wide personal influence. He is sought after to have his name enrolled among the managers of various imposing institutions. He is a patron of fashionable charities. He is called on to preside at public meetings. Therefore, he is a very proper man to be a Bank President! It is not supposed that these distinctions are inconsistent with the most desirable qualifications for the office; but they are too often admitted in substitution thereof.

There is, happily, a saving clause in the organization of a bank, which protects it against many of the consequences of unfitness in the chief officer. The division of labor is such as to compensate in the mere mechanism of the business for want of capacity in the individual; and the Board of Directors have the right to assume, either in session or by committees, the conduct of important affairs. They may limit the discretionary powers of the President by by-laws, or by closer personal attention to the business.

It is not unfrequent that the Cashier of a bank, though nominally subordinate, is practically the superior officer. His duties being to a great extent concurrent with those of the President, it is easy for him to step in and occupy the ground. He may hold the reins of authority, and be the ears, the eyes, the brain and the soul of the institution. The relation works itself into such terms unavoidably, when the President is unequal to his place.

The manual work that is performed by the President in a bank of the first class is but little. A casual observer might think his salary of ten thousand dollars a year, out of all just proportion with it. But his freedom from the annoyance of details leaves his judgment cool, and enables him to give more uninterrupted attention to the causes which affect commercial credit, and which may make it expedient to change the course of the business.

The President of a bank is its personal and moral, as well as its legal representative. If he is known to be high-minded and honorable in his individual relations, the confidence of the community does not stop at the man, but extends to the institution. Its counters are thronged by depositors, and many friends are anxious to become its stockholders. Such a personality is of prodigious account in an active market, where competition divides the patronage of dealers. It acts beneficially in the opposite direction also, by repelling hazardous business. In banking, as well as in social intercourse, "like seeks like." The President who speculates in lands, railroad stocks, and mining shares, attracts around him the plotters in these various schemes; and whatever may be the extent of his private property, however high his standing and successful his adventures, the capital of a bank is not safe in his hands. At one time or another, in one way or another, the institution is compromised by unsafe investments. The solicitation of a personal friend obtains a short loan on good security; the market changes, and the security depreciates while the loan is extended from necessity, and perhaps increased; a substitution of securities is allowed; defective powers of attorney creep in by oversight; the treasurers of the borrowing companies are changed;

the original negotiators die;—a thousand accidents occur to involve and to complicate this class of financial operations. The only rule of safety for a bank is, to discard them altogether; and this is the rule of integrity to the commercial interest also.

The bank officer who is not proof against the temptations held out for the employment of funds in speculative channels is an unsafe trustee.

"What!" says one, "shall I keep idle two or three hundred thousand dollars, which the regular dealers of the bank do not want to borrow, when I can loan it, on call, at seven per cent interest?" Accordingly, he loans it out. This is the origin of the employment of bank capital on the Stock Exchange—a practice which has often been severely criticized by commercial men.

The desire to make the most out of the means of the bank is natural; but this does not always consist in a particular economy, such as transient loans outside of the commercial interest. It may be better economy to let the excess remain as a dead weight, until the renewed activity of trade shall again call it into use. Such, in fact, has been the experience of several of our city banks which have repudiated stock loans altogether. They have found their reward in attracting the best class of merchants to their counters, which gives a more stable deposit, and consequently a more uniform line of discount.

The objections to call-loans on the Stock Exchange are:—that they inflate and sustain fictitious values; that they encourage the speculative market, and stimulate the rates of interest, which commerce has to pay; that many of the securities bought and sold are worthless, and to countenance dealing in them, therefore, tends to fraud; that the system, to a great extent, is mere gambling, in which merchants are constantly tempted to their ruin; and that it corrupts the whole market.

It is well known that the old commission-house of Tumbledown & Co. was for many years a measure of credit. "Will you take some paper to-day?" asks a broker of a Bank President.

"Yes. We'll take fifty thousand dollars, if it's as good as Tumbledown & Co."

The same President was shocked one day to hear that the house had been ruined by speculations in "Erie," or "Harlem;" and the probabilities were as four to five, that his own loans to the stock-market had something to do with it.

In some banks, stock loans have been prohibited by a vote of the Board of Directors. Where they are admitted, the President commonly exercises his discretion as to the kind and amount of securities. There is probably not a Bank Board in the City of New York that would not pass a vote of prohibition, if strongly urged to do so by the President.

Among the duties of the President is, that of constantly reviewing the credits of the bank.

Merchandise is sold from first hands to the *jobber* on a credit of eight months (more or less), for which the latter gives his promissory notes. The jobber sells in smaller quantities (by the piece or single package) to the retailer, on a credit of six months. It is good management for a merchant to have his bills receivable coming due in season to apply their proceeds to discharge his bills payable. But the ability of the retailer to pay the jobber depends chiefly on the punctuality of the consumer in settling his bills. Thus each class of merchants is dependent on another class for the means of liquidation. A large cash capital may enable a man to pay all his notes at maturity, even if his debtors fall considerably in arrears; but the majority of traders of all classes are obliged to carry full lines of credit. This system supplies our banks with promissory notes, the discount of which is their principal source of profit.

The New York city banks do not discount paper until it comes within two or three months of maturity. That which has a longer period to run, is therefore unavailable for direct use. The bank, however, will admit a modification of its rules, when satisfied that the notes are good. It will receive a certain amount of them as collateral security for the merchant's note payable within the required time, reserving in such cases what is called a *margin* for contingent losses. Thus a dealer may deposit twelve thousand dollars of paper, which has from four to eight months to run, coupling with it his own note for six or eight thousand dollars at sixty days. The excess is the margin intended to cover loss by the possible failure of some of the drawers, and the expenses of collection and interest that would accrue, if the dealer himself should fail and oblige the bank to have recourse to the collateral notes. This is a very simple operation in appearance; but it involves the exercise of no com-

"Sit down, sir, and let me look at your collateral notes."

mon sagacity and discretion on the part of the bank officers. They must endeavor to maintain an accurate knowledge of the affairs of the merchant to whom the loan is made, and of the responsibility of the drawers of the collateral notes. The latter are resident in small towns and at trading stations all over the country, from Canada to Mexico. It is impossible for a bank officer to get much specific information about them. It is presumed that the city merchant has sufficient knowledge of his customers to justify the credit that he gives them. But the President or Cashier frequently enters into a particular examination of each note.

"Mr. Jobber, the Board of Directors has referred your offering to me, to ascertain something about these collaterals. Sit down, sir, and let us look over them. Here is Joseph Scott, of Wheeling, four hundred and sixty dollars, seven months to run. What do you know about him?"

"Well, Mr. President, Scott has dealt with me five years, and never failed to pay promptly. He represents himself as an owner of real estate, worth ten thousand dollars. Besides that, his stock averages some twenty thousand over all his debts. I have a correspondent there who confirms his statement, and the Mercantile Agency here says the same thing. Scott's general character is very fair. Church member—very gentlemanly. I sell him about three thousand dollars a year, and he owes me, running, say two."

"That's quite satisfactory. Now here's Zach & Co.,

Chicago, who are they? Nine hundred and fifty dollars, six months."

"Zach & Co. were recommended to me by my brother-in-law, who lives close by one of the firm, a little out of the city. Owns a fine country-seat—made forty thousand dollars by the rise of real estate—one of the early settlers—half owner of a hotel—worth altogether not a cent less than a hundred thousand dollars. We trust him from three to five, but he pays cash half the time."

"Very good. Next comes Stubbs & Brother, of Shreveport, Louisiana, twelve hundred dollars. That's a good way off!"

"Yes, sir, but very responsible men. They have a capital of thirty thousand dollars. Their city references are of the first class, and we have made particular inquiry as to their general habits and capacity for business. This is their first purchase of us."

"Here are two notes—Jackson & Smith of Montgomery, Alabama, and Joseph Tompkins of Galveston, Texas, made payable at your office, Mr. Jobber. We shall decline them, as notes drawn in that way are apt to be protested."

"Those people have always remitted promptly, Mr. President. The reason of making their notes payable in New York is, that they ship cotton to the East and draw against it."

"That may be; but we prefer notes that are payable where the parties reside. You must send us others in their place."

"We can do so, sir, if you prefer it."

"Ezra Cooper, Savannah. Who's he?"

"First-rate man. Owns a plantation with two hundred slaves. Customer of ten years' standing."

The list of collateral notes is thus scrutinized by the President or Cashier. The extensive correspondence of the bank enables the officers often to corroborate or to correct the representations of the dealer. It has collected paper of the same drawers, or had it returned protested. A short inquiry is frequently appended at the foot of a letter to a Cashier in Columbus or elsewhere: "How does Geo. Draper of (or near) your city stand?" The answer would generally be esteemed as more worthy of reliance than the account of a dealer who is an interested party.—"George Draper, in the dry-goods business, is successor to his former employers who failed a year back. Has the good-will of the old store, stock twenty thousand dollars, no paper out in these parts, prompt in his dealings, and is careful how he trusts people, I should say—a man of the upper middling class."

Another sort of answer will sometimes come: "George Draper is just now out on a grand spree. He is a good whole-souled fellow with but one enemy in this world, and he is George Draper. Has real estate, well mortgaged, a fine run of customers who never pay till called upon—and George is not the man to call. Family of five children, two grown-up and expensive daughters, and a son who is the best sportsman in these diggings.—Confidential. Yours truly."

The President wants to verify a statement of the

affairs of Jonas Marks of Toronto, whose note for twelve hundred dollars, at seven months, is among Mr. Jobber's collaterals. He sends an inquiry to the "Commercial Agency" of Messrs. Paul & Pry, and in thirty minutes gets the following answer:

"[CONFIDENTIAL.]

"Jonas Marks, Toronto, U. C., general hardware. Began business, in 1849, with cash capital, $10,000. Not very successful for the first two years—rather fond of frolics—credit at home not good. In 1852, got run over by a railway-car, and lost half a leg. Recovered $5,000 damages. Settled down and begun to thrive immediately. In 1853, married a daughter of one of our wealthiest citizens who has since died, leaving an estate of three hundred thousand dollars to be divided among twelve children. M. is one of the executors. His business has much improved since '52. In '55, he realized a handsome sum by selling off some real estate, and was appointed deacon in the church. Credit is now A 1."

The ledgers of Messrs. Paul & Pry are full of these particulars. Family, social connections and habits, are often traced with great minuteness. Nothing that bears on credit is unimportant; and there are few facts of any consequence relating to it that escape the record. If Mr. John Green of Galveston, Texas, wants to buy goods in the New York market for his notes, he must take care how he keeps fast horses and runs into extravagant expenses.

The time of most excitement and difficulty to the President, is in an extreme financial pressure. If he is then himself free from debt, as he should be, he becomes practically a dictator. The directors, who are quite likely to want money as badly as other people, are often themselves suppliants; and from that moment, their influence at the Board declines. They are subject to the President, because they are dependent on his will for loans; and his will, being governed by a strong sense of justice and impartiality, is in opposition to their desires. Single-handed, he can resist the whole twelve if they should combine against him to absorb an undue proportion of the funds.

A director has a plausible argument in his favor when he urges his claim for larger loans. He gives valuable time to the bank, and is expected to uphold it in emergencies; therefore, he is entitled to precedence before dealers generally when he is himself in an emergency. Besides, if a director should be allowed to fail, the rumor gets abroad and will be believed, that he is largely indebted to the bank, and thus the bank will be more crippled than it would be by sustaining him with additional loans. Against these arguments the President opposes his resolute negative.

"You have as much money out of the bank as you are entitled to, and I will not consent to discount for you another dollar. If you fail, I can't help it; and if the bank suffer in public estimation as a consequence, the fault will be yours and not mine."

This is the language of a President whose experience warns him that it is easier to refuse at the right stage of such a case than at the wrong one; and that a bank always sustains more injury by an officer's departure from sound rules of management than from the misfortunes of an individual director. If the President is publicly known as a man who will not deviate from an impartial and upright course, even to serve a personal friend in great extremity, his institution cannot be hurt by false rumors.

On the other hand, a yielding President, or one who is himself a borrower and embarrassed for the want of funds, can exert no authority over a needy Board of Directors. There is no restraint upon the latter. "Common want makes mutual friends." The convenience of dealers generally is disregarded, and the funds are absorbed by a few. If the institution escapes immediate difficulty and discredit, it does not escape ultimate damage by the loss of the best class of dealers, who transfer their accounts to other banks where a more honorable spirit prevails.

The directors of a bank are frequently solicited by their friends and persons in trade to "speak a good word for them at the Board." It is flattering to their self-importance to be called on, as they often are, by men who are vastly their superiors in social standing, education and manners, and to be begged for "their influence." It gratifies them to prove that if an acquaintance may be considered an honor on one side, it may be of substantial service on the other. But this personal solicitation becomes annoying to them in a tight market. They shift the ungraciousness of a direct refusal on the officers.

"I'll do what I can for you, but you had better go to the President."

The President then runs the gauntlet of incessant

importunity. He appears to be a monster of insensibility. Many who approach him on the faith of long and intimate friendship, go away convinced that all his professions of regard have been false, and that he is "a hypocrite." He is charged with serving his favorites, or using the bank funds to promote his own speculations

It is now fifteen minutes before three o'clock on a panic day.

Mr. Moreton is one of the oldest dealers of the bank, and a large stockholder. He has already appealed to the President, between whom and himself exists a strong personal friendship, and he now returns for a last effort before the dreadful stroke of three.

"I am sorry to see you again, sir."

"You may be assured that the last extremity only has brought me back. Mr. President, if I do not get ten thousand dollars to-day, I shall go to protest and the labor of my whole life is lost. Here are my securities, worth three times the amount!"

"My dear sir, I am powerless both officially and personally. The bank is on the verge of discredit. I have no right to endanger the interests of our stockholders by loaning another dollar. Your case is but one of twenty similar, that have been presented within the last hour, and it has been my painful duty to reject all."

The President is truly in most trying circumstances. His relations with Mr. Moreton are not merely personal, but social. Their families mingle intimately, and their sympathies and enjoyments have been common. The shock of bankruptcy is suspended over the whole circle. Instead of renewing at evening the pleasures in which he has so often forgotten the annoyance of his daily duties, he fancies dark halls, deserted parlors, separated playmates and broken "silver cords."

The two have withdrawn into an inner room, and it is less the merchant and the banker, than friend and friend; nor could an impartial observer tell from the expression of anxiety and despair in their countenances, upon whom the blow is to fall the heavier.

"Must my name be dishonored for the want of a sum comparatively so trifling as this?—Can you give me no suggestion?"

"I cannot."

It seems to Mr. Moreton that he could lay down his life with less pain than he can submit to the forfeiture of his commercial honor. His reputation, the success of his whole life, the labor of thirty years, are slipping from his grasp with the few remaining seconds of the hour; and then they are gone! This is no exaggeration of the real mental suffering of the sensitive and high-spirited merchant on the brink of bankruptcy, nor of the painful interest of the bank-officer in the fortunes of his friend.

In many cases, the disappointed applicant retires cursing, in soliloquy, the bank as an incorporated nuisance, and the President as an unfeeling monster. The last thought that occurs to him is that his own recklessness in trade or expenditure has had anything to do with bringing his affairs into a bad condition; or that a bank with fifteen hundred dealers is liable to have its deposits drawn upon faster than its discounted bills mature, and that in such a case it is more helpless than an individual merchant; it can neither borrow nor create capital.

It has been considered an axiom of financial wisdom to repudiate "indulgence" as inconsistent with sound banking. The man who recognizes only the "pound of flesh," is regarded as an exemplary bank officer. "He is an excellent man, but too sympathetic for a President," is not an unusual remark, when the qualifications of a candidate are discussed. This is practically an assumption of the superiority of capital over trade and labor; but wherever a fair commercial sympathy is allowed to displace the maxim of Shylock, debts are more honorably settled, defaults more promptly repaired, and the obligations of credit more respected. A bank president who can intrench himself behind bags of coin and look on the disasters of the market without involuntary sympathy for the sufferers, is unworthy of public confidence. He is an enemy to commerce.

All the best interest of society are injured by financial pressure. Education is interrupted in families. Private enterprise is stopped, public works are suspended, and wages are cut off. These results have frequently been brought about or exaggerated by the bad management of banks; therefore, to vest such a power in weak hands is a public wrong.

CHAPTER III.

THE CASHIER.

The internal mechanism and order of a bank depend chiefly on the Cashier. For the greater part, his powers are concurrent with those of the President; but they extend specifically to the details of the business, embracing the supervision of the accounts, the correspondence with other banks, and more active intercourse with the dealers.

He keeps a record of the transactions of the Board of Directors, to which he is Acting Secretary.

He signs, with the President, the certificates of stock issued to shareholders, and the bank bills which are paid out as money.

Checks drawn on other banks are usually signed by him. When he is absent, they are signed by the President.

He indorses, personally or by deputy, all drafts and promissory notes which are sent to other parts of the country for collection.

All drafts and notes received from others for payment in New York are indorsed subject to his order; but on these, the official stamp of the bank is mostly admitted as a substitute for his formal indorsement as follows:

Just Elected.

Pay Walter Mead, Esq.
Cashier, or order.
ANDREW MASON, *Cashier.*

	RECEIVED PAYMENT. WALTER MEAD, CASHIER.	

The stamp is generally impressed with a kind of oil-paint or ink which is not easily erasible. The bank records are accessible for legal proof, and every note paid through it could be traced and verified in case of dispute.

The correspondence of the bank is conducted in the name of the Cashier, officially.

In all cases where his signature alone is required, that of the President may be substituted; but the alternate substitution is not allowed.

When the President is absent, the Cashier is the principal executive manager of the business; and he is often so, practically, when that officer is present. In several of our largest city banks, the Presidency is a mere sinecure accorded to wealth, age, or influence, with little reference to capacity, the Cashier being regarded in fact as the superior officer.

He gives bonds to the amount of ten or twenty thousand dollars.

Bonds are intended as indemnity in case of fraud. They do not cover loss by indiscretion, neglect, or errors of judgment, however gross these may be.

Formerly, the Cashier was forbidden to hold stock in the bank of which he was an officer, for the reason, perhaps, that it would place him too nearly on an equality with the President and directors. Possibly it was feared that a desire to increase his own dividends might induce a speculative employment of the funds. It was considered improper also that he should keep his personal account in the bank, a restriction that was extended likewise to the President, under a general impression that it might be a bar to abuses of privilege. These restrictions are still partially in force, though mostly regarded with indifference. They would be a slight obstacle to fraud with men who are not restrained by a sense of right within themselves. At the same time, experience has shown the wisdom of absolute rules in moneyed institutions by which the first approaches to temptation are kept out of sight.

The Cashier receives his appointment from the Board of Directors, who may also remove him in their discretion. He retains office "during good behavior," unless, as it occasionally happens, he is ousted in a personal quarrel.

When a bank officer resigns his place without explanation or obvious cause, such as ill-health or change of residence, it is generally understood that he has been guilty of some impropriety, or has been found incompetent. This would be likely to defeat his application for employment in other banks.

It is so grave a matter to charge a bank officer with default, even if circumstances are strongly against him, and might be so difficult of proof if he should stand on the defensive, that he is mostly allowed to retire without official exposure, unless the amount in question is very large, or his conduct has been unusually atrocious. His bondsmen are personal friends who are anxious to screen him from public disgrace, and they manage to effect an amicable compromise. Besides, a bank has nothing to gain by thrusting its misfortunes out into public view. The conviction of the offender would not shield it from the suspicion of having careless or ill-guarded methods of business.

Although the power of appointing and removing the Cashier is vested in the Board of Directors, he is not unconditionally subordinate to them. He is regarded by the stockholders as their direct representative and trustee. If the President or directors should attempt to use the funds of the bank for improper or hazardous purposes, the Cashier might authoritatively interpose. It would be his duty to do so. He may object to any measures which he deems injurious to the business or character of the institution, without endangering the tenure of his office and without offence to his superiors. If faithful and well qualified, he is their co-ordinate in the administration of affairs.

The salary of the Cashier depends on the peculiarity of his duties. In some of the smaller banks, where he is a mere clerk, it is two or three thousand dollars a year; while in the larger where he is an executive officer of high grade, it ranges from five to ten thousand dollars. The latter sum is probably the highest paid in the City of New York. In some cases he derives perquisites by acting as trustee or treasurer for other companies. His compensation is made liberal, that he may be under no necessity to engage in other business, which, besides distracting his thoughts, might involve him in debt and create conflict of interests.

The Cashier reaches his desk about nine o'clock in the morning. His first care is to examine the contents of the letters received by mail. In the larger banks an Assistant Cashier or Corresponding Clerk attends wholly or in part to this service.

The inclosures of letters consist of bank checks, personal checks, bank bills, drafts at sight or for acceptance, promissory notes for collection, bills of exchange—foreign or domestic, government warrants, railroad coupons, and any other form of document which represents money. Land warrants are often sent to the city for sale, as it is here that the readiest market is afforded by the competition of emigrants and speculators; also, certificates of stock in banks, in mining, manufacturing, and insurance companies; and State, County, and City bonds, which have been issued for public improvements.

The first thing is to compare these inclosures with the record of the letter. In banks of limited correspondence, the Cashier may check off each item, and hand over the documents to the clerks in whose departments they are to be entered; but in those of widely-extended business he requires several assistants. Sometimes the letter is passed successively to the different clerks, each of whom marks his initials opposite to what he takes out, and it is then returned to the Cashier so vouched.

Most of the documents are made subject to the indorsement of the receiving bank, which is an effectual bar to their abstraction and use in other channels, except by a forged indorsement. Bank notes might be taken by a dishonest clerk, without immediate detection; but the deficiency being reported to the remitting bank, suspicion and probable discovery would follow. Bonds and stocks could not be surreptitiously used without discovery. A fraudulent holder would be arrested, when he came forward to receive the interest. The bank correspondence is, therefore, effectually guarded against fraud by the clerks who may be employed in it, unless they have the hardihood to attempt forgery; and this could not long be concealed.

The practice is common among our city banks to add the available checks that are received in the morning letters to the exchanges, before these are sent to the Clearing House. The amount so used, which in some of the banks with an extensive correspondence frequently reaches three hundred thousand dollars, is equivalent to so much deposit of the day before. It is the saving of one day's interest upon it; or, practically, the specie of the bank is increased by the sum so used, although the benefit that results from it is more apparent than real, since other banks use the checks that are drawn against the remittance in the same manner, and neutralize the gain. The hour devoted to the final preparation of the exchanges by the addition of these checks, which must be culled from many letters, is one of the busiest of the day.

The number of letters received by a bank of the first class ranges from one hundred and fifty to three hundred per day. The majority of them are formal, being merely an abridged statement of the inclosures;

and these can be acknowledged by a corresponding clerk. But many relate to matters which require the personal attention of the Cashier; such as the purchase or sale of stocks, the re-discount of bills receivable, errors and misunderstandings of account, special instructions relative to suspended debts, the capital and credit of merchants, and so forth.

The number of letters sent out daily is about the same as received—that is, received and sent, from three to six hundred.

When the money-market is "easy," the routine of the Cashier's employment is very agreeable. The different departments of the bank move along harmoniously, and without haste. The dealers call and transact their business, and go away in good humor. If they want paper discounted, it is done promptly. They mix a pleasant sociality with their negotiations. They often sit down and talk on indifferent subjects, as in the common intercourse of private life. No topic, grave or light, is out of place in the rooms of the Cashier or the President—politics, theology, history, education, public improvements, and personal matters, are all mixed up together. Either officer will discount a note without interrupting the train of his ideas, and without dropping a sentence. "Let us have credit for that?"—"Yes, sir"—is a trifling interpolation, that may give to a highly esteemed customer the privilege of drawing checks to the amount of twenty or thirty thousand dollars. Nothing can be more pleasant than the call of a director to invite the Cashier to an evening party. Sometimes it extends to a bathing or a fishing excursion, the occasional enjoyment of which is not inconsistent with the interests of the institution. The President cheerfully assumes extra duty on such occasions, and takes his turn when he has the opportunity. The hours of attendance at the bank are neither so early in the morning, so late in the afternoon, nor so constant during the day, as to prevent a wide latitude of personal leisure and polite indulgence. There is excitement enough in these concomitants of "an easy market" to make the office of Cashier one of the most desirable that the community affords.

But the time comes for this agreeable experience to terminate. The market shows symptoms of "tightness." The amount of paper offered for discount is suddenly doubled, and the amount discounted is reduced one-half. Merchants are not satisfied with their usual preparations for the future. They are bent on accumulating twice as much ready money as they need; and they begin to call for loans as soon as the Cashier reaches his desk in the morning, before the bank doors are officially opened. Those whose offerings have been rejected by the Board of Directors come to ask for explanation and to make complaints

"What is the matter, Mr. Cashier?"

"Our means are reduced, sir."

"Is my paper too long?"

"No, sir."

"Is it too short?"

"No, sir."

"Then what is the difficulty? Do tell me."

"Our deposits have fallen off, and we are obliged to hold on to our receipts."

"Don't you like the names?"

"We did not look at them. It was not worth while since we had no money to loan."

"But you *ought* to look at them. Now, see here—look at this, and that, and then here" (turning the notes over in his hand), "and there's another—all as good as wheat!—my *dear sir!*"

These two last words are spoken with peculiar emphasis.

"It would give us pleasure to pass them all to your credit, sir. They are not objectionable."

"Then, why not slip them in at once and be done with it."

"Because, my good friend, it is simply impossible. We have not the means."

"Oh, but my dear Mr. Cashier—come, come, don't say so! These are only four little notes—less than ten thousand dollars in all!"

"My friend, you must believe me. Our coin is reduced, and we cannot discount a dollar."

The Cashier is in the midst of an important letter, and writes a word at a time as he answers this shower of questions. The customer is at length satisfied that he can get nothing by further importunity, and goes away, promising to come back to-morrow.

No sooner is he gone, than his place is filled by another, who asks the same questions and gets the same answers. The conversation is varied by the temper and circumstances of the applicant.

One of the clerks comes to him with a gentleman, whom he introduces as Mr. Tarbox.

The Cashier says mentally: "What business have

strangers to come here for discounts? We have enough to do to take care of our old customers."

The clerk adds: "Mr. Tarbox wishes to open an account, sir."

Oh, that is quite another matter!

"Mr. Tarbox, I am happy to see you, sir"—shaking hands. The Cashier is very polite. It is an agreeable transition from being bored for loans, to find a man who really has money in his pocket to deposit in the bank.

The several dealers in waiting give way, and allow the Cashier and Mr. Tarbox to pass to another room, or within the counters, where they may talk without interruption.

It is one of the most important duties of the bank officer to receive new accounts.

"In what branch of business are you engaged, Mr. Tarbox?"

"In the manufacture and sale of clocks."

"Are you a resident of the city?

"Yes, sir. My store is at No. 2000 Pearl street; but my manufactory is at New Haven."

"What is your capital?"

"It was originally thirty thousand dollars; and my profits have now increased it to sixty thousand."

Other questions follow, relating to the extent of Mr. Tarbox's business, and to whatever may affect his credit. He finally refers the Cashier to Mr. Starr, one of the directors of the bank, with whom he has a personal acquaintance.

"That will do, sir. I'll take your signature in this book, and instruct the Teller to receive your deposit."

The Cashier seizes his first leisure moment to post to his Reference Ledger the particulars stated, with any additional information that he may get from Mr. Starr; and when Mr. Tarbox at a future time offers his bills receivable for discount, the whole story is brought out and read to the Board of Directors.

Thus, in the outset of the Cashier's personal intercourse with the dealer, begins that scrutiny of character on one hand and imparting of confidence on the other, which establishes a more intimate relation than exists in ordinary commerce.

It is true, Mr. Tarbox is rather conferring favor than asking it, by opening his account. But he is laying the foundation for years of continual borrowing and lending between the bank and himself; and the general convenience of his business depends much on his relations with the officers. He is preparing the *hinge of success*, on which may turn a thousand good bargains during the next ten years.

It is a serious mistake for a dealer to decline giving to a bank officer a candid statement of his affairs, when asked for it. Confidence fails at once, and it can rarely be re-established.

Eight or ten anxious customers await the Cashier's release from Mr. Tarbox. Among them are some of his best personal friends. They will not be put off by his first assurance that the bank has no money to loan. Each one considers his case entitled to special attention above all others.

"Good morning, Mr. Cashier."

"Good morning, Mr. A."

"I am very much surprised to find that my paper is not discounted, sir."

"Ah, my friend, I am sorry; but you see that others are in the same predicament."

Yes, sir; but that gives me no comfort. I have my notes to pay."

"The Board did their best, Mr. A. Our receipts happen to be very small just now, and we have been sadly beaten at the Clearing House for three mornings in succession."

"Mr. Cashier, this paper is A 1. You have nothing better on your books. The amount is not large, and the time is short."

"It is impossible sir, for the bank to discount it. We are obliged to turn away every application at present."

"Have you looked at my account?"

"I have not."

"Then you must do so and consider whether I am not entitled to all that I ask."

"The Board of Directors have left me no discretion. They decided that it was not safe to loan a single dollar."

"My balance has not fallen below three thousand dollars for months past. I make no unreasonable requests."

"It is true, sir, that your requests are reasonable, and that your account entitles you to a liberal line. But what can we do without the *means* of doing?"

"The whole amount of my accommodations for a year have been exceedingly moderate I do not trouble you with incessant calls."

"That is so, sir, but—"

"Well, Mr. Cashier, I claim to be an exception tc your general rule. You must discriminate between men who bore you to death all the time, and those who are reasonable in their demands. It is seldom that I ask you for discounts, and when I do, I want them."

"No doubt, sir; and I assure you that we have every disposition to treat you liberally. It is a very unpleasant duty to reject such claims as yours; but I tell you again, and I want you to believe me, that we have no alternative. We cannot move an inch."

"But sir, you *must* move an inch! Do you pretend to tell me that you will enjoy the use of my balance of three or four thousand dollars, lending it out to other people, and then when I want to get a little loan myself, you will turn round and say you *can't*, and you have no discretion and no power? What do I care, if you *are* short at the Clearing House? Does that pay my notes? Now, sir, I will tell you and your Board of Directors that I am not a man to submit to such treatment!"

"Mr. A. if you are a reasonable man—"

"*If* I am a reasonable man! I *am* a reasonable man, sir, and that's just the whole case. Because I am so, I want my paper discounted. It is my *right*, sir, and I don't mean to give it up!"

"Well sir, it *is* your right, and I don't want you to give it up. But you must listen to me, while I put the matter to your own judgment—"

"I have settled it in my judgment already. I don't want to hear this stuff about the Clearing House!

"Now, sir, I will tell you and your Board of Directors, that I am not a man to submit to such treatment."

The Clearing House is nothing to *me!* my notes have to be paid—*that's* my judgment, sir!"

"Do you think, Mr. A., that I am made of gold, or that I can turn back the tides of the North River?"

"I know very well that you cannot change the market; but you can discount this paper."

"My dear sir, I cannot do it without endangering more and larger interests than yours. Our stockholders and creditors generally have rights as well as you. A failure to pay our balances at the Clearing House would be a fatal blow to our credit—equivalent to a protest! Our deposits would be withdrawn, and we could no longer keep your present discount line where it is, which we hope to do by a course of mutual indulgence with our dealers. There is no possible remedy for this state of things but to wait for the gradual maturity of our bills discounted. If you will bring me your paper some days hence, you will probably find us in better condition."

Mr. A. yields in a moment of cooler judgment. If the Cashier, however, had treated him with a sullen refusal, making no explanation, he would have gone away in a fit of anger, and his friendly relations with the bank might cease.

This may be called the *science of contact.* In a tight market, bank officers are every hour brought into collision with the most imposing interests of commerce in the hands of men unaccustomed to denial, whom it is very desirable to conciliate, and very easy at such times to offend. Instances are frequent in which the applicant has a large stake in the negotiation. His credit and continued solvency may be at risk. It may readily be imagined what arts of persuasion and earnest entreaty are then employed.

Messrs. B. C. D. and others who have been waiting impatiently for Mr. A. to finish his interview, successively present their claims. Each one withdraws the Cashier into a corner, or to his private room, and insists on the special character of his application. The failure of all who have preceded him does not convince the last one that his chance is hopeless. None will believe that the available resources of a bank can be so reduced as the Cashier represents, and the majority attribute his refusal to the timidity or the caprice, if not to some less creditable motive, of the officers and directors.

The Cashier is again seated at his table, preparing to resume an unfinished letter; but before he can concentrate his thoughts, the Specie Clerk comes in from the Clearing House and announces the result of the exchange:

"Debtor, sir, two hundred thousand dollars."

"What! Debtor again?"

"Yes, sir."

"Is that possible? Have you made no mistake, Joseph? I added more than that from the morning letters!"

"I am sorry to say it, sir, but it is certainly so, and our neighbors across the street are worse off than we are."

All other employment must give way before the indispensable matter of providing for the payment of the Clearing House debt. The President is surrounded by six or eight of his particular friends, who

The Cashier by the Button-Hole.

are endeavoring to find some cause for the sudden stricture of the market. One ascribes it to the excessive importation of dry-goods, consequent on a reduction of duties; another declares it is the competition of the railroad debt with commerce; another, that it is the natural consequence of extravagant living. The discussion is rather disorderly, and well adapted to spread excitement among the dealers who come in to transact business. They see that "the great merchants" are roused; and thus, from many banks, increased anxiety and agitation is propagated through the community.

The Cashier can have no assistance from the President under these circumstances; but leaves him to the brunt of importunity by the dealers while he goes out to seek aid from another bank. He may be so fortunate as to obtain it, and to be again at his desk in half an hour. Borrowing, however, brings no permanent relief. He gives a check for the amount, which will come in against the bank in the exchanges of the next day, and the debt recurs. How to provide for this, is a mental burden scarcely less engrossing than that which he has just discharged. There is but one source from which permanent improvement in the funds can be derived, and that is *the deposits.* If these should increase, the bank would experience immediate relief, but if they continue to fall, the debt of the bank increases from day to day, in spite of all temporary expedients. The anxiety that weighs on the mind of the bank officer in this extremity cannot be appreciated by the dealers. It ought to be a sufficient excuse for any apparent want of consideration for their personal embarrassment.

This state of affairs is in strong contrast with that which existed but a few days before. It is not only in the officers' department that a change has taken place. The number of persons who come into the bank, for one purpose or another, is quadrupled. They crowd and run against each other. Patience, and even civility, is overborne by the urgency of each man's errand. The most trifling circumstances provoke angry disputes between the dealers' clerks, and the book-keepers or tellers. A general excitement of manner is evident, and the shuffling of feet and the confusion of voices do not cease for an instant.

At the moment when the Cashier is again ready to resume his correspondence, a man enters the bank with a hurried step, and manifestly in a violent passion:

"Mr. Cashier, what kind of Tellers do you keep in your bank?"

"We mean that they shall be gentlemen, sir."

Mr. Kight finds it very difficult to control himself. He thrusts his bank-book before the Cashier, and points with trembling hand to an entry which shows that he had that morning made a deposit of fifteen hundred dollars.

"Do you see that, sir?"

The Cashier sees it.

"Well, sir—your Teller has refused to pay my check for that amount, notwithstanding the money is to my credit! He has sent it back to another bank, and my name is dishonored, sir! Isn't this

Mr. Kight up. "Do you see that, sir?"

a pretty tale, that a man's credit is to be ruined by a miserable teller who doesn't know his duty!"

"I think he knows his duty, Mr. Kight. You have probably made a mistake yourself."

The cool manner of the Cashier does not soothe his excited customer. He denies angrily that he has made any mistake, and attracts the notice of all the clerks by the violence of his language and his defiant air, as the two pass to the desk of the book-keeper to examine his account. The ledger shows that his balance was less than fifty dollars on the day before when he drew his check for fifteen hundred, and it is apparent that he had obtained the use of that much money one day in advance of his deposit. The process is well known to bank officers and clerks under the name of "kiting." It is often resorted to as a last expedient to raise funds, by parties who know better. Two parties who keep accounts in different banks may change checks, and each deposit that of the other, if their certification is not required; and then each may draw out the money. Mr. Kight may have supposed that his deposit of the following morning would be admitted to pay his check; but the Cashier explains to him that the exchange for the Clearing House is made up and dispatched before ten o'clock, so that funds coming in after that hour are necessarily unavailable until the next day. He might even go so far as to show him the very bills that he had deposited still unused in the drawer of the Receiving Teller; but Mr. Kight understands it. He now expresses his opinion that "it is rather small business for a bank with three millions of capital to return a dealer's check for fifteen hundred dollars when the money is actually in the bank, even if it can't be used for a single day."

"There is but one way for us to transact business, Mr. Kight, and that is, to pay checks when we have the deposit to pay with, and to refuse them when we have not."

He adds: "It is true, sir, that your check for fifteen hundred dollars would make no sensible difference in our general balance, but every overdraft goes into one sum in the Clearing House exchange, and the aggregate of overdrafts in this way has sometimes reached forty or fifty thousand dollars."

Mr. Kight's deposit is now available to him, since the Teller has received payment for the dishonored check from the bank to which he returned it. He requests that it may be certified, with the intent to redeposit it in the same channel as before, and so rub out the discredit which his good name has suffered in that quarter.

But at this moment a messenger from another bank presents a check drawn by Mr. Wing which Mr. Kight had deposited the day before. It is returned "not good," and Mr. Kight must pay it. This absorbs his deposit and leaves him with his own dishonored check in hand. The whole transaction is now fully exposed. Mr. Kight and Mr. Wing had exchanged checks, each trusting to make his account good by an early deposit on the following morning; but their plan was thwarted in both banks by the vigilance of the Paying Teller.

If the Teller, instead of returning Mr. Kight's

Mr. Kight Down.

check had charged it against the morning deposit, he would now have Mr. Wing's dishonored check on his hands without any means of securing its payment; and it might be a total loss to the bank.

The quarter of an hour given to this tedious explanation is not entirely thrown away, since it affords the Cashier a reason for closing Mr. Kight's account, and thus getting rid of a dangerous customer.

Intelligent dealers have occasionally contended that the true presentation of a check through the deposit channel, is at the moment when the exchanges are brought to the bank counter from the Clearing House; and that if the deposit is there by that time, it is all that could strictly be asked of them. But if required, would the check be *certified* by the bank on which it is drawn, *at or before three o'clock of the same day?* That is the test of right in the case. In fact, a check is paid to the holder at the moment that it is allowed in his account so that he can draw the money for it, no matter by what bank allowed. On Mr. Kight's process overdrafts might be propagated from day to day for any time or any amount, by persons without a dollar of capital.

Once more the Cashier returns to his desk. A new throng of disappointed dealers presses upon him. Mr. Tarbox is whispering confidentially in one ear, and Mr. Jones in the other. The Corresponding Clerk thrusts a score of drafts under his pen for indorsement. Dealers in manifest trepidation come in hastily, and finding him pre-occupied, go out again. A dozen or twenty wait in the lobby for a more favorable opportunity. One cries out from the doorway:

"Mr. Cashier, can you draw on Boston?"

"I'll ascertain sir.—Mr. Jones I will listen to you in a minute.—Mr. Tarbox, I must refer you to the President.—Mr. Crook, see if we can draw on Boston."

In answer to as many different questions which are spoken in a confidential tone, the Cashier answers aloud. "Yes, sir.—No, sir.—Out of the question.—By no means.—It must be paid, I can't help you"—and so forth.

Mr. Crook reports that the bank can draw on Boston for twenty-five thousand dollars.

"How much do you want, Mr. Bell? Did you say twenty thousand? Send us a certified check."

"Won't you take A 1 paper at ninety days?"

"No, sir."

A very confident-looking personage, who evidently thinks his claims are of superior consequence, walks directly to the Cashier, and lays down a bundle of stock securities. He communicates his business in a whisper, meets with a flat denial, and retires in a flush of anger.

Mr. Sweatem, of the long-established firm of Sweatem, Sore & Co., seizes the opportunity for which he has been watching an hour or more, to urge his particular necessities. Single words and parts of sentences only are heard, which indicate a decided difference of opinion between him and the Cashier. His expostulations might be rendered in a connected form, as follows:

"It will not do, Mr. Cashier, to cut down our line at present. We are all right, and doing a profitable

The Cashier in a State of Siege.

Mr. Sweatem convincing the Cashier that his affairs are in a very prosperou
condition.

business. I come to you as our last resource. We have tried other banks, and tried our friends all round, but everybody is hard up. We are nearly through our heavy payments. A few days more, and we shall be in smooth water. To be cut down now—I tell you it won't answer! We have offered at the Board four times in succession, and you have not given us a cent. Now, Mr. Cashier, there's reason in all things, you *must* give us this accommodation. We are entitled to it on every principle of right and justice."

To all this the Cashier answers: "I cannot, my dear sir, act in opposition to the Board of Directors;" and Mr. Sweatem retires discomfited.

It is now what may be called "high 'change" in the rooms of the President and Cashier. Both officers are beset with remonstrance and importunity. The attacking column lengthens and shortens, and disappears and comes again; and the tail lashes itself into an angry growl at the tardiness of the head. A stranger would suppose the bank to be in a state of general disorder, from the multitude of dealers at the different desks, and the incessant murmur of conversation.

Some of the applications for money must be granted notwithstanding the condition of the bank funds. There are dealers who have kept large balances, and ask loans for the first time. There are also current loans in a critical state which must be indulged to save the bank from loss. Seeing that some are successful in their applications, dealers take offence, and charge the officers with partiality.

"It is not true, sir, that your means are exhausted!

I have seen you discount paper for several of your favorites since I have been waiting.

"Those are special cases which we cannot refuse. If your account were as good as theirs without a cent of loan, we would discount for you too."

Greater freedom of expression is commonly indulged in by dealers in conversing with the Cashier than with the President, whose official dignity imposes more respect in tone and manner. The former therefore, is more likely to get the brunt of an outburst of personal irritation. He receives it however in *an official capacity*, and does not allow it to interrupt the general suavity of his intercourse. Mr. Boyle has tried persuasion in vain, and finally broken out into violent abuse of the bank.

"Damn your institution, sir! The only thing you do is to supply your directors and a few favorites with all the money they want! Public good indeed! Public good!! It's all damned nonsense!"

"Mr. Boyle, if you are not satisfied with what I have told you, go to the President. He is in his room, and happens just now to be alone."

Mr. Boyle takes off his hat, which he had not thought of before, and although his manner is not free from excitement, it is reduced by many degrees, so that he would hardly be identified as the same person.

"Mr. President, I have some most unquestionable securities here, amounting to twenty thousand dollars, on which I want a loan of twelve or fifteen for thirty days."

"My dear sir, you have come to the wrong shop. I'm *very* sorry!"

A bad Bank Statement. The Board adjourns " without discounting a dollar

"Mr. President, can't you squeeze out that much?"

"It would be a greater gratification to me than to you Mr. Boyle, if I could. You can hardly imagine the pressure that is on us now."

"But consider Mr. President, what a humiliating extremity this is! Here are securities just as good as United States stock! I could have sold them at a hundred and twenty only thirty days ago and now they would hardly bring par! I want an advance of but little more than fifty per cent on them—the paltry sum of twelve thousand dollars; and I am told by my bank that it can give me no help with its capital of five millions! What am I to do, sir?"

"My friend, with all my heart I wish I could assist you. It gives me pain when merchants of your high standing in the community appeal to me in this manner, and the more because I am helpless. Surely you can borrow from some source on that class of securities!"

"No, sir. I believe there is not a bank in the city that is not very much in the same condition as you are. I *must*," says Mr. Boyle with great emphasis, throwing his securities upon the table, "Mr. President, I MUST have five thousand dollars this day if it is only till to-morrow."

"Wait a moment, sir. I'll consult the Cashier."

The consultation may result in giving Mr. Boyle the privilege of drawing for five thousand dollars as a loan payable on demand, or at one day's notice. He gladly accepts it, though it leaves him at best in the uncertainty that a condemned man feels when his hanging is put off for a few days. His other obligations continue to mature, and the notice may come on the top of them when they are of themselves as much as he can bear. This kind of "relief" is very deceptive. It is bad policy both for the bank and the merchant. The former may be forced to sell the securities in a depreciated market, and the loss sustained by the latter is so much out of his capital at the moment when he most needs it.

Bank officers are not always insensible to alarm when respectable merchants, failing in their best endeavors, are driven into a corner and assume an air of desperation. They know all the danger that hangs over the market. Credit is prodigiously expanded; everything in a state of extreme tension; the public excitement is wrought up to a high pitch of apprehension, and there needs but a single failure of a "great house" to explode the "mighty bubble!" Who knows that it is a bubble? Who knows that the highest point of the pressure is not reached to-day, and that to-morrow the waters will not begin to subside? And then, gradually, things fall into their old channels, confidence revives, and it is proved that there was no bubble to burst after all! Now if the leading and rich commission or importing house of Cottonade, Fabriqué & Co., can only get through this last day of the pressure, the credit of the forty jobbing merchants whom they have been compelled to assist will remain untarnished, and payments will go on as usual; but if they fail, the forty will fail, and the forty have each on an average not less than two hundred thousand dollars of bills payable out, making eignt millions scattered through the various banks, which instead of being paid, will go to protest and drag on for many months in a course of troublesome liquidation. If the whole picture were painted on canvas, it could not be plainer than it is to the President and Cashier as they confer together on the propriety of lending twenty thousand dollars to Mr. Fabriqué, who sits in an inner room waiting for their decision.

"I don't see how we can safely do it?" says the President, shaking his head, "and yet it will have a terrible effect on the market!"

"And his securities are of the highest class too!"

"Yes, yes—the very best. If these are not safe there is nothing safe in the market."

"Mr. Fabriqué is well nigh desperate. I wish we *could* devise some way to help him!"

"So do I, with all my heart. But we have run behind at the Clearing House for several days in succession, and we have every prospect of doing so again!"

The Cashier being the younger man, has naturally more energy of feeling than the President. He trusts that they "may not be so unfortunate." Less gloomy thoughts float in his mind. He catches at contingencies which are too remote for the President to appreciate. "Let us risk it!" he proposes with a sudden renewal of hope and courage "This is too important a house to be allowed to go down in an hour. We have a large amount of bills depending on their customers being kept up, and if they lose their main prop—"

"True, true! But it will be the same to-morrow. We would only be getting deeper and not save them at last!"

"Mr. Fabriqué assures me that this loan will put them through; and to tell you the truth, Mr. President, I fear the consequences of denial more than I do the Clearing house. He will make no other effort to-day!"

"Well, Mr. Cashier, if you think you can manage the Clearing House debt to-morrow, I will consent."

The house of Cottonade, Fabriqué & Co. may, in such a case, be the key-stone of the arch by which the whole market is sustained. And after the danger has passed away, no one is conscious that it was kept in its place by a single bank cashier who had overcome the "conservative" counsels of his president.

An act of courage begun, inspires the mind with *more* courage, even if the consequences of it are yet in the future and very doubtful, especially when a sense of justice is at the bottom of it. Both President and Cashier now agree that it would have been *a great commercial fault* to let the house go down, and their fears of to-morrow are measurably lightened.

The Cashier is frequently applied to by the clerks for instruction in disputed matters, and by dealers who have real or imaginary causes of complaint. The general book-keeper reports several country banks overdrawn perhaps a hundred thousand dollars; whence he concludes there must be a failure of remittances or miscarriage of letters, or special understanding with the officers. The Cashier has given no authority to overdraw, and the telegraph is employed to have the matter explained. It is found that letters are missing; and the Porter is dispatched to the Post Office, where he finds them just returned from another bank to which they had been inadvertently delivered.

"Mr. Cashier, why can't I have my collection paper credited when it is past due?" says a petulant dealer, exhibiting his note-book.

"You can, sir."

"Well, I don't get it! Here's a note of twelve hundred dollars due at Mobile a week ago, and another of sixteen hundred at Baltimore which was paid the day before yesterday; and all the satisfaction I can get out of your book-keeper is that he supposes they are not heard from. I wish I could be saved this annoyance of having to run to the bank every day to keep your books straight!"

"The clerk is right, Mr. Krabb. We have no advice of the notes, but I think we should get it by to-day's Southern mail. Walk in, sir. Here is the Porter with the letters now."

The Cashier finds a notice of protest in both cases, which he hands over to Mr. Krabb, who vents some additional bitterness on banks generally, as if they were responsible for his misfortunes. It is often ludicrous to witness the manner in which people of a certain temper seem to derive the greatest comfort, when their affairs go wrong, in "blowing up the bank."

Mr. Krabb gives place to a complainant whose country checks have been refused on deposit by the Receiving Teller, for which on inquiry the Cashier finds there was ample ground. Then follows, from a profitable dealer who cannot be turned aside, an application for a clerkship on behalf of a young relative whose qualifications and even genealogy must be stated at length, notwithstanding the assurance that there is no vacancy, and none in prospect. An officer of a distant corresponding bank consumes an hour in talking about the details of his account. A country stockholder is disturbed about the misfortunes of trade, and " drops in " to have his fears quieted; another to ask advice whether it is not a good time to sell or to purchase stock. The interruptions are endless, often for trifling cause, and often vexatious. This is the common experience of the Cashier of an active city bank.

Whilst the Cashier has been thus occupied, his assistant or corresponding clerk has prepared most of the outgoing correspondence for the day, consisting of acknowledgments, checks and notes to be forwarded to other banks for collection, the return of protested paper, and other formal matters.

The Southern mail brings a new batch of letters from Philadelphia, Baltimore, Charleston, Mobile, New Orleans, and elsewhere. Those which require his particular attention are separated from the rest, and he disposes of them as he finds opportunity. During the last hour before three o'clock he is liable to increased pressure and annoyance from dealers, according to the condition of the market.

The banking business of New York is generally active throughout the year. A short term of relaxation occurs in midsummer, but it bears no proportion to the relaxation in trade. The period immediately following the panic of 1857 was one of unprecedented prostration, and wholly exceptional. For the previous ten or fifteen years, there was probably not more than an average of a single month in the year when the absence of either the President or Cashier would not have devolved an inconvenient burden on the other.

What has been said of the personal character and influence of the President is in every way equally applicable to the Cashier. There is perhaps more necessity on his part for the exercise of patience and forbearance, for the reason that the dignity and public estimation of the higher office secures it against many annoyances of the smaller accounts.

To gain confidence, the bank officer must deserve confidence. He must possess the real qualities of character that call it forth. Many of the circumstances of trade are of a kind that tend to weaken and corrupt the moral sense. When men are sorely pressed for the want of money, they find some person with whom to exchange notes—commonly one in like condition; and thus a fictitious obligation is created. The ebb tides of commerce are always floating downwards men who, yesterday, were floating up. There are solvent merchants always drifting towards insolvency. In their efforts to stem the current, they resort to every possible expedient—to speculation in land, or in guano companies—to gambling at the Stock Board, or at the faro table. The bank records

contain many instances of men suddenly breaking down after a long and successful career, with scarcely a vestige of property left unmortgaged. These histories are all freshened up in the memory of the bank officer, when the money-market becomes tight and dangerous. They excite his distrust, and he scrutinizes notes and securities, perhaps with undue severity, while the needy applicant for money overrates their value, and strives to conceal the weak points of his business.

Why treat with such cases on any terms? Why not discard them at once?—Because the parties are already indebted to the bank, and it is the duty of the officer to extend indulgence where the debt may be saved.

The Cashier is necessarily in frequent contact with the different clerks in the bank, and a description of many current incidents of his office will be embraced in an account of their duties.

Although it is not possible for him to maintain a personal supervision of all the books of a bank in detail, it is his duty to keep them in constant general review. In the first place, it is indispensable that he should have a perfect acquaintance with the theory of the accounts, so that when his eye falls on any page he shall comprehend it immediately, whether it consists of a mere record of the notes lodged for collection, the postings of an individual account in the Ledger, the entries on the Paying Teller's Cash-book, or anything else. One of the principal peculiarities of bank accounts is the daily transfer of original records by many different persons to different books, and their final concentration in one book which furnishes the proof of the whole. This includes many long and laborious additions which grow so rapidly into vast accumulations and various dependence, as to defy the vigilance of any one person. The Cashier cannot make the additions, but he can in a few minutes satisfy himself of the accuracy of transfers to the general proof. He is not expected to examine the separate accounts of a ledger of fifteen hundred pages, but he can in an instant compare the footing of its proof-sheet with the general ledger. If he wants to test a particular point in any part of the system, he knows what books and accounts to refer to without the aid of the clerks themselves, and how to ask them for explanation if he sees cause for it. To his practiced eye, a single glance is enough to inform him whether a ledger is properly kept or neglected. He can examine it as rapidly as he can turn over its leaves. The observation for five minutes, of the manner in which a clerk transacts his duties, is enough to satisfy him of his competency. It may readily be conceived that a Cashier so skilled shall exert a very effectual supervision over a company of clerks by his mere presence; and on the other hand, it is apparent that one who is deficient in such knowledge of accounts may be blinded to any extent of error and imposition.

The Cashier has it in his power to commit fraud without limit, and to conceal it for a time, in spite of all the vigilance of the President, clerks, and directors. By collusion with others, and especially with the Paying Teller, it is difficult to say what he might not do. A case like the following occurred within a few years in the State of New York.

The Cashier of a bank with a capital of four hundred thousand dollars became interested in a railroad, and was appointed its treasurer. In the course of the negotiations and disbursements which he carried on, the road became indebted to the bank by overdraft. To conceal this from the President, who was a stern disciplinarian and a near connection of the Cashier, the latter obtained credit from a corresponding bank by the re-discount of bills receivable which had been forwarded to it for collection. This involved the necessity of falsifying the accounts, so that the collection paper should appear as part of the assets of the bank, after it had been virtually sold to another institution. Thus was established a threefold fraud—first, by the overdraft, second by forgery of records, third, by breach of confidence with his superior officer. The Cashier had been associated with the President for twenty years, and during that time was faithful and efficient. The family connection existing between them, served most effectually to aid him in a system of concealment, which resulted before discovery in the embezzlement of two hundred and fifty thousand dollars.

As the embezzlement grew, it caused a corresponding depression of the discount line of the bank, which constantly passed under the eye of the President. He was deceived by a fictitious statement of bills discounted, which was kept up continuously as the case required. The accounts of the bank with its corresponding banks in other cities were overdrawn; post-dated certificates of deposit were issued, and being illegal, they were kept in negotiation by outside confederates, and in surreptitious channels; the unemployed circulating notes of the bank were secretly hypothecated for loans; the absorption of its resources in one direction necessarily withdrew accommodations from the regular dealers, and the consequent decline of deposits was concealed by the withholding of individual checks and by false ledger entries; drafts on other cities of which no entries were made were sold, and the proceeds abstracted; to provide against the discovery of false additions where a page was likely to be examined, the component entries were falsified, and after the examination was made, the falsifications were erased; these, with many other processes, were kept up for a year and a half without exciting the suspicion of the President. Five successive quarterly statements were sworn to, and forwarded to the Bank Superintendent at Albany, in which the overdrafts were stated, in four of them at less than two thousand dollars, when they were in fact from one hundred to one hundred and seventy thousand dollars, and in the fifth at ten thousand, when they exceeded two hundred thousand dollars. The amount of illegal certificates and post-dated checks negotiated within the time named, was more than a million of dollars.

During the entire period of this systematic embezzlement, the President of the bank assisted in the daily management of its affairs, and was almost hourly in contact with the Cashier and the clerks. He was an experienced banker, both in theory and practice, and gave perhaps more attention to the details of the business than is usual for bank presidents who are associated with active and skillful cashiers. It seems hardly credible that such various and extensive frauds could be carried on so long, without the exposure of some weak point. But it is explained by the collusion of clerks, and by the completeness of the watch that was secretly kept upon all his movements. His daily calls at the Post Office were anticipated by the Cashier, who intercepted all letters which would excite suspicion, and there were many written to him for this express purpose. The Post Office clerk was bribed to withhold any that might come at an unusual time. In fact, the President was dogged and blinded at every step and hour of his existence, as any other man would have been in the same position. Any ordinary fraud would have transpired through an honest clerk, but the clerk was not honest. No avenue was left open by which suspicion could enter.

Such an extraordinary case as this is not necessary to prove to an experienced banker, the utter impossibility of preventing fraud by any combination of sagacity, watchfulness, and supervision. There is perhaps no record of a bank fraud extant of which the perpetrator was not honest *yesterday*. The man who has been faithful for twenty years is faithless on the next day. What is to prevent it?

CHAPTER IV.

THE PAYING TELLER.

The Paying Teller of a bank stands at the head of the clerks' department, and next in the usual order of promotion to the Cashier. He is frequently called also, the First Teller.

His duty, as signified by his title, is to pay out money. No other clerk—not even the President or Cashier—interferes with this function.

The nature of the banking business calls for direct individual responsibility in the clerk. Money occupies but little space and is easily abstracted. The opportunities of fraud are frequent and beyond the reach of vigilance. Each clerk is therefore required to give bonds for his integrity; and it is necessary in the division of labor to assign specific duties, that one may not be liable to suffer for the default of another.

The Paying Teller gives bonds, according to the magnitude of the trust confided to him, to the extent of ten or twenty thousand dollars. The latter sum is the highest required by any of our city banks. It is usual to divide this between several persons, the guarantee being considered stronger in a moral point of view; and in case of default by the Teller it is redeemable with less hardship than it would be if the entire obligation rested on one. The bondsmen must be

5*

men of established character and pecuniary ability. Their names are submitted to the Board of Directors, or to a committee of which the President is mostly chairman. If they are not satisfactory, the Teller must procure others.

A Director is not allowed to be bondsman for a clerk in the same bank, nor one officer for another, as such an obligation might be used to obtain an undue influence over the favored person. A book-keeper might hesitate to expose irregularities in the account of a director to whom he was partially indebted for his salary.

The use of bonds as a guarantee of integrity has been questioned, because they will not be violated by honest, nor respected by dishonest men; and they are apt to be regarded as formal instruments, merely to answer a by-law or to maintain an old custom. There are, however, indications in their requirement which could not safely be dispensed with. The ability of a person to find security for so large a sum as twenty thousand dollars, is a strong proof of his good repute, which is further attested by the character of the guarantors. They are his commercial godfathers. They cannot be banished from his memory when temptation knocks at the elbow. They must frequently cross his footsteps on his first wanderings from the path of rectitude.

The most responsible and critical service in the bank is that which embraces the custody and disbursement of its funds. This is assigned to the Paying Teller. There is some incidental exception in the custody, to be hereafter noticed.

The amount of money in his keeping may be several millions of dollars, consisting of coin, bullion, bank bills, stocks, bonds, and other documents. There are generally three or four apartments in the vault, of which one is appropriated to his exclusive use. He holds the key, locks and unlocks it in person, goes to it during business hours at discretion, unattended, and is the sole trustee of its contents. He is jealous of the charge, and shares it with nobody. He is sensible that the key of his vault is also the key of his character, and he will not give it to the keeping of another for an instant—not even to the President or Cashier, without satisfactory explanation. If they should officially require him to surrender it, distrust would be implied, or perhaps dismissal from office.

On the other hand, there are possible circumstances under which a Teller, conscious of his own rectitude, would refuse to deliver his key even to his superior officers. The terms of his bond make him contingently independent of them. A suspicion that they were in collusion for dishonest purposes would not only justify such refusal, but make it an imperative duty. Besides, his bondsmen have legal rights in the premises which might be compromised by allowing the custody of his vault to pass into other hands. His own rights also, and his character, might be involved by the unconditional surrender of his key on any demand.

Again, if the Paying Teller, without obvious cause, such as sickness or necessary absence, should tender the custody of his key for a single night to the President or Cashier, or to another clerk, it would be declined. The tender might be made for the express purpose of creating a divided or doubtful responsibility for a default.

The statement of these details is necessary to show the exact relation of the Paying Teller to his trust. There is no apparent obstacle to his abuse of it, nor are the means of detection so immediate as to prevent escape. Neither would his arrest necessarily insure the recovery of money abstracted, which might greatly exceed the amount of his bonds. His position is more vulnerable than any other in the bank. It is the only one that is out of the reach of daily observation by other clerks, and in which fraud may be practiced without collusion or risk of immediate discovery. Nor does it seem possible to devise any method of supervision to prevent abuse, or adequate indemnity to cover it.

This close custody of the vault does not, however, limit the right of the officers to enforce the most rigid examination of its contents. They may require him, in their presence, to weigh every bag of gold, count the silver and bank bills, and test the accuracy thereof by his books, to their full satisfaction. Or they may call in the aid of other clerks to perform this service. It is impossible that he should know at what time the officers, or a committee of the directors, may wait on him to make the examination. His accounts must therefore be kept in such order as to stand the test.

The necessary qualifications of a clerk in this post can be better understood by following him through his daily routine, than by any other mode of description.

The plan of his accounts is entirely simple. He has a certain amount of cash on hand from which to pay checks. The amount of the latter subtracted from the former must agree with the remaining balance. The only modification of this process is the debit and credit of the exchanges through the Clearing House.

The Paying Teller reaches the bank about nine o'clock in the morning. He unlocks his vault in person, and the Porter assists in carrying to his desk the trunks and trays containing as much money in bank bills and coin as he will be likely to want during the day. He locks the vault, and retains the key in his personal care.

The bills of the issuing banks are technically distinguished from those of other banks by the name of "Office Notes." The money-drawer is divided into boxes, in which the different denominations are distributed. To facilitate payments, the smaller denominations are usually kept counted in packets of fifty bills each. A packet of fives contains two hundred and fifty dollars; a packet of tens, five hundred dollars, and a packet of twenties, one thousand dollars. The bills below five (consisting of threes, twos, and ones) are generally kept in packets of fifty dollars gross, and mixed together for the convenience of dealers. A check for the precise amount of any of these packets, is paid in an instant without recounting the bills. For intermediate amounts the packets are opened, and they must of course be recounted.

The theory of the bank accounts requires that all

payments of money must be made by one Teller. The result is, that all money received must appear on his books.* The *Exchange* sent to the Clearing House is money paid out, and it must therefore pass through the accounts of the Paying Teller. The particular description of this exchange comes appropriately under the head of *the receiving department* of the bank, where it originates. It is sufficient here to state, that it is composed of the checks and bills on other banks taken in deposit, and each day sent in for redemption at the Clearing House counter. It is officially delivered in a prepared state to the Paying Teller by the Receiving Tellers, on each morning following its receipt. The former takes cognizance of it only in the aggregate, responsibility for its accuracy in detail resting on those by whom it is prepared.

To dispatch this Exchange to the Clearing House is the first duty of the Paying Teller every morning. This is generally done by half past nine o'clock; and at ten precisely, the Teller opens his little gate in the counter railing, and is ready for the current business of the day.

The payment of checks begins immediately. A stranger presents one for five hundred dollars, with a request for certain denominations of bills. He wants "two hundred dollars in twenties, one hundred and fifty in fives, and the balance in ones, twos, and threes."

---

* There is an accidental modification of this rule, which will be found explained elsewhere.

Here is a requirement for rapidity and accuracy quite above mediocrity. The Teller must pass through his hands forty single bank bills and three packets.

Another applicant wants "five hundred dollars in twenties, two hundred in tens, one hundred and fifty in fives, and forty in smaller bills." This will require the counting of more than one hundred bank notes.

These are the simplest transactions of the desk; yet, following rapidly in succession, they call for presence of mind, precise tact, and no common skill in mental arithmetic.

The debit Exchange from the Clearing House is brought in by the Porter about half past ten o'clock; and although the chief labor of its examination devolves on an assistant, the Paying Teller will not pass it into his accounts until satisfied by personal revision that it is correct. It amounts frequently to a million of dollars or more,* consisting mostly of the checks of dealers. The signature, indorsement, and other peculiarities of each, must be scrutinized before it is charged to the drawer. This examination is protracted from one to two hours, subject to the current accidents of the business. It is dropped on the instant, remitted for two or five minutes, resumed, immediately dropped again, and again resumed, with constant interruptions.

Some of the large banks have made the receipt and examination of the Clearing House Exchange the

* In some of the larger banks, more than two millions.

work of a separate department, as a better guarantee against mistakes.

"Will you certify that, sir?" It is a check for thirty thousand dollars, drawn by Slater & Co. They have not half that sum on deposit in the bank, but usage justifies the certification on certain terms, of which the Teller takes instant cognizance from memory. These relate to the capital, manner of business, character of the men, and other circumstances which may make it safe for the bank to pay checks in advance of the deposit.

"Are Slater and Co. sufficiently reliable to justify my loaning them thirty thousand dollars without special security? May I trust their ability and honor to restore their account before three o'clock?"

This is one of the most interesting and critical emergencies of the Paying Teller's desk. If he should refuse the certification, the credit of Slater & Co. would be shocked as with an electric discharge. Even if he holds it in suspense an instant, as though a doubt troubled his mind, the doubt is communicated to the owner of the check and is reflected against the drawers. He certifies it without hesitation. This is the best possible proof of the high standing of a dealer with his bank.

The discretion of the Teller in certifying checks is for the most part independent of the superior officers, and they are averse to interfering with it. In doubtful cases, he refers to them for special instruction. Dealers apply to them also to reverse his judgment, though not often with success. Either of them would be likely to answer—"the Teller understands his business better than I do." Such is the influence acquired by a competent and judicious clerk in this post, that he obtains a degree of respect from the customers of the bank little less than is accorded to the President or Cashier.

The Paying Teller alone is authorized to certify checks. His name written across them, ordinarily on the face, pledges the bank to pay them when subsequently returned through the exchanges or otherwise, if the indorsements are correct. Any city bank will receive on deposit certified checks on other banks in good standing, without reference to the drawers, and pay out its own bills, or gold, for drafts against such deposits.

Under the old special charters, our banks were allowed to issue currency to twice the amount of their capital stock, and bills of the higher denominations of one, five, and ten thousand dollars were in common use. Checks were then mostly paid in bank bills, and certification was rather exceptional. But since the enactment of the General Banking Law in 1838, the old charters have gradually expired, and their circulation has been withdrawn. There is no fact that better indicates the improved character of our banking system, than its diminished paper issues. The old laws would give to our present city capital an issue of more than one hundred and twenty millions of dollars, whereas we have now (in 1858) less than the one-tenth part of this sum registered, and less than the one-fifteenth part in actual circulation. The result of this decrease of bank currency is that business is transacted mostly by checks. In an average market the daily exchanges of the Clearing House alone are near twenty-five millions of dollars, and our entire city circulation is but seven millions, which is principally absorbed in the retail trade. The amount of bank bills redeemed daily through the exchanges does not average over two or three hundred thousand dollars; the balance consists of the checks of individuals, and of bank checks on each other.

Certified checks are mostly returned in the debit exchange of the following day, through the Clearing House. They are used either for deposit, or to pay notes in other banks than that on which they are drawn. Being of nearly equal credibility with bank drafts, they are used also in remittance to distant parts of the country, in which case they do not appear for redemption for several days. They are, however, charged to the drawers immediately, certification being equivalent to payment. The Paying Teller's record of certified checks is a *fac simile* of the Receiving Teller's deposit book in its rulings, extension columns, postings, and method of proof—the one being a *credit*, and the other a *debit* entry to the dealer. See example on page 115.

This manner of posting certifications is of recent origin. The *certification check list* is a new book not yet generally adopted in our city banks. The aggregate is posted to *Certification Account*, which balances the separate charges to individuals. When the checks are finally redeemed, they are carried to the debit of this account, which thus always shows the balance of certified checks remaining out. This,

CERTIFICATION CHECK LIST.

			A to F.		G to L.		M to R.		S to Z.	
	$	c.	$	c.	$	c.	$	c.	$	c.
Slater & Co.	30,000								30,000	
Jno. Adams	5,000		5,000							
William Gordon	500				500					
E. West & Co.	10,000								10,000	
Jno. Rogers	1,000						1,000			
Brown & Green	1,850	75	1,850	75						
Green & Brown	1,400	50			1,400	50				
Norton & Co.	1,250						1,250			
King & Brothers	15,000				15,000					
Carpenter & Wood	6,000		6,000							
Wood & Carpenter	4,875								4,875	
Joseph Benton	1,240	31	1,240	31						
E. Denny	10,500		10,500							
Oakley & Ford	975						975			
Gray & Co.	250	40			250	40				
John Porter	195	73					195	73		
	90,037	69	24,591	06	17,150	90	3,420	73	44,875	
A to F.									24,591	06
G to L.									17,150	90
M to R.									3,420	73
Proof.									90,037	69

E. S.

or some equivalent plan, is indispensable to prevent fraud or error by the duplication of checks. On the old plan, the dealer's ledger account was not actually charged with certified checks until they were returned. They might be in transit long enough for the memory of the Teller and the Book-keeper to become dim, or for other transactions to throw them out of sight. A pencil memorandum on the Ledger (a usual method of noting them) might easily be effaced by accident or design. In fact, it was such abuse and accident that led to the adoption of the present plan of posting certifications.

The Teller has resumed the examination of the Exchange checks, after certifying that of Slater & Co. Those which are defective, or of doubtful character in any respect, are laid aside for more particular inspection; the immediate pressure being to charge the mass of them to their respective accounts in the Ledger; for these are liable to be drawn against continuously, and it is important to know their actual condition.

Meanwhile, the current transactions of the business are going on. The presentation of checks at the counter is more frequent as the day advances, and some require correction or explanation. One is not indorsed, or improperly indorsed. Another is post-dated. The date of another has been altered, and the Teller must be satisfied whether honestly or not. Another is drawn against an uncertain account, and is referred to the Book-keeper to be assured correct before payment. These various accidents are modified by the disposition of the holder of the check. A crabbed customer will block access to the Teller's gate, contesting his right to be paid in spite of informalities, until six or ten new comers crowd behind him and become impatient of delay. Being unacquainted with the exact liabilities of a bank, and the various tricks attempted on the Teller, they often regard his precautions as mere "stickling" at trifles.

Of what consequence is it if a check drawn to the order of John C. Brown is indorsed John Brown? The consequence might be the repudiation of the payment by the dealer, and loss of the whole amount by the bank. There is as much difference between these two names, legally and in bank usage, as between the names of John C. Brown and Abel Dodge. Yet, if the Teller knows that John Brown is the man to whom the money was designed to be paid by the drawer, he might pass over so slight a discrepancy as the omission of the letter C. And the drawer could not then avail himself of such discrepancy to dispute the rightfulness of the payment.

Of what consequence is it if a post-date is altered to an anterior date? It does not make the signature less genuine, nor does the dealer pay more than he has promised!

No. But a check paid before due is not chargeable to the dealer until the true date transpires. He might withdraw his balance meanwhile, and fail to provide for it subsequently, thus throwing the loss on the bank. It is therefore hazardous to admit of dates that have undergone any apparent alteration.

The post-dating of checks is regarded by bank officers as a commercial misdemeanor. A dealer who persists in the practice after being warned of its impropriety, would lose credit, and probably receive notice to withdraw his account.

There are ordinarily some checks in the Exchange that are rejected for want of funds, or other cause. These are returned to the sending banks by a messenger, who brings back to the Teller the bank bills or coin. The bank returning them has a right to demand gold, since it has paid gold for them in the Clearing House settlement.

Unfortunately, the same condition of the market that makes it difficult for the banks to maintain a creditable average of specie for the weekly statement, is fruitful in overdrafts; and the reclamations in gold are sometimes large—reaching many thousand dollars.

All the checks that pass the Teller's examination are given to a clerk for entry on his Check List, whence they are charged to their respective accounts in the Ledger. The bank bills, and the amount received for reclamations, go into his general cash. The Clearing House Exchange is then wholly incorporated in his accounts.

THE PAYMENT OF CHECKS.

There are three facts of which the Teller must take special cognizance in the payment of checks. *First*, Is the signature genuine? *Second*, Is the account of the drawer good? *Third*, Is the person who presents the check entitled to receive the money. Generally, the last occurs only when indorsements are to be verified; although an accomplished Teller never loses sight of it, even when checks are drawn payable to the bearer. Forged checks are almost uniformly so drawn.

There are many points of exposure under each of the three heads named. First, of the signature:

The tricks of forgery are so ingenious as to constitute a standing terror to banks; and so loose are the habits of many merchants in the custody and writing of checks, that the temptation to try experiments in this direction is frequently presented.

Check-books are left open on the desk within sight of casual and unknown visitors. They might be abstracted for half an hour—long enough to give the forger some of the most material points of success: the style of writing, the color of the ink, the number next, or near in order, and above all, a leaf of blank checks with the name of the merchant engraved on the end.

"There's no danger in our office. Somebody is always there. Our name was never forged yet. And besides, if it should be, the loss won't be ours. That's the bank's look-out."

The last suggestion is probably not the least influential. If the Teller pays a forged check, the bank, and not the merchant, is the loser. And so a careless security on the part of dealers opens the door and invites the forger to come in.

Instead of allowing his check-book to be as public as a newspaper, the merchant should guard it with the same care that he does his cash-box or his bills receivable.

The Signature-Book contains the autograph signature of every dealer in the bank, in alphabetical order, so that the Teller may compare a suspicious signature with the original—an hourly necessity, in consequence of the dissimilarity of writing by the same hand at different times. The first thing required of a new customer is, to write his name and residence in this book; and if a stranger, the name of the person by whom he is introduced. The signature of a firm is written by each member, with his individual name opposite. The names of foreign correspondents are often cut from letters and pasted on the page.

There is nothing in bank history more remarkable than the unfrequent and comparatively trifling loss by forged signatures. It would seem almost miraculous to a spectator standing by the counter of one of our active city banks, to witness the rapidity with which the Teller pays checks (often at the rate of three in a minute), whilst at the same time he is subject to perpetual interruptions from within and without. At the end of the day, he has paid from four to six hundred checks amounting to more than a million of dollars—a large proportion to strangers. In the fifty-three city banks, during the same six hours, there have been paid from fifteen to twenty thousand checks, covering thirty millions of dollars—and not one forged signature! The records of the Clearing House show that the amount of payments for a year through that channel has reached the prodigious aggregate of seven thousand millions of dollars.

Another large amount, not represented in the exchanges, is paid over the counters—making a grand total of probably eight thousand millions in three hundred days; and yet it is seldom that the community is startled by an announcement that a forged check of any impŏrtance has slipped through the hands of the paying Teller in our city banks!

It is doubtless to the terrors of the law, partly, that banks are indebted for this fortunate immunity. But these are operative mostly on a single instant of time —when the check is presented. That passed, the forger is comparatively safe. He may set rewards and telegraphs at defiance. It is, therefore, the skill and discernment of the Teller, first and last, that keeps the forger at a respectful distance—skill, not only in detecting false signatures, but in reading men at sight by the most obscure of all characters written upon the manner, and covered by practiced dissemblance, more quickly than you would read Roman capitals. The value to the bank of this detective faculty can hardly be exaggerated.

Again, the forger seldom appears in person at the counter. He employs, to draw the money, an innocent agent, who will exhibit none of the signs of conscious guilt. The teller is alive to this hazard, and questions strangers in such a manner as to dispel or confirm his apprehensions.

"Do you wish to pay this money out for wages in the city?" Or,

"Is this for your own use sir?"

"No, sir; I am drawing it for another."

"Who?"

"For a stranger, who requested it?"

"Where is the stranger?"

The answer would make it clear whether there is ground for suspicion. An innocent person would answer promptly, and betray no symptoms of fear. The forger or an accomplice would fly at once.

The time chosen by the forger to present checks is generally between two and three o'clock, when the counter is crowded by applicants, and the Teller is obliged to pay as quickly as possible. He has a choice of days also, preferring Saturday or the day before holidays, when the business of two or more days is crowded into one. On these "double days" the vigilance of the Teller is particularly roused, and it is not unusual for the President or Cashier to give him a passing admonition to "look out for forged checks."

The researches of the forger have been carried so far as to discover that the fourth of the month, and especially of certain months, as of March, October, and November, is what bankers call "a heavy day," and is more favorable for his tricks than most others.

Confidential marks independent of the signature have sometimes been agreed upon between the merchant and the Teller, as a further aid to the latter in distinguishing the genuineness of checks—such as a pin hole in a certain letter, or the omission of a usual feature in writing; but these distract attention from the more essential points to be guarded, and if discovered by the forger, would greatly improve his chances of success. One of his first steps is, to obtain a genuine check, and subject it to microscopic examination. The following instance, which came under the immediate notice of the writer, shows how ingeniously this is sometimes done.

A stranger made a small purchase at a produce store after the banks were closed for the day, and tendered in payment a genuine bill of one hundred dollars. The merchant having deposited all his money, could not return the difference, which was over ninety dollars. Neither could he get the bill changed by his neighbors. The stranger, seeing the difficulty, said carelessly:

"No matter, sir, about bank bills. Give me your check for the difference.

It was given without hesitation.

On the following morning, it was paid at the counter of the bank; and immediately after, another check for six hundred dollars with the same signature was presented by a boy. There were no appearances of irregularity in the latter, but the intuitive precaution of the Teller against fraud suggested the question, suddenly and sharply spoken:

"Where did you get this?"

"A man gave it to me."

"What man?"

"At the corner."

The boy took instant alarm, and escaped before the Porter could be called to intercept him.

The check was a forgery. It had been traced over glass from the genuine signature, as became evident when the two were applied together.

Unsuspecting boys are sometimes induced by the promise of a dollar or two to present a forged check, while the rogue lies in waiting. In such a case, the money has not unfrequently been paid, the boy followed, and his employer arrested in the act of receiving it.

The forger works in the dark. He has ample time to prepare every circumstance that can favor his purpose, and to study all the contingencies of failure.

The following case shows how one bank may be used to facilitate fraud on another. It will also enforce what has been said on the proper care of checks.

A leaf of blank forms was stolen from the check-book of a wealthy merchant who was a director in one of our city banks. A small business transaction was then contrived by which a full genuine check was obtained.

The forger might now practice on the signature at pleasure. When satisfied that he could produce a *fac simile* check, he filled up one of the stolen forms with an odd sum under three thousand dollars, and presented it at the bank. To avoid suspicion, that might be excited by so large a check if drawn payable to the bearer, he made it payable to his own order in an assumed name, and requested the Teller to certify it, saying, that the indorsement would be guaranteed by the bank in which he intended to deposit it. The deliberation and coolness with which he referred to the manner of satisfying the rule of the bank with respect to indorsements, and his possession of the auxiliary points of number, apparent consecutiveness with previous checks, and especially the check itself with the name of the merchant engraved on the end, procured him the genuine certification of the Teller without suspicion.

He then opened an account in another city bank, using the name of a well-known Cashier in Albany as introductory to the officers, and exhibiting the check, the certification of which vouched for the signature. He indorsed it in their presence; and thus every formal requisition in bank practice was complied with.

There was now no obstacle to his drawing his own checks against the deposit, which he did for the entire amount within an hour; and although some suspicion was excited by this summary use of the whole, it was allayed again by the unquestionable genuineness of the certification.

This forgery remained undiscovered for a fortnight; and was brought to light only by the apparent overdraft of the merchant's account, which led to a comparison of his check-book with the bank ledger. The difference being the exact amount of the fraudulent check, it was easily detected.

The overdraft of an ordinarily well-kept account raises an immediate presumption of error or forgery. Either a deposit may have been omitted, or a check wrongly paid. The book-keeper sends for the dealer's bank-book, balances it, and returns the checks cancelled, in which process the discrepancy is explained. It is by no means improbable, however, that forged checks sometimes elude detection both by Teller and dealer, in which case the latter is the loser. In neither of the instances given was the dealer himself able to distinguish the fraudulent from the genuine signature; and but for the experimental question of the Teller in one case, and the collateral evidence of the merchant's cash-book in the other, both might have gone through the accounts, and the dealers been so much poorer, but no wiser.

Is it possible that men in business might incur these serious losses without such sensible inconvenience as to excite suspicion and search, or without the ability to trace and detect them?

Yes. No fault is so common among merchants as that of keeping an inexact and slovenly cash-book. Instead of a daily test balance, the cash account is often suffered to run for a week, more or less, until the current disbursements and receipts are so jumbled together as to defy all analysis or proof. A balance is then forced—supposed to be "not far out of the way—nothing to affect the general results of the business." Not hundreds merely, but thousands of dollars are lost, both by slow abstraction and in the lump, through the little opening between an exact balance and the difference of "a few dimes!"—and the loser is unconscious that this may be the chief cause that urges him towards insolvency.

There are circumstances under which it may be impossible for the Paying Teller to detect forgery.

Some years since, the financial clerk of a wealthy importing house presented a forged check for ten thousand dollars at the counter of one of our principal banks, and it was paid without hesitation. He had long been in the service of his employers, was known to enjoy their full confidence, and to hold the custody of their private papers. It was a usual circumstance for the house to draw checks for that or larger amounts, and the fraud was consummated without presenting a single point to excite suspicion. It was discovered by the report of an overdraft in the account, and the simultaneous elopement of the guilty clerk.

The following singular case came within the knowledge of the writer.

The bank account of a highly respectable house was reported overdrawn two thousand dollars; and one of the firm denied the genuineness of a particular check for that amount. A number of his checks were so arranged as to conceal all but the signatures, and he was requested to point out the forgery. He acknowledged his inability to discriminate between that and any other. On close inquiry, it appeared that he had been in the habit of signing checks in blank to the order of his book-keeper, to be used in his absence, and the one in question was of this description, excepting that it was payable to bearer. He was asked if he could swear that the signature was not his own—to which he answered in the negative. Yet it was not made subject to order in his usual form, and he had no recollection of having signed it. Under these circumstances, the bank insisted that it was genuine, and the house submitted to the loss.

There are circumstances under which a bank might be exempt from liability for the payment of forged checks. A want of due care by the merchant to guard his own affairs against attack, though a vague ground of defence, is entitled to some weight. The employment as clerk of a person known by him to have committed forgery would be a good defence in equity, if not in law.

It would be tedious to describe all the ingenious devices of the forger to blind the Paying Teller. When an old trick wears out, a new one is invented. While he is on the watch against new tricks, an old one is suddenly revived.

The signature and indorsement of a check being genuine, the Teller must be satisfied that the account of the drawer is good.

Some of our larger banks have fifteen hundred accounts open in the ledgers, all of which are liable to draft without notice. It rarely happens that more than one-fourth of them are checked against on any single day. Some will remain unused a week or a month, and then suddenly start into great activity. Some show regular daily receipts and payments, with one deposit and from two to five checks. Some will have a single deposit at long intervals, with checks once or twice a week to pay family expenses. Some will accumulate rents and dividends for several months, and be drawn against in one large sum for investment. The account of an active merchant will show from five to fifteen checks in a day, while that of a broker or private banker will have over one hundred. Some will always have a respectable balance on hand, no matter how many checks are paid, and others a small balance, no matter how few are paid.

The question occurs,—How can the Teller remember

the balances of fifteen hundred different accounts while paying or certifying checks at the rate of three or four in a minute?

From a careful examination of the deposits and checks of a dealer, it is easy to judge whether they belong to a legitimate business, or whether they are mostly mere transfers between different persons and accounts; also to what extent his balances are maintained by loans and transient accommodations. It is not difficult to ascertain whether a man uses his credit excessively or with prudence; nor to get information of his personal habits, associations, and general character. The contact of the Teller with merchants in all branches of trade affords many opportunities of inquiry which, with those in possession of the bank officers, enable him to classify the dealers, and thus assist his memory.

In the first-class stand those of known large capital, who never give out their own notes. They may sell on credit, but they buy always for cash. Their deposits in bank are generally far greater than their immediate wants. When their checks are presented, the Teller may safely pay them without reference to the condition of their accounts; for if they should even appear overdrawn at the moment, he knows that they will make an ample deposit before the close of the day. In addition to this, they are likely to have a considerable amount of promissory notes lodged in the bank for collection which are a collateral security.

The middle class of dealers are the most numerous. Less independent as it regards capital, and relying on the bank for loans, they are yet generally safe and trustworthy. They will not transgress its rules, lest they forfeit its confidence. The Teller pays their checks commonly without examining their accounts, depending on their integrity and self-interest to rectify possible errors by overdraft or otherwise.

Next come the retail shopkeepers, mechanics, and small manufacturers. Many of this class keep accumulating accounts, and seldom call for loans; or if so, to a very moderate extent. Separately, their deposits are not large, but in the aggregate, they add materially to the loaning facilities of the bank. They draw but few checks, and their accounts are not liable to sudden changes. The Teller soon acquires such a knowledge of them as to remember which need watching; and the Book-keepers aid him in this by an alphabetical list of balances. An old bank gradually expurgates its ledgers of troublesome accounts, while a new bank, from competition for business, or non-acquaintance with the character of dealers, is likely to fall heir to them.

By this, or some similar classification, the Paying Teller is able to "keep the run" of his customers with surprising closeness. But there is still room left for accidents and irregularities, which are a source of perpetual annoyance to him. The number of depositors who lack mercantile training is very large. They have never learned the value of time or rules in business, and "hot water" seems to be their "native element." They can seldom tell what money they have on deposit without asking the bank Bookkeeper. They make mistakes of addition in their check-books, or omit entries, or give out checks without recording them. It is not unusual for people of this careless character to meet in a bank lobby to consummate street bargains, and to take from their hat crowns loose checks which they exchange for hundreds or thousands of dollars; they post-date them a week or a fortnight; the printed title of the bank is often erased, and that of another illegibly substituted; the signatures are carelessly written, and blotted by folding, and they are stuffed in a pocket-wallet, to be forgotten, or remembered by accident. They give notes to each other drawn payable at banks where they keep no account. All these documents, when due, are presented to the Paying Teller, who is thus made the focus of many irregularities by total strangers. There is not an hour of the day free from their annoyance. He must examine them to ascertain what they are, and his time is taxed, often when he is most occupied with pressing duties.

A man offers a promissory note of Thomas Brown, for certification.

"Mr. Brown keeps no account here."

"Dont you think he'll send the money to pay it?"

"I dont know anything about him."

"Wont you take the note and hold it till the money comes?"

"No, sir. It's contrary to our rules."

"What shall I do?"

"I can't give you any help, sir."

Jacob Grimes keeps no bank account, but he takes the liberty of making his notes payable at the

Commercial Bank. He brings a handfull of bills or gold, and offers it to the Teller.

"What is that for?"

"To pay my note due to-day."

"It is not our practice to receive money from persons who keep no account with us."

This is something new to Mr. Grimes. "What are banks made for," he thinks, "if not to accommodate the public."

He considers the Teller churlish, and the bank "a nuisance"; but he does not consider that his own case would be but one of twenty or thirty if the practice were admitted, and that it would then be a serious interference with the regular duties of the Teller. Neither does he reflect that the bank would be responsible if a forged note should be paid instead of the genuine one, which might easily occur, since the Teller is unacquainted with the signature of the drawer.

Mr. Grimes may be obliged to wait at the counter of the Paying Teller half the day before his note is presented—involving a loss of time, and perhaps of temper also, for which nobody but himself is to blame.

Merchants in distant cities frequently make their notes payable at a bank in New York, and remit the money within a short time of their maturity. To send it back would cause the note to be protested, and injure the credit of the drawer. The letter of instruction with the inclosure is therefore handed over to the Teller, who pays the note when it is presented. It is then cancelled and returned to the remitter. Instead of bank checks, drafts on other parties, and sometimes on other cities, are sent, which adds both labor and risk to the gratuitous service. Bank officers have occasionally advised this class of correspondents that their letters would not be taken from the post-office if they continued the practice: but it has grown into a permanent annoyance, and is mostly submitted to.

The common idea that banks are public institutions is probably the ground on which they are expected to serve the public without compensation. It should be remembered that they are private associations, organized for the special benefit of the stockholders, and not for that of the people at large. They have as much right as an individual merchant to refuse service that yields no compensation. They cannot escape legal responsibility to their accepted dealers, for any omission or neglect of proper forms; but they cannot be forced to assume responsibility against their choice or judgment.

If non-residents and parties who keep no bank account were required to pay a small commission for this kind of imposed service, it might become an acknowledged function of the business.

There are many cunning and unscrupulous persons who maintain the appearance of respectability in their bank dealings until an opportunity offers to secure some advantage by trick or accident. They may obtain an introduction through other dealers with whom they are connected in trade, and who are themselves deceived as to their real character. By adroit management, and strict propriety of conduct, they gradually win the confidence of the officers and clerks, and obtain considerable loans, with the usual indulgences that are enjoyed by good customers. An overdraft of account by cross deposits with dealers in other banks may first expose them in their true colors. If money should be credited to them by mistake, they would not hesitate to use it. Instead of reporting errors in their favor, they would adopt them, and keep silence. They change their accounts from one bank to another as their tricks fail, or when they have gained all they can hope for. Against these, the combined vigilance of the Teller and other clerks is not always successful.

"Do you know," asks the Book-keeper of the Paying Teller, "that you overpaid Samuel Filibuster's account a thousand dollars yesterday?"

"No. But he is an honorable man, isn't he?"

"He has always kept a fair balance; and I have never seen any proof of his being tricky."

"Well—send for his book, and write it up. There may be a deposit or a collection omitted!"

The examination discloses no error of the kind. The Teller thinks that Mr. Filibuster may continue to make deposits as usual, and afford him an opportunity to reserve the amount of the overdraft. If it is an unconscious error on his part, he will do so. But the day passes without such fortunate accident. It is certain Mr. Filibuster knows that he has checked out of the bank a thousand dollars more than he had a right to, and that he means to make the most of it. This is the very "accident" that he has hoped for, and in view of which he has long and carefully observed the rules, to win the confidence of the bank.

It is the duty of the Teller to report such a transaction to the superior officers; but as it will weigh against his character for vigilance and sagacity, he first attempts to recover the amount by personal negotiation with Mr. Filibuster. That gentleman protests that it is "a most unaccountable error" and one which he exceedingly regrets; but he has no means in possession to rectify it at present.

"I trusted to your honor, Mr. Filibuster. You know it is an injury to a dealer to examine his accounts before paying his checks!"

"Yes, sir—and I am very sensible of your gentlemanly conduct in the whole course of my dealings with you. I must say you have treated me with great politeness, and I feel the more regret for that reason."

"Cant you deposit part of the sum to-day, and the rest to-morrow?"

"Indeed, sir, that is quite impossible."

"I dont want to report this to the President and Cashier, for that would injure you in their esteem. But I shall be obliged to do so, unless you make your account good."

These considerations, urged with very conciliatory manner by the Teller, in spite of the indignation which he feels burning within, almost impelling him to a personal assault on "the scoundrel" for his "villainy," are without effect. He steps into the Cashier's room, and tells him of the misfortune.

"Mr. Filibuster has overdrawn his account a

thousand dollars, sir, and now refuses to make it good."

"What! Filibuster?—I thought he was an honorable man!"

"So did I, sir. He has kept up a good show in his account—I suspect for this very purpose."

"Send him to me."

The Cashier considers it a piece of extraordinary luck if, after a fortnight's negotiation, he can bring Mr. Filibuster to give his notes at six, nine, and twelve months, for the amount of his overdraft. A civil suit would yield but a barren judgment, if successful, besides increasing the loss.

The identification of indorsers gives more annoyance to the Paying Teller than any other part of his business. The object of making a check payable "to order" is, on the part of the drawer, that he may have the indorsement of the person to whom it is given as an additional evidence of the payment; and the receiver of the check desires it as a security in case of loss. The risk of the indorsement is thus thrown on the bank. If it should pay a lost or stolen check with a forged indorsement, the person to whom the money is due may claim the payment over again. There is no apparent commercial propriety or justice in dealers throwing this risk on the bank, as it really belongs to their own business. A check drawn payable "to bearer" is as legal and complete payment as if drawn payable to the order of the receiver. It is a reasonable precaution in the transmission of checks by mail, to make them subject to the order of those to whom they are sent; but this is unnecessary in direct personal transactions. It is a source of annoyance and frequent dispute to the holder of a check as well as to the Teller. He is frequently a stranger, and can offer no positive proof of his identity.

John Gilpin, of Maine, presents a check at the counter payable to his order.

"Who is John Gilpin?" asks the Teller.

"That is my name, sir."

"I have no doubt of it; but our rules require that we should have some proof of it."

Mr. Gilpin has not a single acquaintance in New York who happens to be known at the bank. He returns to the maker of the check, at the suggestion of the Teller, and requests him to vouch for the indorsement, or to change it for another, payable "to bearer" instead of "order." This being refused, he presents it again at the bank, and complains that he is subjected to such trouble and loss of time. He thinks the Teller is "more nice than wise." But there is no reason why the bank should assume a dealer's risks, when the dealer himself is afraid of them.

The certification of the check may improve the holder's chances of using it in another channel. The bank is then bound to pay it when the indorsement is properly verified.

Indorsed checks paid through the Exchange, are understood to be guarantied by the bank from which they are received; and any that are unsatisfactory or informal are immediately returned for correction. Any bank will guarantee the indorsements of a dealer in whom it has confidence.

In many cases, the Teller trusts to his skill in physiognomy and in the discernment of character, and pays checks without positive identity of the indorsers.

The most acceptable form of check to the Teller is, that which is printed payable "to bearer." His only responsibility, then, is for the genuineness of the signature and the state of the account. If such a check should be lost, and subsequently paid to a dishonest finder, neither the bank nor the drawer of it would suffer—but only the person who lost it, as in the case of a bank bill. The vigilance of the Teller is alive, however, to be assured that "the bearer" is the right bearer. Any remission of personal scrutiny of all who approach his counter, would be to abandon the outer wall of his defence against forgery.

The practice of certifying checks for the better class of dealers, before they have made their deposit, is common in our city banks. It is a measure of the credit which the bank is willing to give. A customer who thinks himself entitled to it, takes offence at its refusal, and withdraws his account. A wholesale merchant would deal more cautiously with a jobber, if his checks did not command this credit in his own bank.

This advance certification is an indispensable economy in our method of banking. The funds which compose the deposits of a dealer, are the product of sales or collections made at different hours of the day, and they cannot be brought together in one sum until near the close of it. Their deposit in several sums would add immeasurably to the labor of the clerks by multiplying entries; and if the Teller should withhold certification until the credits are actually made, the transactions of the day would be crowded into the last hours, causing much inconvenience and increased risk of error. The aggregate certifications of a bank in full business may reach several hundred thousand dollars before the deposits begin to come in—all depending on the discretion and judgment of the Paying Teller. At the close of the day, the Book-keepers report to him whether any dealers have failed to make good their accounts.

When the market is growing tight, the Teller becomes more watchful of his certifications. The failure of two or three usually prompt dealers to cover their checks seasonably, is perhaps the first warning for this necessity. All but the first class of customers are told, that it is "against the rules to certify in advance of the deposit."

"Then you have constantly violated your own rules!"

"It is safe to relax them in an easy market; but our experience proves it to be unsafe in a tight market."

Reflecting men see the reason for this, and conform to it, while others get angry and denounce the bank and all its officers and clerks as "arrogant" and "undeserving of public confidence." It is not far wrong to set the latter down as among the weaker class, towards whom extra caution will be prudent. A merchant of sound capital has a common interest with the bank in clipping the widely-spread wings of credit, by which commerce generally is endangered.

A great service comes to the trading community from the periodical contraction of bank facilities. The collection of debts is more diligently urged, and wild speculation is arrested.

When the return Exchange is brought in from the Clearing House, it is counted on a separate table, and proved by an *Assistant*. The checks and bills of which it is composed are incorporated with the accounts of the Paying Teller. The checks must undergo the same inspection as those which are paid over the counter. The signature, date, and indorsement of each one is separately examined, and the accounts drawn against ascertained to be good. Among these are many checks of distant banks and correspondents, often with six or eight transfer indorsements, for the general accuracy of which the last remitting bank is held. The Teller particularly observes that the course of transfer from one to another is correct; and requires a special guarantee indorsement of the city bank to which it is paid, for any informality or omission. If at any subsequent time it should be discovered that one of the indorsements is fraudulent, it claims repayment from said bank, which claims in turn from its correspondent, and so on, until the first victim of the fraud is reached, on whom the loss falls. If the forms of transfer appear to be correct, the guarantee against forgery is valid by custom without special writing.

While the Teller is pursuing this examination, the current business of the day goes on with increasing pressure from the outside. So long as he can dispose of the applications uninterruptedly, as they are presented, the lobby is comparatively quiet and free from obstruction; but even a momentary stoppage causes the crowd to gather, and soon ten or a dozen persons are waiting to be served in turn. Expressions of impatience are not uncommon. The Teller is pronounced "slow"—"indifferent to the convenience of customers"—"incompetent" and "tantalizing," by his deliberation of movement. Deliberation is the secret of his accomplishing so much. In truth, there is hardly a moment when he may not be said to be doing two or more things at once, and yet with such a habit of concentration on each at the juncture as to avoid confusing them together.

The interruptions to which he is subject are almost incessant. The Cashier has just received advice of the issue of a number of duplicate checks by a corresponding bank, to replace the originals which have been lost in the mail. He brings the letter and list of duplicates to the Teller, who is occupied several minutes in obtaining a clear understanding of the case. Some of the originals might be in the hands of persons then waiting to be served, and he must be able to detect them at sight.

"Will you pay me this check, sir? I don't want to be kept here half a day!" growls a hot-tempered customer at the gate.

"Yes, sir," answers the Teller, "if you will have the discrepancy corrected between the figures and the writing."

"How did your exchanges come out the day before yesterday?" asks a messenger from another bank.

"A thousand dollars over."

"That's lucky! Our Teller is short a thousand—that must be it!"

"Well, if he can establish his claim, and no other bank contests it, I'll pay it."

It is a mutual obligation between bank tellers to afford each other every facility for discovering such errors. One who does not answer truly and promptly, can hardly expect to be so answered in his turn.

The Teller might appropriate this thousand dollars to himself; but he is too well aware of the hazards of detection. He cannot know that it has not been designedly placed in his way, and that the bank officers are not in the secret. However dishonorable it may seem to resort to such a plan for detection, none other is so easy, effectual, and harmless; for the dishonest only can be injured. It is objectionable on the ground of laying temptation, and inducing a first fault. Yet what is to be done, when suspicion has been awakened, and where fraud may be practiced so secretly as to defy all ordinary vigilance?

"I want five thousand dollars in gold for that check—not good," says another bank messenger.

The Porter or Specie Clerk, who keeps the coin prepared for such demands, is absent, and the Teller may be obliged to go to the vault for it.

In the next moment, a check which had been sent to another bank through the exchanges, is returned for a written guarantee of indorsement. If satisfied of its correctness, the Teller gives the guarantee

Otherwise he pays the money for it, and returns it to the dealer who had deposited it.

A stranger offers to the Teller five hundred dollars in bills, to pay a check which he had drawn on the bank. Keeping no account, his money is refused, but he persists in an altercation about it, to the hindrance of those behind him.

A dealer wants thirty or forty thousand dollars in coin, to pay duties at the Custom House.

Another hands in a memorandum of a check that he has given out, but of which he wants to arrest payment.

Another inquires whether a lost check, of which he had previously given notice, has been paid.

A Porter from the Merchants' Bank presents a dozen notes of different parties for certification, and he is immediately followed by one from another bank, with a bag of gold which he reports ten dollars short, and which may be the occasion of some dispute.

The other clerks have frequent necessity to communicate with the Paying Teller with respect to the state of accounts, and he with them.

A noisy colloquy occurs with a dealer whose check has been refused, because of his deposit having been credited to another party; and with another whose account appears deficient, because a promised discount of paper has not been entered on the books.

"Here!" says Mr. Bungle, returning a handful of

rumpled bank bills and coin, "that money which you paid me is twenty dollars short." The Teller examines it, and satisfies Mr. Bungle that the error was in his own counting.

Many persons who present checks are so ignorant of bank usage as not to know when an indorsement is necessary; some forget it until they have reached the Teller's gate, and are then obliged, after filling the omission, to take their place again at the foot of a line of twenty, and wait their turn. In character and disposition, the applicants are as different as in their features—boys, workmen, sailors, doctors, knaves, and drunkards. Some want "half gold and half notes," some "half silver and the rest in small bills," some "all bills," and some "all gold and be damned to you."

The Teller is often obliged to break away from a line of impatient customers to prepare his settlement balance of two hundred thousand dollars (more or less) to be sent to the Clearing House, or to receive the same. If he has not the whole sum in coin certificates, he pays part in gold.

There are three other channels through which checks may be paid by the bank, simultaneously with their payment by the First Teller. The Note Teller may receive them in discharge of a note; the Deposit Teller may take them in credit, and the Runner in settlement of a draft—each without the knowledge of the others. For example, if Alexander Jones has a balance of one thousand dollars in the bank, he

Transacting business at the Paying Teller's Desk.

may draw that amount in bills or gold from the Paying Teller; he may give his check for it to another dealer for deposit in the same bank; he may take up a note with it at the Note Teller's desk; and he may pay a sight draft with it to the Runner: so that he may draw out four thousand dollars, while he has a balance of but one thousand. There are two guards against this, as it respects the Tellers, viz.: their mutual advisements, and the good faith of Alexander Jones. The Runner has the latter only to rely upon; for he cannot tell whether the check is good or bad until he returns to the bank. It is a creditable fact, both to the integrity of dealers and to the watchfulness of the clerks, that fraud is seldom attempted by the duplication of checks in this manner. The bank owes its security, no doubt, to the power of credit. If men are not governed by correct principles, they are restrained by the fear of being cut off from facilities which are essential to their success in trade.

If a dealer deposits checks on other banks, which prove not good when sent through the exchanges, they are chargeable to his account directly, or he is bound to redeem them. But a check *on the same bank* is as actually paid when taken in deposit by the Receiving Teller, as if paid by the First Teller in bank bills; and if it should not be good, the recourse of the bank is to the drawer of it—not to the depositor. Likewise, if a dealer takes up his note with the check of another dealer on the same bank, the recourse of a bank is to the drawer of the check, and not to that dealer.

The proportion of checks liquidated through the several other channels together, is small compared with that paid by the First Teller, and it is confined to receiving them in account. It does not extend to the actual disbursement of gold or bills to the applicant.

There are times when the Paying Teller would seem, to an outside observer, to be almost helpless against threatened losses.

It is one of those "panic days" on which men are driven to desperation by the utter failure, one after another, of all their resources. Employers as well as clerks are seen hurrying along the streets to borrow, or to beg a respite from their obligations. Merchants who were never known to be "short" before, are now seen to enter the bank in great agitation, and after fruitless intercession with the officers, to go out again with hopelessness and discredit impressed in every feature. The President and Cashier themselves manifest extreme anxiety. All the counters are thronged by dealers in a high state of excitement. The clerks are deeply engrossed in examinations, mutual inquiries and messages, hurrying from desk to desk, amidst the general confusion of voices, the rattling of specie and the perpetual reverberation of banging doors. There is a prevalent sense in the bank of apprehension and alarm. But the Teller goes on impassively with his certifications and payments, not suffering himself to be flurried by what passes around him, and exhibiting not the slightest discomposure of manner.

The Cashier lays an open note on his desk:

"CASHIER COMMERCIAL BANK:

"DEAR SIR: Please certify no more notes of our firm after receipt of this. Mar. 4, 2½ P.M.

"Yours, respectfully, SKAREM & Co."

"Too late, sir. I have already certified forty thousand dollars!"

"The deuce you have!"

"Yes, sir—but they are honorable men. I have no doubt they will protect the bank."

More notes of Skarem & Co. are brought in for certification.

"No funds to pay those notes."

"*What* do you say?"

"I have a written notice not to certify any more of their paper."

The messenger hurries off to communicate the intelligence to the officers of his own bank. It has already found currency in "the street," and the number of firms heretofore in good standing, that are seriously involved, is a subject of free speculation. The liabilities of "Skarem & Co." are variously stated at from two to five millions of dollars, and all the probable consequences of their failure are exaggerated by public rumor.

Three o'clock. The Paying Teller closes his gate. A few straggling notes and checks for certification concludes the day's business, and leaves him at liberty to look after the *indulged accounts.* A string of twenty depositors yet wait their turn.

Skarem & Co. have made a deposit sufficient to cover all their certifications; but the Teller finds that Wilkins & Smith, for whom he had certified near seventy thousand dollars, have not yet made their account good. He is alarmed, and communicates the fact to the Cashier. While they are in consultation, the clerk of Wilkins & Smith hands in their book with twice the required amount of funds.

"That," says the Teller, with manifest relief, "makes us right for the day."

EXPLANATION OF THE PAYING TELLER'S PROOF.

The business of the day begins with the balance of cash on hand, $3,100,728.37.

The money received on the previous day by the Deposit and the Note Teller (here called second and third) consists of three kinds of funds: office notes, specie, and exchange funds. All must be added to the above balance.

The title "Commercial Bank" is adopted to simplify the explanation of some terms.

Office Notes means, the bills of the Commercial Bank in distinction from those of all other banks. Uncurrent bank bills, and checks that cannot be used in the Exchange, are classed under the same head, and constitute the *Office List.*

The items numbered 1, 2, 3, and 4, are the unexchangeable portion of the funds, and with some

A.

	$	c.	$	c.
Balance of cash brought forward from previous day............	....	....	3,100,728	37
Received:				
From 2d Teller, Office List....(1)	13,938	71		
" 3d " " ....(2)	9,275	87	23,214	58
" 2d " Specie.......(3)	3,884	95		
" 3d " " .. ....(4)	29,520	06	33,405	01
" 2d " C. H. Exchange (5)	554,982	99		
" 3d " " (6)	323,075	03	878,058	02
" " " Checks from letters added to the Exchange.(7)	....	....	91,876	18
Exchange from Clearing House (8)	....	....	870,463	27
			4,997,745	43

	$	c.
Paid:		
Exchange sent to Clearing House...................(9)	969,934	20
Bills and Checks to 2d Teller..(10)	6,327	48
" " 3d " ..(11)	3,408	32
Total amount of Checks paid..(12)	1,021,571	31
Total Payments................	2,001,241	31
Balance of Cash carried forward to next day.............(13)	2,996,504	12
	4,997,745	43

B.

		$.	c.
Cash on hand:			
Office-notes (See particulars*)........		140,843	
Bills of other banks redeemed........		9,786	
Sundries.........................			
Specie:			
In vault...............2,827,000			
In trays...............	18,875.12	2,845,875	12
Total agreeing with balance............		2,996,504	12

* Amount of different denomination of Bills:

1,000	$15,000
500	7,000
100	58,100
50	41,150
20	8,000
10	8,020
1	1,760
3	597
2	286
1	170
	125,083
Mutilated Bills,	15,810
	140,843

exceptions, are incorporated in the Paying Teller's general cash. The items 5 and 6, make the Clearing House Exchange, amounting to $878,058.02.

The checks that are added from the morning letters must be credited to the remitters on the books of the Third Teller, and are transferred by him to the Paying Teller—$91,876.18.

The exchange received from the Clearing House in return for that sent to it—number 8, $870,463.27, completes the entire amount of the Paying Teller's cash—$4,997,745.43.

The payments are as follows:.

The exchange sent to the Clearing House, which is the precise amount of the items 5, 6, and 7, on the other side of the account—number 9, $969,934.20.

Numbers 10 and 11 are, respectively, portions of the items numbered 1, and 2, returned to the Second and Third Tellers. They may consist of country checks, or checks that remain unpaid for some cause, or uncurrent bank bills, the responsibility of converting which into exchangeable funds belongs to the Tellers who received them, and not to the Paying Teller.

Number 12, is the whole amount of the dealers' checks paid in this department during the day.

The sum of these payments being subtracted from the footing of the opposite side of the account, calls for the balance in cash of $2,996,504.12.

So much for the books.

The Paying Teller now counts up all the office notes, or bills of his own bank, by denominations, and finds them to be $140,843. He has redeemed bills of corresponding banks to the amount of $9786. He counts over the specie (that in the vault by bags or certificates), and on adding these sums together, finds the whole to agree with the Proof.

If there is a discrepancy, he mostly discovers it by revision. Errors of surplus or deficiency that cannot be explained, must be marked on the Proof, and reported to the Cashier. Their solution may come about by accident after the lapse of weeks or months.

The short summary marked B. is the most important statement in the whole history of the business. It is exclusively in the keeping of the Paying Teller, is out of the reach of all the examinations and tests of the general accounts of the bank, and no clerk has any necessity or right to look into it. The President, the Cashier, or a committee of the Board of Directors may investigate it when they think proper; but they rarely do it with any thoroughness—the President or Cashier perhaps not once in twelve months. In some banks, the Board of Directors is divided into standing committees of three or four members each; and these committees rotate as examiners for stated periods. In others, special committees are appointed for the service; but not one bank director in twenty has enough practical acquaintance with accounts to give real value to his certificate of accuracy. All the bank frauds that have been perpetrated in New York have been carried through repeated directorial examinations, and not one within the author's knowledge, has ever been discovered by them. Discovery has almost uniformly been the result of accident, of self-conviction, or of unmanageable magnitude in the default. The methods of concealment in the hands of a skillful clerk, are too many and too intricate to be detected by common scrutiny.

A better method is, for the Cashier to select two or three intelligent clerks who are not connected with the Paying Teller's department, to assist him in the examination. This is the practice of several banks which are under the best discipline.

The *office list* in this statement has frequently been used to cover the embezzlement and misuse of funds. Under the specification of "sundries," or "cash items," or "mutilated bills," any deficiency could be concealed. The Teller may carry on false figures for years, and no after-examination could prove them false.

The *office list* has also been used by bank officers to conceal their improper application or abstraction of funds. The President or Cashier may make loans on "traps,"* seal them up, mark on them a fictitious value, and instruct the Teller to "put them in the office list." Such abuse is not discoverable by the Teller. He commonly obeys the instructions of the officers without inquiry, and may thus be made the involuntary instrument of fraud. In case of discovery he would be held blameless. But with just views of his own duty and responsibility, he might object to receiving from the President or Cashier, any sealed securities or vouchers to be counted as funds. If they

* This is a common term, signifying uncommercial, and worthless documents, such as depreciated railroad bonds, land grant bonds, railroad acceptances, bad or accommodation notes, broken stocks, &c.

should offer him securities of an improper kind, it would be his right and duty to refuse them; nor would any bank officers dare resent such refusal.

The modern improved discipline of banks, together with the various legal reports of their condition, has lessened the facility of fraud by the *office list.* Large sums under the head of "sundries" or "cash items," are regarded with distrust.

The substitution of copper for gold in the sealed bags is a very hazardous experiment, and yet it has occasionally been resorted to with success by a dishonest Teller. The difference in bulk of the same weight of gold and copper would be too obvious to the experienced eye of the Porter, to escape detection; and the difference in weight of the same bulk would be discovered in the handling of it.

Certification is the most dangerous and least guarded function of any person connected with the bank, whether officer, director, or clerk. It is, in fact, the power of bank issue; and it is vested exclusively in the Paying Teller. By simply writing his name across the face of a check, he gives it the credibility of an official bank draft. He can do this at his own house as well as at the bank counter, and for people who keep no account with the institution as well as for those who do.

The use of the Certification Check List, is to prevent dealers overdrawing their accounts by the duplication of checks. It cannot prevent the Teller from certifying beyond the record.

The Paying Tellers of New York disburse daily near twenty-five millions, and in the course of a year eight or ten thousand millions of dollars; and the aggregate of all losses incurred through them by mistakes or by abuse of trust, is not, at the highest, as much, perhaps, as the one ten-thousandth part of one per cent! This is strong testimony in favor of their general fidelity as a class, in view of the extensive powers with which they are intrusted; and especially, in view of the power of certification, which in the manner of its use up to the present day, has been without any other protection than their own sense of propriety and honor.

Various changes have been proposed by bank officers in the method of certification. When an example of its abuse is made known, the subject is freely discussed by them, and it is felt to be the weakest and most unguarded point in our banking system. Some institutions have adopted a stamp in red or blue ink to accompany the signature of the Teller; but the stamp could be duplicated or secretly used without difficulty. Others have proposed to conjoin the signature of another clerk with that of the Paying Teller; and others, to create a certifying department with an exchange issue of checks.

The plain truth is, that the power of certification is too easily abused, and too destructive in its abuse, to be vested in single hands, without effectual supervision.

The following example shows how checks fraudulently certified may be kept alive from day to day, and assist a large default, without causing any irregularity in the books of a bank, and without exciting the suspicion of the officers and clerks.

The Paying Teller began by certifying a check in advance of the dealer's deposit; and on the following day certified another, that it might be negotiated, and the means thus obtained to remove the first out of sight; to provide for the second, a third was certified, and so continuously on, the negotiations of one day furnishing the means to redeem the checks of the day before. The amount was gradually increased, until twelve or fifteen checks, for amounts between four or five thousand dollars each, were afloat in the various channels of negotiation. They were drawn for irregular sums, that they might wear a business-like appearance. No entry of them was made on any of the books, and no apparent deficiency was caused in the Teller's daily cash. An examination of his statement, similar to that marked B, on page 149, would have developed no clue to the fraud, which consisted entirely of *floating certifications.* There were two confederates in the plan—one a dealer in the bank, and the other a broker whose account had been closed for irregularity several months before the exposure came about. As the fraud could be maintained only by a complete daily renewal and negotiation of the whole of it, the three met in the evening at the office of the broker, and the Teller was advised of the banks in which the checks had been deposited, so that he could lay aside those particular exchanges in the morning, and thus prevent them from passing into the hands of the Assistant Teller. It was then also ascertained what amount of checks must be negotiated on the following day, and they were written by the confederates, and then certified by the Paying Teller. Subsequent developments proved that this process had been carried on for many months, the amount gradually increasing until it reached seventy-five thousand dollars. There had been, in the mean time, five or six examinations by committees of the Directors, and the usual certificate of accuracy in the accounts was recorded.

The Teller who perpetrated this fraud was a very accomplished clerk. His self-possession, when all around him was excitement and hurry, seemed to increase with the emergency. He manifested an extraordinary faculty for detecting the slightest indications of fraudulent or dishonorable purposes in others; and the bank owed to him many fortunate escapes from loss by the various tricks and impositions which are practiced by dealers in extremity. To all these qualifications, he added such diligent habits of business as to attract, in an unusual degree, the personal attention, respect, and confidence of every director, as well as of the officers of the institution. It was subsequently found that he had been a regular attendant at a gambling-house, even before his appointment as Teller. The discovery of his fraud caused an immediate examination into the accounts of many other Tellers in the city banks. In two cases each, a deficiency of more than one hundred thousand dollars came to light, and in a third, one of seventy thousand.

Fraud and collusion may always be presumed from the use of certified checks as collateral security for loans. There can be no honest reason for not drawing the money for them, as they are charged to the account of the dealer when they are certified, and *he* —not the holder of the checks, is the man who must pay them. In fact, they are already paid. The hypothecation of certified checks is like the hypothecation of gold; and when one deposits gold as security, agreeing to pay interest on it, the presumption is, that it is a surreptitious transaction. The only possible excuse would be, an expected advance of premium enough greater than the interest, to justify the hoarding. No dealer in money is so ignorant as not to know these facts. A broker who receives certified checks as collateral security for loans, becomes a party to the fraud, because the tacit if not the expressed condition is, that he shall withhold them from the bank.

The Paying Teller, to a considerable extent, holds in his hands the commercial fate of the merchant, in the power to certify checks. He is therefore likely at times to be tempted and embarrassed by personal relations. Old companions and friends are shaken by the financial storm, but he must prefer his own duty to their interest. He must be unapproachable by bribes of feeling, as well as of money. His greatest danger is in the first exception to rules, which draws after it a second exception. A Teller of one of our city banks once made the following confession to the author:

A personal friend and a highly respectable merchant called at the bank after three o'clock, and requested him to certify his check for six thousand dollars. He represented, that by paying off a loan for that amount, he would release collaterals which he had already negotiated for nine thousand dollars, and that he would deposit the latter sum within half an hour, thus making his check good. After a long resistance, the Teller yielded—not to the merchant, but to the friend, on the express condition that the check should be used for no other purpose. He was met on the way to redeem his promise, by a creditor, who overcame his purpose by the force of a superior will, and obtained from him the certified check. Finding that the borrower did not return, the Teller became alarmed. He had delayed charging the certification until the deposit should be brought in, and now withheld it to avoid inevitable exposure on the following morning, and consequent dismissal and disgrace. After a week's labor and suspense, during which he suffered the most painful anxiety, and withheld the check, he secured the money, and then informed the officers of the transaction. They were satisfied that the lesson would make him more watchful in future, and their confidence in him was rather improved than abated.

The Paying Teller is the natural successor in office to the Cashier—a very influential consideration to make him deserve the good opinion of the Directors, and the esteem of the public.

He generally proves his cash within half an hour after three o'clock. The Porter assists him in carrying his trunks and trays into the vault, which he locks, and with the key in his pocket, leaves the bank for the day.

CHAPTER V.

THE DEPOSIT TELLER.

THE accounts of a bank are divided into two classes, known as *individual* and *general.*

The former are personal, belonging to individuals or firms. The latter are those of other banks, and such as show the aggregates or results of the business; as Stock, Expenses, Bills Discounted, Profit and Loss, Cash, Interest, Exchange, and some others.

The original entries of the former, called Individual Deposits, are made by the Deposit Teller, and the latter by the Note Teller. The Note Teller also receives the money paid in for notes lodged for collection on personal account. Both of these clerks are Receiving Tellers, and are distinguished also as Second and Third Tellers, in the order named, from the rank which they hold with respect to promotion. If the place of the First or Paying Teller becomes vacant, the Second or Deposit Teller takes it, and he is succeeded by the Third, or Note Teller, the qualifications of the clerk in each case being undisputed.

The duty of the Deposit Teller is to receive all direct deposits of money brought by the individual dealers of the bank. The book in which he enters these is called the Second Teller's Cash-book. While in use, it lies open before him on the desk, with such conveniences of blotting-paper, pencils, eraser, and India-rubber as may be required. There are commonly two of these Cash-books open at the same time, for alternate use by the Teller and the Book-keepers. They have the same rulings precisely as the Certification check-list, on page 115. The name of the depositor, and the amount of his deposit in the first column, is the Teller's original entry, corresponding in the figures with that which he makes in the Dealers' Bank-book. A form of the Bank-book is given on page 161. It is the Teller's receipt to the latter for his deposits. The letter A is the initial of his name, and identifies the receiver of the money. The example shows a succession of deposits, and other entries, which, with the extension columns of the Second Teller's Cash-book, will be more appropriately explained under the head of *Book-keepers.*

The deposits of merchants consist of bank bills, coin, personal and bank checks, certificates of deposit, and other documents which represent money. The dealer is required to state them in detail as in the form on page 161. The banks generally furnish printed tickets with blank spaces for the name of the dealer and the figures. These are not only a help to the Teller, with whom small economies become great gains, but to the depositors also, many of whom stand in need of instruction as to order and system in their accounts. They may commit any number of mistakes in their cash-book at home, but the tickets will always set them right with respect to their deposits in bank. The Teller will not receive money without them. If his cash does not prove at the end

FORM OF DEALER'S BANK-BOOK.

Dr. *The Commercial Bank in a/c with* SLATER & Co. *Cr.*

			$	c.				$	c.
1855									
June	18	To Cash,......*A*	30,000		June	19	By Cash...	960	
	19	" " ......*A*	19,240	60		20	" " ...	14,240	15
	21	" " ......*A*	6,352			24	" " ...	30,000	
	22	" " ......*A*	10,051	42		28	" " ...	2,240	16
July	1	" " ......*A*	1,275	60	July	5	" " ...	500	50
	3	" " ......*A*	21,000			6	" " ...	15,045	
	10	" " ......*A*	17,001	10		10	" " ...	25,000	
	11	" Bills discounted	22,363	18		12	" " ...	16,840	75
	12	" Jones, 2,500				16	" " ...	8,750	
		12.50		50			" Balance.	18,819	84
			2,487						
	"	" Brown........	1,625						
	14	" Cash,.......*A*	1,000						
			132,396	40				132,396	40
		To Balance.......	18,819	84					

DEPOSIT TICKET.

Deposited in COMMERCIAL BANK,

By *Slater & Co.*

New York, June 18, 1855.

	$	c.
Bank Bills..................	1,250	
Specie......................	41	50
Checks......................	1,655	72
"	10,940	
"	2,740	16
"	5,000	
"	8,372	62
	30,000	

of the day, he re-examines them, first by comparison of their footings with the book entry, and then by checking off each item, and revising the additions. They enable him to trace and identify all the checks on other banks, and so assist his memory that he can recall most of the transactions of the day. After proving his cash, he rolls them into a compact bundle, marks the date on the cover, and puts them away for future reference, in case of necessity.

The Exchange Drawer is a drawer divided into as many boxes as there are banks. The bills and checks of each bank are separated by distribution, each kind in its own box. The following example shows a complete list, excepting in the length of it, which is about eight inches. It is a statement of all the bills and checks of the Mechanics' Bank, received by the Commercial Bank during one day.

MECHANICS' BANK.

COMMERCIAL BANK, JUNE 18, 1855.

$	c.
1,550	
640	72
6,284	26
1,000	
275	46
160	16
1,546	90
2,500	
4,542	60
2,740	65
*21,240	75

* See this amount transferred to the Proof, on page 163—No. 4.

Every bank in the city has one such list against every other bank; that is, fifty-two lists, its own *Office List* making the fifty-third. When the footings of these fifty-two are copied on a general list, called *The Second Teller's Proof*, and added together, they constitute the Deposit Teller's portion of the Exchange which goes to the Clearing House. It appears in gross on the Paying Teller's Proof of the next morning, as a part of his receipts, as on page 149, $554,982.99.

THE COMMERCIAL BANK.

SECOND TELLER'S PROOF.

June 18th, 1855.

1	Bank of New York	$21,154.42
2	Manhattan Company	15,000.00
3	Merchants' Bank	30,150.75
4	Mechanics' Bank	21,240.75
5	Union Bank	10,142.14
6	Bank of America	14,972.16
7	Phenix Bank	11,243.60
8	City Bank	16,800.19
9	North River Bank	
10	Tradesmen's Bank	5,204.17
11	Fulton Bank	6,315.90
12	Chemical Bank	14,510.80
13	Merchants' Exchange Bank	18,260.01
14	National Bank	16,210.40
15	Butchers' & Drovers' Bank	1,745.00
16	Mechanics' & Traders' Bank	4,520.72
17	Greenwich Bank	7,240.65
18	Leather Manufacturers' Bank	16,752.40
19	Seventh Ward Bank	7,265.10
20	Bank of the State of New York	27,566.70
21	American Exchange Bank	41,317.62

22	Mechanics' Banking Association.........	$1,500.25
23	Bank of Commerce....................	27,005.16
24	Bowery Bank...............(*Suspended.*)	
25	Broadway Bank......................	8,742.10
26	Ocean Bank.........................	5,740.00
27	Mercantile Bank....................	4,960.11
28	Pacific Bank.......................	1,950.00
29	Bank of the Republic............	18,100.05
30	Chatham Bank.......................	1,750.82
31	People's Bank......................	1,200.06
32	Bank of North America...............	16,200.60
33	Hanover Bank.......................	1,850.00
34	Irving Bank........................	3,200.00
35	Metropolitan Bank..................	38,716.94
36	Citizens' Bank.....................	1,325.60
38	Grocers' Bank......................	1,300.02
40	Nassau Bank........................	6,240.14
41	East River Bank............(*Suspended.*)	
42	Market Bank........................	15,270.65
43	Saint Nicholas Bank................	1,201.10
44	Shoe and Leather Bank...............	14,964.10
45	Corn Exchange Bank..................	5,317.69
47	Continental Bank....................	12,572.64
48	Bank of the Commonwealth............	9,214.00
49	Oriental Bank......................	1,625.50
50	Marine Bank........................	1,100.16
52	Atlantic Bank......................	2,560.08
53	Importers' & Traders' Bank............	22,540.13
54	Park Bank..........................	19,378.96
55	Artisan's Bank.....................	1,842.65
		$554,982.99
	Office List........................	13,938.71
	Specie.............................	3,884.95
	Checks.............................	64,387.92
		$637,194.57
	Footing of Cash Book..............	**637,194.57**

The foregoing list presents an exact proof of the cash with the Deposit Book.

The manner in which the several items, excepting the checks, are incorporated with the cash of the Paying Teller, may be seen by comparing them with the entries of the Proof on page 149. The item of $64,387.92 is the amount of checks on the Commercial Bank itself, and they are charged to the accounts of the drawers.

It is not unusual for depositors who receive large checks by their morning letters, to send them to the bank for addition to the Exchange before it is dispatched to the Clearing House, in which case the Deposit Teller passes them over to the Paying Teller. This would require some additional entries at the foot of the Proof, which would complicate it to the general reader.

The whole duty of the Deposit Teller is performed when he finishes this Proof. He locks up the fifty-three packets or lists of money in a trunk, and deposits it in the vault, when he is at liberty to leave the bank, which he does mostly from half-past three to four o'clock. He is expected to be at his post in the morning in season to deliver his Exchange to the Paying Teller, and to assist in the incorporation with it of the Proof List of the Note Teller.

There are no complex calculations in the accounts of the Deposit Teller. Simple addition and subtraction embraces all the arithmetic required. It is the understood rule of the bank to avoid needless conversation, and to never speak to a Teller when he is engaged in counting money. In truth, the mere mechanical performance of the duties of this desk is compatible with a very moderate degree of intelligence. It will be seen, however, on looking behind the machinery, that a dull brain might easily prove a very bad investment for the bank.

By far the larger part of the deposit of our city banks consists of merchants' checks, given to each other in payment of debts, or for mutual accommodation. Without the certification of the bank on which they are drawn, these are no more than personal obligations, of the validity of which the Teller can have but little knowledge. The stated rule is, that they must be certified before deposit; but this would be attended by so much inconvenience and loss of time, that it is relaxed with dealers of good standing, who are supposed to be responsible for any that may be returned dishonored, and who, in self-defence, are not likely to deal with unsafe people. And so it happens, from usage, that a large proportion of all checks received are uncertified.

Mr. Tarbox may deposit twenty checks amounting to five thousand dollars. They may be drawn on as many different banks, and it may take one or two hours' running and waiting to get them all certified. The Teller has no definite knowledge of the personal responsibility of the drawers; but Mr. Tarbox himself is a man of capital, prudence, and honor. He therefore receives the checks, although he knows that they will be drawn against immediately, and that a day must elapse before they will reach the banks where they are payable, whence any of them that are not good will be returned to him for redemption. It is not unlikely that one or two of the twenty may be sent back. If so, they are immediately presented to Mr. Tarbox, who pays them by his own check. The Teller might have recourse to his account in the bank, the current balance of which is probably sufficient to cover them; but this would be leaving Tarbox in the dark as to the dishonored checks, the collection of which might be endangered by delay. Moreover, if not apprized of their debit to his account, he might overdraw that by his own checks. It is, therefore, not only courteous, but necessary to the safety of both bank and dealer, that he should be advised without delay of any default in the checks that he deposits.

Abel Dodge might prove to be less honorable than Mr. Tarbox. He may not have given the Teller any reason to think so as yet, and his deposit is received in the same way. He draws his own check for the whole amount within an hour, and presents it for certification. If the Paying Teller should want confirmation of the deposit having been made, he has only to ask the Book-keeper, who answers in the affirmative; and Dodge thus gets his own check certified, against a deposit which consists of the uncertified checks of other people. If the latter should prove bad, the bank can have recourse only to Mr. Dodge. To trace such a transaction, we may suppose one of them to be returned from the bank on which it is drawn. A messenger presents it to the Paying Teller about midday, and demands the money for it.

"Joseph Pine's check not good, sir. I'll take the gold, if you please."

It is paid, and passed over to the Deposit Teller, who, wishing to avoid censure for unwatchfulness, sends it to Mr. Dodge by the Porter, with instructions to get the money for it. The Porter returns, with information that Dodge has failed, and can't pay.

"Did you tell him it was a debt of honor?"

"I did."

"What did he say to that?"

"Said he knew it, and was very sorry, but could'nt help himself. Would be very happy to pay it, and wishes he had the means."

"That's consoling. Did you ask him about Pine?"

"Says Pine's failed too."

"What? Both on the same day?'

"So it seems."

"Hang the pirates! I'll go and see 'em after bank hours, and try if I can't squeeze something out of 'em."

In such a case, the Teller may prove a better negotiator than the officers of the bank. If he should be able to make any kind of arrangement by which the bank will receive final payment, he submits it to the Cashier for his approval. Otherwise, he has the mortification of informing that officer of the casualty, and of the failure of his attempt.

Bank officers are not apt to be censorious when satisfied with the general method and accuracy of the Teller's desk. They know that losses are incident to the business. But if they are of frequent occurrence, or if they manifestly result from incapacity or carelessness, the Teller loses his place.

An accident of this kind stimulates his vigilance.

Like small misfortunes in any business, it doubtless wards off larger. He looks more closely into the ledger balances, scrutinizes with a sharper eye accounts, check, and persons, and consults his fears. Other Able Dodges may turn up any day. He enforces his rule of certification with more vigor, and perhaps needlessly in many cases, giving offence to thin-skinned dealers and lazy clerks.

"Now, where's the use of my traipsing all over the city to get checks certified, when I know they're good?"

"Well—I can't help it. You know the rule of the bank, and ought not to require me to break it. Here's one large check of five thousand dollars, which I will *not* take on my own responsibility. If you get the Cashier's consent, very good. I'll take the rest of your deposit to-day, but hereafter you must get all checks over a thousand dollars certified."

The dealer obtains the Cashier's consent, with an admonition, however, that it is better to observe the rule of the bank than to give the Teller an opportunity to refuse his deposit. If he has any doubt of the check being good, or of the ability of the dealer to redeem it if bad, he refuses at once. "No, sir. It is the Teller's province to decide that point, and I will not interfere with him." The Teller understands this to be an approval of his course.

The risk of neglecting certifications falls back on the merchant. The rule of the bank is, therefore, his best protection, and should be appreciated as such, rather than be deemed offensive to credit or standing. Yet it is not unusual for a dealer or his clerk, when asked why he does not get his check certified, to answer, pettishly: "Because there's no need of it. What do you want me to run my legs off for, when 'tis no use?"

The Teller of a bank may have reasons which are unknown to the dealer, for requiring certain checks to be certified, and which he is not at liberty to communicate. He may have received the same from other parties to such an amount as to create suspicion of kiting. This is the most vulnerable part of his business—the easiest and most specious method of overdraft. It is that at which the Able Dodges are sure to aim; and when the market is troubled, the aim is frequent.

It is the Teller's duty to keep alive and always fresh his knowledge of the general state of accounts, by asking the book-keepers how they stand, what is their average "run," and so forth; by examining the ledgers in person; inspecting the character of the deposits and checks, just as the Paying Teller does; consulting that officer; comparing notes and experiences; clearing up doubts, or confirming suspicions; and so on, incessantly. In fact, he has much to do in determining the character of the whole business. If he is gifted with brains, vivacity, patience, and a civil spirit, he may sift out the wheat from the chaff—separate the sheep from the goats, and exert a most practical influence over the success of the institution. A conceited, pompous fool (a character not unknown in the New York banks) repels the better class of customers from the counter, and attracts those who are not above flattering him one day to cheat him on the next.

"Why do you reject this check from my deposit."

"Can't you see, without asking? What do you try to walk over the rules of the bank for, putting in uncertified checks?"

"We shall not draw against our deposit within five times the amount of that check, sir, so that you will run no risk by taking it. Besides, we know it to be good."

"Well, I don't; and that's the point to be settled here"

Such a Teller will lose business, by losing the respect of dealers. Clerks tell their employers, and the contagion of disrespect spreads. It is less common, however, to meet examples of this kind now than it was formerly. Civility is found to be a commercial investment. A surly, ill-mannered Teller, would be complained of to the officers or directors, and, if found incorrigible, would be dismissed.

The Deposit Teller has the same need to examine signatures, indorsements, dates, and other peculiarities of checks, as the Paying Teller. Dealers who are entirely honorable and above practicing imposition themselves, may be imposed on by others with fraudulent or kiting checks. The name of the depositor must be indorsed below all others on the back of each. In the hurried reception of deposits, he takes special cognizance of this last indorsement, as the key to discovery if any thing should prove wrong. He cannot always examine at the moment the whole history. That is sure to be done at the counter where final payment is made, and the error, if any, comes back thence for correction.

Reclamations between the banks are of every day occurrence. A check is dated ahead, or the date is obscure, or omitted; it lacks an intermediate indorsement, or is indorsed "by attorney," without proof that the attorney is authorized by the principal; the filling up in the body does not correspond with the figures, or is entirely wanting. Singular as it may seem, a check will occasionally slip through the hands of a Teller, without signature: he recognizes a familiar style of writing, and the absence of the name does not arrest his attention.

In the hurry of distribution, checks are thrown into the wrong box, which takes them to the wrong bank. All these errors come back to be corrected, by the same channel through which they go out. New modes of error are turning up every day. No Teller has ever yet reached the end of them, and never will, while the firm of Cunning, Carelessness & Co., does half the world's business.

Merchants frequently keep accounts in two or more banks. They draw checks on one to deposit in another. This is a mere changing of balances; and as nothing is easier than for a man to sign his own name, the Teller regards it with suspicion. Unless well satisfied of the integrity and safety of his dealer, he insists on the certification of all such checks. The shifting of balances is sometimes unavoidable by a merchant. He may draw on one bank in expectancy of funds which he designs to deposit therein, and fail to receive them; in which case he writes a transfer check on another, to restore his balance.

There is a protective feature in many accounts

which keeps the bank safe against overdrafts; that is, when dealers have notes deposited for collection. As these are paid, they are posted to the credit of their owner, and may make up his deficit. Bank officers will sometimes admit temporary overdrafts in anticipation of the maturity of collection notes; or, what is better, make transient loans, holding them as collateral, by which the irregularity of overdraft is avoided. The Deposit Teller takes no cognizance of this source of recuperation, unless he finds necessity to resort to it.

The financial connection of merchants in good credit with an inferior class, tends to drag the former down, and to confound them with the latter. "How comes it," says the Teller to himself, "that our friend Blunt is getting hooked in with such a fellow as Dodge?" Blunt, thenceforward, becomes himself subject to closer scrutiny. His account is more narrowly inspected; and if it should appear that there is any thing like an established connection, he sinks a degree in commercial standing.

The word *foreign* applies to banks out of the city. Most of the New York city banks receive on deposit, either at par, or at a small rate of discount, individual checks on banks at a distance. Merchants in Buffalo remit their checks on banks in that city, to their creditors in New York; and here they are received as cash, deducting enough to cover the exchange and expenses of collection. They may be returned not good after several days, when the depositor must promptly redeem them. The interval between their deposit and their return, is long enough to allow the dealer to close his account and leave the bank in the lurch. It follows that the Deposit Teller is practically discounting paper all the time. The aggregate amount of checks in transit for collection may often reach one or two hundred thousand dollars, for the security of which, the main reliance of the bank is on his judgment.

Drafts on individuals and private bankers in the city, are received to a limited extent, in deposits; but this throws on the bank the trouble of collecting them, and makes it responsible for indorsements in which it has no interest. Dealers are therefore mostly required to collect them on their own behalf.

The ingenious methods of counterfeiting bank bills by photographic and other processes are such as to defy any ordinary powers of detection. Besides making entirely spurious bills, there are many tricks of alteration and substitution which are very successfully practiced. A genuine plate of a broken bank is changed in its title to conform to some existing bank. The lesser denominations of bills are altered to the higher —three to ten, or one to fifty. The ink is extracted chemically, and other titles and figures are neatly executed with a pen. The genuine dies, stolen from the engravers, are imprinted on false bills. A small and different portion is cut out of each of ten or fifteen genuine bills, and a new bill made of the pieces, neatly pasted together. The chances of success in these various processes, are in proportion to the number of different kinds of bills in circulation. The notes of near two hundred banks are receivable in deposit in New York. If each one issues six denominations, it gives a total of twelve hundred different imprints.

The attention of the Teller is not so much directed to confirm the genuineness of each bill, as it is to detect unusual appearances—like one in a crowded street, who does not observe common peculiarities, but at once distinguishes a man in Turkish or other singular costume. But he might often be deceived by fraudulent bills in his rapid counting, were it not that other eyes than his own are bent upon their discovery. No sooner is a counterfeit launched upon the community, than some one of the several thousand clerks in our banks and brokers' offices detects it, and it is immediately announced in the public papers, with such a description as to make its subsequent detection easy. He has another guard in the watchfulness of his dealers, who, it is presumed, will not knowingly present spurious bills. Notwithstanding these defences, however, he is always on the alert. The counterfeiter employs workmen of equal skill with those who produce the genuine bill; and although engravers periodically announce a new improvement or device which cannot be successfully imitated, they are as often cheated by a *fac simile* that puts them to the necessity of another trial.

The Teller acquires an instinctive faculty for the detection of spurious bills. To stand by and observe him counting, it might be supposed that he could hardly get a glimpse of each, so rapidly do they pass through his hands. He looks as if he were trying how many times he could strike the ends of his fingers together in the twentieth part of a second; but you see a steady stream of bills issuing beneath them, and gradually gathering into a pile.

There goes one aside, without perceptible pause in the swift handling! He checks the item on the list, and with his right hand thrusts the pile into a drawer, whilst with the left he tosses the single bill back to the depositor.

"Counterfeit—five dollars off!"

He makes the entry, deducting it from the list, hands the book to the dealer, and takes the next in order, in which there is a package of mixed denominations of several hundred dollars. He gives it a smack on the counter to loosen the bills, and a peculiar toss, which makes them fall over like the leaves of a book, affording an instantaneous glance at their ends. His eye has caught in that instant an old acquaintance!

"Where did you get that altered bill?" he asks of the customer, meantime counting—"twenty, thirty, fifty, fifty-five, sixty," and on he goes like lightning. The dealer looks astonished, not thinking it possible that the question could have reference to a bill in his money. The Teller repeats, without ceasing his count for an appreciable instant—"one twenty, one thirty, two, five, one forty-five—say, where did you get that altered bill — sixty-five, one seventy, eighty, two thirty—*that*," he says, tossing it in his face—"two, altered to ten—two eighty-five, two ninety-five, three, five, ten—three thirty-five—ten off, right." And the deposit is entered, and the dealer's book is returned before he knows it, and the Teller is in the midst of another count for the next customer in order.

This is very curious to an inexperienced observer. But there are certain well-known spurious and altered bank bills which are distinguishable by a quick Teller, as readily as the countenance of his landlord who approaches to ask for his quarter's rent. Counterfeits in general have their run, and then mostly disappear. To-day, it is a new ten, with which, if it is a close imitation, the Teller may be caught—but only once. He studies over its peculiarities, comparing every part with a genuine bill, and he would sooner mistake a parasol for a hat than be cheated by it again. Next week, a spurious five has its run, and there may be an interim of a month before another appears on the stage. The bank counter, however, is the last place for counterfeits to be presented. They are generally set afloat in country places, or among the small shops, where they are more likely to escape immediate detection. A few days, and often a few hours, is enough to spread the alarm, and to give all the peculiarities of the forged bill to the public papers, so that Bank Tellers are apt to be forewarned.

CLAIMS FOR DIFFERENCES.

While the Deposit Teller is pressed with the current business of his desk, the Paying Teller comes to his elbow, and waiting for a pause, shows him one of his Exchange lists of the day before. "Claim of twenty dollars short in that item," says he.

"Don't believe it. Didn't differ a cent."

The messenger who brought the list from the claiming bank speaks up: "It is so, you may depend on it. Mr. Sharp counted it himself, and is very positive."

"Don't care if he is. My cash was right. Did he prove his exchanges?"

"Yes, sir."

"Well—give my compliments to Mr. Sharp, and tell him he'll not get the first red cent of his twenty dollars out of me."

Mr. Sharp may find his cash correct at the end of the day. Having, as he supposed, discovered an error, he made the claim at hazard, rather than allow the proper moment for so doing to pass without it.

A specific error should be reported to the bank in whose money it is found—either a deficiency or surplus, with equal promptitude. Formerly, it was customary to claim the deficit, but to say nothing of the excess unless it was called for. If a careless Teller was one or two hundred dollars "over," he reserved the amount from his cash, trusting that it would be claimed by the bank to whom it belonged; and if not claimed, it made a loose fund without an owner, thus opening the door of temptation. But the explanation of such differences was likely to be forthcoming at any moment within one or six months.

The customary rule has been, for the sending bank to admit a claim of deficiency on the statement of the receiving bank, if the Teller's proof for the day calls for that precise amount. This gives a dishonest Teller an opportunity to abstract money from the exchanges of another bank. He has only to insist on the deficit, and usage gives him the advantage over the opposite party, who claims with equal obstinacy that the money was correctly counted by him. Such reclamations have occasionally excited suspicion, and a small excess has been made up in the Exchange, as a bait to detect where the supposed dishonesty lay. During the several years, preceding 1855, the number of city banks increased from twenty-five to more than fifty. Tellers were appointed Cashiers, and Book-keepers succeded Tellers. Many new and inexperienced clerks were employed, and reclamations for differences became so common, and were occasionally so large as to be quite serious. Bank officers consulted together, and imposed stricter rules on their Tellers. It was even suggested to make them personally accountable for differences which they could not explain. Frequent disputes arose between banks where the contesting Tellers were equally skillful, honest, and obstinate. The old plan of exchanges by Porters, who were out of sight and knowledge for one or two hours every day with the money in their possession, left the door open for suspicion or dishonesty among them also. But the present method of settlement by the Clearing House, together with improved bank discipline, and the refusal of some banks who were confident in their own accuracy, to pay claims unaccompanied by proof, have greatly reduced the number of such claims; and the wonder now is, that such a vast amount of business as is transacted by our city banks, should be carried on with few and unimportant errors.

It was suggested, when the Clearing House was first organized, that the packets of money should be sealed up, and the amount indorsed on the outside. This method has been partially adopted. It relieves the transit of suspicion, and reduces the question to one of honesty and accuracy between the exchanging desks—a very desirable issue. There might yet be duplicate envelopes and seals, but with such hazards of detection as few persons would be willing to encounter.

Differences in the money department of a bank sometimes spring up very mysteriously. A Porter occasionally goes round with an inquiry of each:

"How did your cash come out on the 24th?" several days after that date.

"All right. Why?"

"Our Receiving Teller is a thousand short, and can't find it. He has looked everywhere, too."

The next day, a note will be written on each exchange list: "Please send lists of the 24th."

The Teller makes a general and thorough revision of all his figures, checking them off by the deposit tickets, and going over the additions. If he fails to find it by this method, he sends a personal inquiry to each dealer in whose deposit it may possibly have occurred; and still failing, he communicates his misfortune to the Cashier, by whom it is made known to the directors at their next meeting. The search is not given up as hopeless, perhaps for several weeks. The unfortunate Teller is annoyed by the daily question of one or other officer of the bank, or by a director, or fellow clerk: "Have you found your difference?" It is finally considered as lost, and no more referred to.

Bank officers are slow to entertain suspicion of a clerk, unless there is some ground for it in his character or habits of living, which may then form a subject of conversation in the Board of Directors.

There is a looseness of practice with some banks as to the deficit or excess of cash in the daily accounts of the Tellers. Small sums accrue, which are thrown together in a box or drawer, and applied to the restoration of small deficits, it not being deemed a matter of sufficient consequence to be noted on the face of the day's transactions. The chief objection to this is, that it is a departure from exactness of record—a small wedge that might be driven further in. Nothing short of exactitude should be allowed in commercial accounts, and especially in a bank. There should be a ledger account opened with each Teller, in which the surplus, if any, should be credited under its actual date, or deficiency charged; and this might be periodically balanced by a transfer to Profit and Loss.

The Deposit Teller is, to a great extent, the absolute judge in his department, as to what measure of confidence may be safely reposed in individual dealers. He has therefore much need to study character. He must be able to read the manner, the countenance, the general bearing of men. If he is fully equal to the position, he is the first person, of clerks and officers, to catch indications of trick or weakness in the dealer, which are most likely to appear in his deposit. The Paying Teller, the Book-keepers, or the Officers of the bank, see only the aggregate sum set down to his credit; but the Deposit Teller handles every check, and from long experience discriminates between those which are borrowed, and those which represent the real transactions of trade. He frequently asks questions, to satisfy himself of the credibility of checks. If a dealer who is apparently hard pressed in a tight market, offers unusual checks, he wants to know who the drawers are, in what business, and so forth. The bank officers depend on him to communicate whatever intelligence he receives that may affect the credit of customers; and not unfrequently consult him in reference to discounts.

"How do the deposits of Sweatem, Sore & Co., look now?"

"Rather scaly, sir. Composed of an inferior class of checks, to a considerable extent."

"Well, you are careful to have them certified?"

"Oh, yes. I have been obliged to hold them up pretty closely on that tack, because I see they are generally in the borrow."

"Deposits not so good as formerly, eh?"

"No. Nothing like it. Very much larger proportion of accommodation checks. Mr. Sweatem comes himself, occasionally, and looks annoyed. I can't help feeling sorry for him; at the same time, it won't do to take his deposits as we used to."

The Cashier returns to the Directors' room.

"Gentlemen," says he, "I don't feel satisfied to discount Mr. Sweatem's paper without another name. From what the Deposit Teller informs me, I think that he is becoming embarrassed; and his line is already higher than it ought to be."

"We'll let it slide, then," says the President.

The Deposit Teller causes dealers to be expelled.

Nathaniel Jones has several times deposited kiting checks, and undertaken some sleight-of-hand tricks inconsistent with fair and honorable dealing. The Teller communicates this to the Cashier, and expresses his opinion, that Nathaniel is an unsafe customer. "When he comes to make another deposit, send him to me. Or, stay! Have you examined the Discount Ledger, to see if he owes us anything?"

"Yes, sir. His last note runs off in a few days. I concluded to get along without betraying any distrust till that is paid, and then we'd better close him out."

"Very well. Refer him to me at the proper time, and I'll put him through."

The Teller does so.

"Mr. Jones," says the Cashier, "it appears that you have deposited kiting checks several times lately, and practiced some irregularities which conflict with our rules!"

Mr. Jones attempts an explanation, which proves altogether unsatisfactory. The Cashier expresses his regret at feeling compelled to advise him to withdraw his account from the bank.

"I can do that, sir. It has not been so useful to me as to make it much of a hardship to break the connection."

Mr. Jones takes it in dudgeon, nevertheless. His sensibilities are not so blunt but that he can feel this sharp sting of discredit. The Cashier informs him, that it is both the interest and the duty of the officers to cultivate a good understanding with their dealers; but it is, likewise, their interest and duty to get rid of dangerous accounts. He politely requests him to draw a check for his balance of deposit, and to leave his book for settlement.

An account cannot always be closed immediately when it ceases to be honorable and safe. There are often unmatured discounts, which might be endangered by unfriendly terms. The officers and clerks must be patient till these are paid.

The Deposit Teller is much less liable to interruption than the Paying Teller. When the ticket is properly made out, he receives the deposit, makes the entries, and returns the book to the dealer, without speaking a word. A slight nod of recognition is all that passes between them, and so he may go on by the hour. At other times, the dealer will stop for conversation about the business, or on indifferent subjects. One whose office-cash is wrong, calls to ask if any error appeared in the Teller's accounts of the day before.

"Yes. I was a hundred dollars over, and found it in the addition of your ticket."

He unrols the packet of tickets, shows the error to the dealer, and either returns the amount or places it to his credit.

"Don't you keep a copy of your deposit tickets?"

"No."

"Well, you ought to. It would save time."

"That's true. This mistake has cost me two hours, and a good deal of anxiety."

Nobody knows better than a bank teller the value of strict habits in these apparently small points, or is better qualified to give instruction about them. He has a decided advantage over a careless and disingenuous customer, who puts his inquiry in the shape of an assertion:

"Your cash must have come out a hundred dollars over yesterday!"

"Why so?"

"Because I made a mistake in my deposit."

"If you had, I think I would have found it. My accounts balanced within two cents."

The dealer's ticket is produced, and the Teller shows the marks of his pencil, by which he distinguishes the character of every item on it—whether it was a foreign check, a city bank check, bills, silver, or gold, and its agreement with the book-entry.

"You had better examine your own figures a little better before you make such a claim of me!"

If this dealer should come later in the day and request the Teller to enter his deposit, while, to save time, he transacted business at another desk, he would get for answer:

"No, sir. You must wait here till I count it. I will take no such risk from a man who may come to-morrow and claim to have given me a hundred dollars more than I have credited to him!"

Honorable dealers, whom the Teller knows to be exact, will occasionally leave a large amount of checks and bank bills for him to count at convenience, and return for their books after an hour, or on the following day, which saves them the time that would be lost by falling in at the foot of a long row of depositors and waiting their turn. But the rule, to count the funds in the presence of the dealer, is generally adhered to. It is not unusual to receive packets of money at the dealer's mark without opening them; his name being written upon the strap; in which case he abides by the Teller's count, and makes up any deficit. Small coin in bags or packets, marked on the outside, are received without opening, subject to the examination of the Specie Clerk, or Porter, at his leisure. Deposits are not unfrequently received with a ticket only, the dealer's book having been mislaid, or left with the book-keeper to be balanced. The omission is supplied by a subsequent entry. There are many careless dealers and illegible writers among bank customers, who find it difficult to count money, or to make the simplest addition correctly. It is generally easier for the Teller to rectify their mistakes, than to require them to do it. Instruction gradually improves them. But some who blunder from sheer carelessness get a very short lesson.

"Here. Take your money and book back. Go to that desk, and make out a decent list of the checks in proper order, and the bank bills separately, and then I'll receive it—not before."

The Deposit Teller is not liable to be cheated by forged checks. He transacts business with those persons only who have been admitted as dealers by the bank officers, and who are therefore presumed to be worthy of some confidence. As they have, mostly, fixed and known residences, any attempt at ordinary fraud would return upon them.

Towards the latter part of the day, depositors begin to crowd in upon each other's heels. "First come, first served," is the rule of reception. Each takes his place in the row, and moves up as those before him complete their deposits.

The *Assistant Teller* is generally released from his duties in the department of the Paying Teller, about noon, from which time forth he is an auxiliary to the Deposit Teller. He begins immediately to assort the money and checks as they are deposited. There are near one hundred different kinds to distribute into upwards of fifty boxes, the country bills falling to those banks by which they are redeemed. Long habit gives great facility and rapidity in this process. The Assistant is awake to the detection of counterfeit bills, especially in the unopened packets, the examination of which is transferred to him by the Deposit Teller. He carries forward the "making up" as fast as possible, keeping the counted portion *under* the slip in each box.

All the checks on foreign banks are handed over to another clerk, who returns for them a charge-ticket against the bank to which they are to be remitted for collection; and these tickets, together with the *office checks*, are charged to their respective accounts, making the *Second* Teller's check-list, of which the item $64,387.92 in the Proof, on page 164, is an example.

Between two and three o'clock, there is mostly a great pressure of depositors, with apparent hurry and confusion. Every thought of the Teller is fixed intently, and he seldom speaks a word, except to give or ask a necessary explanation of things. On tight days his vigilance is exerted with an intensity that soon becomes painful. The character of the deposits shows him, from day to day, that certain dealers are "hard up," and he looks suspiciously at their checks. Mr. Jones has a list amounting to six or seven thousand dollars, in which there is a check of twenty-five hundred. The Teller deducts it from the footing, gives him credit for the balance, and returns it with a significant glance, which that gentleman does not wish to have more publicly explained. Mr. Jones' certifications are proportionably limited at the counter of the Paying Teller.

The last deposit is entered, and the Teller before closing his little gate, shakes his head ominously, and not unsympathizingly, at a man who had been standing at the railing for the last hour, holding a check in his hand. To the inquiry of the Cashier, he answers:

"He is a poor shoemaker, with Jacob Screw's check for ninety dollars, and he is watching for a deposit that he may draw the money before anybody else gets it."

"What! Is that our Screw who owns so much real estate?"

"Yes, sir."

"Well, if he makes a deposit, try and save the poor man, and then close his account. I'll have no such scaly fellow in the bank."

The Exchange slips are all counted up like the example of the Mechanics' Bank, on page 162, and entered on the Proof. With the Office list, specie, and checks added, it must agree with the Cash-book. See examples, page 164.

CHAPTER VI.

THE NOTE TELLER.

THE Note Teller (or Third Teller) receives the money for all promissory notes liquidated at the bank, and hence his title. This office was formerly included with the duties of the Deposit Teller, and still remains so in banks of small business; but such has been the growth of commerce, and the consequent increase of financial methods, that the division has been found, in the larger institutions, both convenient and necessary.

There are two classes of notes: those which are discounted by the bank, and those which are merely deposited by the owners, for payment to their credit. They are called *bills discounted*, and *collection notes*. The book in which the former are entered has the title of *General Accounts*, and that appropriated to the latter is called the *Third Teller's Cash-book*, or *Note-book*. Both classes of notes are filed in neat packets, each note numbered on the end to correspond with the number in the *Tickler*.*

The Teller takes up the Collection Note Tickler,

* This is an arbitrary term, derived probably from the practice of *ticking* or *checking* off figures in commercial accounts. A particular description, and a page of the book, is given under the head of the Note department.

and draws out, by the number, the notes due on a particular day. To be sure that they are the right ones, he checks them off by the name of the drawer, and the amount. He enters them on his cash-book in the alphabetical order of the indorsers' names, writing the names of the drawers next, and then the amount, as in the example page. Those which belong to foreign banks are entered in the book of *General Accounts*, which differs from the individual book in having no extension rulings, as all the postings go into one ledger.

When all the notes are entered, they are arranged in the alphabetical order of the names of the *drawers*, and placed in a pile on the counter, with a weight on one end, so that any particular note called for can be slipped out, leaving the others still in order.

The discounted notes are drawn from the files in the same manner, and placed alphabetically under another weight. They are not entered separately on the cash-book, as they are to be posted in gross to *Bills Discounted;* the amount is transferred from the Tickler page at the close of the day.

The Teller is now prepared to receive payment for the notes as they may be called for. This preparation is always kept one day in advance, to avoid confusion with other duties in the morning.

The bank notices of the discounted notes are filled up with red ink, and those of the collection notes with black ink, which indicates at once in which pile the note is to be found.

The Note Teller reaches his desk by half-past eight

PAGE OF COLLECTION NOTE-BOOK.

Indorser, or Owner.	Payer.			A to F.		G to L.		M to R.		S to Z.	
		$	c.	$	c.	$	c.	$	c.	$	c.
John Adams	W. Stimson	250									
	S. Ackley & Co	1,242	75								
	T. Watson	1,500	10	2,992	85						
Thos. Barton & Co.	E. Sickles	4,000									
	Bell & T.	152	70	4,152	70						
Samuel Chambers.	Corse & Noxon	1,600	00	protested							
Wm. Jackson	T. Thomas	1,050	75			1,050	75				
Lindley & Murray	S. Wilson	542	30			542	30				
Parker, Starr & Co.	O. Jones	2,000						2,000			
Richardson & Ott.	G. Roberts	1,750						1,750			
Stout, Rose & Co.	L. Jackson	5,040	24								
	P. Alexander	10,001	42							15,041	66
Truman & Webb	A. Davis	1,450								1,450	
Waterman & Co	R. Still	375	10	protested							
Joseph Young	P. Stark & Co	1,640	70								
	Johnson & Swift	2,500								4,140	70
		33,120	96	7,145	55	1,593	05	3,750	00	20,632	36
				A to F						7,145	55
				G to L						1,593	05
				M to R						3,750	00
				Proof						33,120	96

o'clock, or in season to make the entries of remittances received by the morning's mail. The following is the usual form of a letter, with abbreviations:

"PHILADELPHIA BANK.

"PHILADELPHIA, June 18, 1858.

"H. MORSE, ESQ., Cash'r.

"DEAR SIR—Inclosed, find for our credit:

Peters,	Cash'r., on	Com.		L.	$9400.00
Ruffin,	" "	Am.		L.	10000.00
Luther,	" "	Am. Ex.		L.	1575.60
Simpson,	" "	Met.		L.	14263.70
Corse & Co.,	" "	Nat.		L.	1800.00
Kerr,	" "	Phx.		L.	2740.00
Brown,	"	Thompson,	3 ds.	P.	1250.00
Green,		Burr & Co.	10 ds.	P.	3263.20
Wilson,			3 mos.	P.	2249.75
White,			90 ds.	P.	242.90
Kent,		Alby.	2 mos.	P.	506.00
Mather,		Buffo.	45 ds.	P.	1000.00
Gray & Co.,		Hartfd.	Sight,	P.	2600.00
Roberts,		Port.	10 ds.	P.	1050.00

"Market tight—no change in rates—business active, &c.

"Yours, resp'y, T. BARKER, Cash'r."

The open letter is given to the Teller, who writes his initial, L., as his receipt for all checks that he takes from it for credit to the remitting bank. In like manner, all letters containing cash documents are passed into his hands, and the proper entries made from them.

Both the discounted and collection notes are classed into *domestic* and *foreign*. The latter are payable in various towns and cities over the country, and those which belong to the accounts of the Note Teller, are transferred to him, when paid, from another book.

The payment of notes begins as soon as the bank-doors are open for public business. Generally the Runner's notice is handed in, with a certified check, or the exact amount in bank bills. It is one of the best habits of a Teller's desk to preserve the notices and memoranda of transactions in the order of their occurrence, until the cash is proved at the end of the day. They serve as hints to the memory, and although apparently trifling, often supply a link in a chain of investigation. Even if the Teller's cash should prove on first trial, it is still better to preserve his old file for several days, until the last probability of error shall have passed. Each bank has its stamp to imprint on notes when paid, of which the following is a common pattern.

The ink being in oil colors, cannot be readily removed from the face of the note, without at the same time obliterating the writing; and it makes a permanent record to the payer, by which the transaction may be traced, if necessary, at any subsequent time. It is also a substitute for the Cashier's indorsement, to which the payment is generally subject.

Up to one o'clock or later, payments are made

deliberately, and the Teller mostly has time to enter, and prepare his notes for the following day. He is obliged, however, to answer many questions, and to make examinations, which are not always connected with his business.

A dissatisfied face fills the gate in the railing:

"Is there a note of J. Freeman, six hundred dollars, due here to-day?"

"No, sir."

'Won't you look again? I've been to half the banks in the city, and can't find it."

"Have you no notice?"

"No, sir. I never get any, and always have to run about two or three hours to hunt up my notes."

On looking over the Tickler, the Teller discovers a record of J. Trueman, $600, due three days later, and on producing the note, Mr. Freeman identifies it as his own. The signature is carelessly written, and hence the error in copying it. Besides, there are ten or a dozen different J. Freemans and J. Truemans in the directory, so that the chances of the Runner finding the right man were as twenty to one. Mr. Freeman had himself omitted to allow for the three days' grace, in calculating the maturity of the note, so that he is entirely the author of his own perplexity. The Teller advises him to write his name more distinctly, and to mark his residence under it, by which he will avoid all trouble in future. If he had applied at a later hour, when the Teller could not spare the time to help him out of his trouble, the note would have been protested.

It is common for tradesmen to count sixty days as

two months, by which they get a wrong date of maturity for their notes, and often spend hours in searching for them, without success. Many persons keep no record of their notes, depending on the bank to serve them with notices. Some ask for a note or draft by the name of the indorser or drawer, instead of the *payer*, which is always the distinguishing name in bank records.

The delivery of a bank notice to a wrong person of the same name, incommodes both. One is obliged to hunt his note from bank to bank till he finds it, and the other is disturbed by a call to pay a note that he doesn't owe. As there is a chance of his having given one without a record, he hurries off to the bank to examine the original. On its being shown he says, angrily:

"Not mine!—I wish you wouldn't be bothering me with other people's notes. What have I got to do with that?"

"An unavoidable mistake, sir, by our Runner. He can't always hit the right man, when there are a dozen of the same name in the directory."

The customer thinks more angrily still that he "*ought* to hit the right man. It has cost him an hour's time and interruption to look up the matter, and it isn't the first, nor the twentieth wrong notice that has been served on him by different banks within a year."

He might save himself from all annoyance of this kind by the simple rule, which no merchant or tradesman ought to neglect—to record bills payable before signing them. No prejudice can then arise from disregarding the mistakes of others.

Mr. Fosforus hands a certified check to the Teller and wants to know "why he can't have notices sent. The Runner of any bank ought to be kicked out of it head foremost for such willful neglect."

The Teller calls the Runner to explain. Mr. Fosforus flashes out again in a general abuse of bank clerks, and "supposes none of 'em ever heard of the old silk house of Fosforus, Pine & Co."

The Runner declares that he delivered the notice to Mr. Pine in person, as he stood in his store door. "Has a distinct recollection. Knows Mr. Pine perfectly well. Been in his store a thousand times. Bushy hair—wears gold specs. Must have put the notice in his pocket instead of giving it to his clerk."

These altercations assume every phase that can be given by irritable temperaments, and are liberally interspersed with other accidents of the desk.

A dealer who has collection-paper coming due, and depends on its payment for his own liquidations, applies to know what portion of it is paid.

Another inquires whether certain protested paper with his indorsement has been taken up. Some want to withdraw paper that will not be paid.

The counting of bank bills received in remittance from correspondents in the country, is one of the common occupations of the Note Teller. These are to be distributed in his drawer, and recounted in the exchange lists to which they respectively belong.

An Express-agent brings a bag of gold, or a box of silver, to go to the credit of a country bank.

The President or Cashier comes along and looks casually at the various books and documents on the

Teller's desk, and inquires whether his payments are going as favorably as usual.

Many merchants write their notes payable at the bank where they keep their account. The Teller reserves the presentation of these until the latter part of the day, when the deposits are made to meet them, and then sends them by the Porter or other messenger, to the different banks for certification. When returned, he stamps the accepted ones paid, and distributes them in his exchange drawer.

The last half-hour of a busy day is full of excitement at the Teller's desk. A line of twenty or more note-payers is formed along the outside of the counter, pressing on each other's heels, and impatient that those before should crowd up. A new face is thrust into the little railing-gate every second. Some of them are in desperate haste, and the moment they receive their notes, rush off to other banks to make other payments. The Teller has not time now to answer questions, or to give explanations of anything. His attention must not be distracted for an instant from the process of receiving, counting, and stamping.

After the last payer is dismissed, he closes his gate, erases from the Cash-book and Discount Tickler the notes that remain unpaid, and delivers them to a Notary Public for protest.

The protest consists in presenting the note at the place of business of the drawer, or wherever it is made payable, and demanding the money for it. If still refused, it is attached to a printed legal form which recites the facts, and returned to the bank on the following day. The Notary sends notice of the protest to all the indorsers, and to the drawer of drafts, which advises them of their liability for the payment, in case of continued default of the first debtor. If the notes should be paid when presented by the Notary, he returns the money to the bank on the next morning.

The remaining labor of the Note Teller is to complete his Proof, which is a list precisely similar to that of the Deposit Teller. His money-drawer is of the same construction, and his manner of distributing the bills and checks the same. On the following morning he transfers the entire receipts of his department to the Deposit Teller, who incorporates them with his own, in a list called "The Settling Clerk's Statement," of which an example will be given in the account of the Clearing House. The receipts of both desks are then transferred to the Paying Teller, and all the exchangeable portion thereof sent by him to the Clearing House.

This is the complete theory of the Cash Department of the bank. All the receipts pass every day into the hands of the Paying Teller, leaving no open account with either of the receiving tellers.

A tight day at the Discount Desk.

CHAPTER VII.

THE DISCOUNT CLERK

The profit of the banking business consists, in general terms, of interest on money. Strictly, it is composed of interest, discount, and exchange.

Interest is simply the rent of money. It is payable at intervals, as agreed on between borrower and lender, and is not ordinarily considered due until the principal has been enjoyed.

The difference between interest and discount in bank practice is, that the former is payable at the end of a given term, while the latter is reserved from the principal at the beginning of the term.

When a note is discounted at bank, the interest for the period which it has to run before maturity is subtracted immediately, and the merchant receives credit for that much less than the total. This admits, to some extent, of compounding interest.

One hundred thousand dollars loaned on mortgage for six months, would yield at the end of that time, at the rate of seven per cent, a profit of three thousand five hundred dollars to the lender. The same amount discounted according to bank usage, would give the lender the same profit at the *beginning* of the term, with which he could discount another note of thirty-five hundred dollars for the same period. This would yield an additional profit of one hundred and twenty-two dollars and fifty cents; and this sum again loaned for the same time, would give a profit of about forty-three cents more. The difference between the two methods of operation on this amount is one hundred and twenty-two dollars and ninety-three cents, for six months.

The loan on simple interest would give this advantage to the borrower. By the method of discount, it is reserved to the lender.

A bank of several millions of capital derives a proportionably large gain by the same process; and the reduction of the discount period from six to two months, gives the opportunity of compounding the interest more frequently. The average period in our city banks is about forty days, which makes nine compounding terms for the year.

The general practice of Bank Board Directors in New York is, to meet on two stated days of the week, to act on the notes offered for discount. These are called *Discount Days.* Those immediately preceding are called *Offering Days*, because the notes are then sent in for preliminary record and examination.

The term *Offering* is applied either to a single note, or to the aggregate amount offered at a time. When bank officers meet, and wish to ascertain the general current of the market, they ask: "How are your offerings?" The same expression is used in the newspaper reports to indicate the activity of demand for money "The offerings at bank are heavy—or light."

In a bank of the first class, the number of dealers

who apply for discounts on the stated days is from seventy-five to one hundred. Some offer a single note, and others a dozen. They are usually enclosed in a letter sheet, with a brief description, embracing drawer, date, and amount, with or without special communication.

FORMS OF LETTERS ENCLOSING OFFERINGS FOR DISCOUNT.

New York, June 18, 1857.

Thos. Brown, Esq., Cash'r:

Dear Sir—We offer for discount notes enclosed, as follows:

John Snowden,	Jan. 10,	6 mos.	$1245.60
Wm. Wilson,	Feb. 25,	do.	1400.00
S. Cannon,	April 4,	4 mos.	2340.75
			$4986.35

Yours, respectf'y, John Jones & Co.

We beg to say that our account will show a fair running balance, and that our discount line has been materially reduced within the last month.

J. J. & Co.

New York, June 18, 1857.

Thos. Brown, Esq., Cash'r:

Dear Sir—Enclosed, find our note at sixty days, for $10,000, with fifteen of our business notes as collateral. By discounting the same, you will oblige,

Yrs., Resp'y. Cobb & Bro.

New York, June 18, 1857.

To Pres., Cash., and Directors, Commercial Bank:

Gentn—Pleas discount My note herein, Jno. Jones, $275, it is a one and No mistake.

Obt. P. Stanley.

New York, June 18, 1857.

Thos. Brown, Esq., Cash'r:

Dear Sir—we enclose again our offering for discount, which you rejected last day. See memo., with particulars.

Our need is somewhat pressing, and you would do us a great favor to pass the whole. The paper is good beyond casualty. If you desire reference, or further explanation with regard to it, we can satisfy you. The general run of our dealings with the bank entitles us to more liberal consideration than we have yet had. Our balance of account has seldom fallen below $3,000, and our line has not averaged over $8,000. It is now reduced to about half that sum. We therefore make this application with confidence that it will be accepted.

Yours, respectf'y, Sergeant, Wilkes & Co.

New York, June 18, 1857.

Cashier Commercial Bank:

Put to my credit $1800 as inclosed.

Yrs., &c. M. Wessells.

The Discount Clerk records them in the Offering Book, in the alphabetical order of the dealers' names, and numbered to correspond with the margin. In the first column (see page 203), are the names of the offerers, followed by their average balance of deposits, the amount which they have already under discount, the names of indorsers, if any, or statement of collateral securities, the names of the payers, the time to maturity, and lastly the amount. This record presents an abstract of the whole Offering, with the state of each account, enabling the directors to judge of its value and desert. The footing of the column shows the total amount offered.

PAGE OF OFFERING-BOOK.

	Offered by	Average Balance.	Amount under Discount.	Indorser.	Payer.	Time.	Amount.			Discount.		Net.	
		$	$				$	c.		$	c.	$	c.
1	Joseph Adams........	1,200	4,500	....	W. Stimson............	45 days	1,206	72	A	10	42	1,196	30
2	Askew & Physick.....	2,200	6,000	I. Hicks..............	S. Ackley & Co........	2 mos.	1,500		Ref.	to	of	ficers	..
3	Jno. Bullock & Co....	4,000	7,000	Collaterals with their	own note..............	90 days	5,000		A	86	30	4,913	70
4	Cobb & Brother.......	250	1,500	T. Watson.............	O. Jones & Son........	4 mos.	750	16	R	....	..	......	..
5	Foster & Sons........	none	800	R. Owen...............	Peter Smith...........	60 days	300		R	....	..	......	..
6	Thos. Larkin.........	600	1,200	....	Jesse Gauze...........	30 days	655	40	A	3	77	651	63
7	Mitchell & Clark.....	overdr'wn	2,000	....	L. Jackson............	3 mos.	375		R	....	..	......	..
8	Joseph Scott.........	900	2,300	Enoch Lewis...........	Robt. Hunard..........	75 days	1,650	34	A	23	73	1,626	61
9	Thompson & Co........	1,500	none	....	D. Thorn..............	120 days	3,425	90	A	78	85	3,347	05
10	James Wilson.........	6,000	2,400	Cyrus Newlin..........	S. Griscom............	90 days	10,243	72	A	176	81	10,066	91
11	Robert Young.........	1,400	3,000	25 shares bank stock as	collateral to his own note	60 days	1,600		Ref.	to	of	ficers	..
12	Zabriskie & Co.......	4,500	5,000	15 business notes, as per	letter, amounting to.....	....	7,400		A	162	40	7,237	60
							34,107	24		542	28	29,039	80
					Amount accepted...............		29,582	08				542	28
												29,582	08

The form of the Offering Book is not the same in all banks. Some dispense with the balance column, and some add another, showing the liquidations before the next discount day. Others enter loans also on this book, to the credit of the borrower, on the theory that everything in the nature of a discount ought to be shown in one consecutive history. The Directors have, then, before them when they meet, a statement of every transaction that has taken place, without the necessity of referring to other books.

The old-fashioned Offering Book was a mere blotter of abbreviated entries, from which the accepted paper was transcribed either to a General Register, and from that to the Discount Books, or direct to the latter. This method is still in use, and in banks which have much paper of an inferior class offered, the transcription is necessary to a neat record.

After preparing the Offering Book, the clerk refolds the envelopes, so that the notes can be conveniently examined, without being separated therefrom.

The preparation of these details occupies considerable time; and therefore it is required that the offerings be brought in before two o'clock. They are dropped in a box at the desk of the Discount Clerk.

Dealers seldom appreciate the value of time to bank clerks. They are apt to say: "That's what he was put there for—to wait on customers. He gets a good salary—who cares if it is after two?"

An addition to the offerings after they are partly recorded deranges their alphabetical order—which embarrasses every subsequent use of the book in transcribing or posting. The Ledger accounts are opened in the same order, and not only the facility, but the accuracy of the system is greatly aided by its preservation. Each dealer should reflect how much easier it is for him to observe a stated rule, than it is for the clerk to overcome the inconvenience that results from the concentration of many irregularities on one point.

The Offering Book and the packet of notes are returned to the Discount Clerk, after being acted upon by the Board of Directors. He finds the letter A (accepted), scored opposite to each offering that is to be discounted, and the letter R (rejected), opposite those which are refused. Any that are otherwise disposed of, are marked accordingly.

The record of the accepted paper is now transferred to *Discount Books*, of which there is one for each dealer's ledger, embracing the same letters of the alphabet. The discount and net proceeds of the notes are extended in the additional columns on the Offering Book, of which the footings must agree with the aggregate footings of the Discount Books. From these latter the credits are posted to the accounts in the ledgers.

Another plan is, to transfer the discounted paper from the Offering Book to a Register, whence it is posted to the personal accounts.

There are also *Discount Ledgers*, which are opened in the same manner as the personal ledgers, but embrace the accounts of those dealers only who get notes discounted. They show each note that has been discounted for any dealer, the date of its discount, the indorser or security liable for it, if any, and the time of its maturity. The whole is kept footed in pencil, being subject to frequent change by the payment of notes as they mature, and the addition of new entries. They exhibit also the liability of each dealer as indorser for others on discounted paper; this being one of the most important points to guard in the banking business. If any two dealers should exchange notes or indorsements, and put them in the same bank, these books would expose the fact. They are placed on the Directors' table on discount days for reference, as may be required.

It is from these auxiliary Ledgers that the clerk ascertains the amount of discounts set down in the Offering Book. He keeps daily supervision over them, cancelling the paid notes as fast as they mature, by a ruled line across the figures, without obliterating the record.

The notes are numbered on the back and end with red ink, and filed in neat packets. They are also transcribed on the Discount Ticklers, each under the date of its maturity, with the number, name of the payer, and amount. The Ticklers continue to receive accessions by new discounts, up to within a few days of the transpiring date. They are kept added in pencil until that time, when they are finally closed in ink.

In some banks, the notes are filed without numbering, those of each day being kept in a separate packet, and the packets in the consecutive order of the dates. This plan is thought to be more convenient where the number of notes is very large, and it has the advantage of easier reference to all that mature on any single day. It also brings the department more within the reach of an extempore examination without the aid of the clerk himself.

The Discount Clerk makes a proof of his books at the end of each month. The addition of his Ticklers ought to show the exact amount of bills discounted, corresponding with the balance of this account on the General Ledger. The final and conclusive test is, by checking off the Ticklers with the notes, which proves them to be in actual possession of the bank.

The Discount Clerk holds in his immediate charge the greater part of the bills receivable, in which the means of the bank are invested. He deposits the trunk containing them in the vault at the close of the day, and resumes the personal care of it on the next morning. The officers may change or regulate this custody, but they do not interfere with it so as to impair his direct responsibility for its contents. If they wish to examine particular notes, they do so in his presence, or require him to produce them. Their own meddling, or that of other clerks, would justify the defence that he is no more accountable than they, if any should be lost or stolen; and it might exonerate his bondsmen from their liability.

Next to the officers, the Discount Clerk shares most in personal intercourse with the customers of the bank; and in some respects, on terms more favorable to the observation of character, on which so much depends in the business. They apply to him after the adjournment of the Board meetings to know how their Offerings have been disposed of, and he witnesses their extemporaneous expressions of anxiety and disappointment when they are rejected. He is the stated medium of communication between the officers and the dealers respecting the business of his desk, and in the majority of cases there is no need of any other. In a season of severe pressure, when personal solicitation with the officers becomes common, a half confidential tone is maintained with the clerk. He is "near the throne," and if not specially instructed, is supposed to have more or less influence, and to be capable of giving some useful hints.

The stated meetings of the Board usually begin at nine o'clock, A. M., and occupy from one to two hours. The customers, or their clerks, then call to know the result of their applications. When the market is very stringent, they not unfrequently throng at the desk before the adjournment, taking their places in succession to push forward as soon as the books and notes are given to the clerk. The letter A enables him to answer, either by an affirmative nod, or the monosyllable "done," and the letter R, by reference to the number, to return the rejected notes in the original envelop to the owner.

The first crowd of the morning is composed of the most anxious dealers. It is important for them to know early, whether they must seek elsewhere the bread of commercial life for the day. They are followed by the less needy, or the more deliberate, who know the value of "deportment" in a tight market.

"Notes done, sir?" is asked by the applicants, either verbally, or in pantomime.

The affirmative causes a bright gleam of sunshine

Consolation. Better fare than at the Discount Board.

in the face of the questioner. But a negative to the next comer substitutes a scowl of disappointment.

"What is the reason of that, sir? Has the bank stopped discounting?"

"Market tightened up, sir. Deposits down. Offerings very heavy."

The customer departs with an audible growl of indignation at what he conceives to be "a denial of rights."

Number Twenty. "Good morning, Mr. Smith, what have you to say to me?"

"Nothing very encouraging, sir. The Board discounted one of your notes."

"What—only one out of ten?"

"That's all. Very good proportion, I do assure you."

"A single thousand! And I want five to-day! Where's the President?"

"In his room, sir. But I don't believe you'll gain anything by talking to him. Our receipts are very small just now, and the Porter brings bad news from the Clearing House."

Number Twenty-one fills the little gate in the railing with a grum and threatening visage, but does not speak. The clerk knows him as a frequent applicant, and seldom a fortunate one, the character of his account, as well as of his paper, being inferior, and presenting no claims worthy of consideration by the Directors. He receives back his offering without remark, and departs in sullen silence.

Number Twenty-two. "Well, Smith, don't tell me my notes ain't done?"

"Wouldn't if I could help it, sir. Board did mighty little this morning."

"Hang the Board! Isn't there any explanation? Dont they know the paper? Is it too long?"

"No explanation given to me. Bank's short. Can't help it. Majority in the same boat."

Twenty-two leaves an oath behind him.

Number Twenty-three. "My paper done?"

"No, sir."

"What's in the wind now?"

"Market tightened up."

"Don't they do *any* thing?"

"Not much."

"Well, they do *some!* Why the devil can't they distribute the thing impartially?"

"I s'pose they try to do it; but it's not an easy matter to satisfy an offering of four hundred thousand dollars with about one fourth of that amount of means."

Number Twenty-four is a man in his shirt-sleeves—a carman or laborer, with a small debt on his house to discharge.

"Mr. Clerk, will you be good enough to hand me the proceeds of that note?"

"What name, sir?"

"Axletree is my name."

"Mr. Axletree, I am sorry to return your note. The Board couldn't discount it."

Outside. Two per Cent. a Month.

"What! Can't give me the money for a note of five hundred dollars?"

The explanations of the clerk are nothing to him. He sees only a bank with three millions of capital on one hand, and his trifling call for five hundred dollars on the other.

"Now, what shall I do?" he asks. "I have no other place to get this money. I've kept an account in this bank for five years and never asked a favor; and now I want this little accommodation, and can't get it! Do you call that fair?"

The Discount Clerk steps over to the Book-keeper's desk and examines Mr. Axletree's account. He finds that his average balance for several years has seldom fallen below three or four hundred dollars. On communicating this fact to the Cashier, Mr. Axletree is recalled, and the merits of his application appearing sound, the note is passed to his credit.

Attention to these small and comparatively obscure accounts is one of the best traits in a bank officer or clerk. They are liable to be overlooked in the pressure and importunity of more important business.

"Mr. Gray sent me to ask if his notes are discounted."

"No, my lad, they're not. Tell Mr. Gray that his paper is too long." At the same time, the Clerk hands back the offering, which the boy declines, saying that "Mr. Gray told him to leave it, and he would see the President about it.

Three out of four of all the applicants are disappointed. They leave the bank, knitting their brows into frowns and nervous distortions. Some mutter oaths of indignation at "such infamous treatment." Boys express themselves indifferently by a suppressed whistle, or with a "Pooh! governor won't relish that!"

The last thought that enters the mind of any, is, that there are twenty applicants for every thousand dollars that the bank has to dispense.

Number Thirty gets an affirmative nod from the Discount Clerk; and the smile of satisfaction with which he leaves the bank is like a sunbeam in the midst of winter clouds. He is such a profitable customer, keeping a large balance on deposit, while asking for comparatively moderate accommodations, that the Directors dare not refuse him.

Number Thirty-one.—"What luck!"

"If you'll make a note for twenty-five hundred dollars instead of five thousand, and put it forty-five days instead of ninety, it'll go through."

"The deuce! That will only put me to the necessity of coming again next week; and that's what I wanted to avoid."

"You are very fortunate to get any, I assure you. The great majority are disappointed entirely."

"Well, I reckon a fellow must be satisfied with half a loaf."

These examples of conversation and incident are sufficient to give a general notion of the daily experience of the Discount Clerk.

Inside. The Consequences of Two per Cent. a Month.

The Discount Clerk handles no money. He has no occasion to touch a bank bill or a piece of coin. His business is exclusively with the bills receivable, and with the accounts. The only most obvious method by which he could perpetrate a fraud, would be, by abstracting notes, and negotiating them through other parties—an operation in which discovery would threaten him at every turn. There was an instance in the old Bank of the United States, of a Clerk abstracting notes after they were discounted and filed away. He selected those which in his judgment would be least likely to be called for, or referred to, before maturity, and by the help of a friend outside of the bank, hypothecated them in an obscure channel, for a loan of money. When they were near due, he selected others of longer date to substitute for them, and restored them to their proper place in the files. The trick was discovered by the maker of one of the hypothecated notes calling at the bank to pay it before its maturity. In banks of effective discipline, such abstraction of paper could not long be concealed.

Discounted notes, which are payable in other cities, are transmitted by mail; and when advice of their payment is received, a Journal entry is made, charging the collecting bank, and crediting bills discounted, in the usual commercial form. A remittance for the balance liquidates the account.

The same end is answered equally well by other methods of entry.

CHAPTER VIII.

THE NOTE DEPARTMENT.

Commerce, in its broadest sense, is carried on by promissory notes. The multiplication of this form of credit is beyond all control. It loads every department of trade, from pins and needles up to cargoes of grain and cotton. It represents ships, railroads, manufactories, public and private contracts. The "pass-book" of the housekeeper is balanced by a note at three or six months. The retailer purchases goods of the jobber, and gives his note in settlement. The jobber gives notes to the wholesale merchant, and he in turn to the manufacturer or producer. The manufacturer gives notes for the raw material. The factor is already under acceptance to the grower, and the grower's notes are given to the banks long before his "fields are white unto harvest." The sugar that reaches our wharves from Havanna or New Orleans has two or three sets of notes predicated on it before the first hogshead is discharged from the vessel; and it continues to accumulate notes as it passes through the hands of the refiner into those of the grocer. Even after it has been swallowed in confections, its notes are still floating, unliquidated, in the market. The market carries millions of notes for what is already consumed, and millions more for what is not yet sprouted in the furrow. The United States Government has lately settled thirty millions of debt by promissory notes, and is rapidly creating the necessity for a further indefinite issue.

The bank is the principal channel of liquidation for all this mass of notes. Those which are not discounted are first entered on the Dealers' Book by the clerk, after careful examination. Informality of indorsement, obscurity of date, or other accident, might make the bank liable to the holder, although it is merely the collecting agent. It is the duty of the Clerk to scrutinize every note narrowly before entering it, and especially to see that the owner is the last indorser, that it may not be placed to a wrong credit, when due. Banks generally will not receive for collection notes which have been disfigured, or changed after issue by the drawer; nor will they receive them from strangers on any terms, even if they are correctly drawn in every respect.

Promissory Notes are commercial currency. They are transferred, by indorsement, from one merchant to another, in settlement of debts, the same as bank bills: differing only in this—that they mature at a stated subsequent time, and that the other indorsers are liable to the owner, in case of non-payment by the drawer. An owner may transfer a note to another, by special agreement that he is to be held exempt from such liability. This is expressed in the indorsement by the words "without recourse," above the name of the exempt indorser.

The *Collection Register* is a book of record ruled in columns, so as to describe the note in a single line. See form on page 217.

The Clerk marks on each note the date of its maturity. If he should mark it one day too late, and the drawer fail to pay, the bank would be liable to the owner, because the notice of protest to the indorsers would be out of legal time. Hence the importance of accuracy in this record. A careful clerk is not satisfied without such revision of his "timing" of notes as to give every possible guarantee against error.

Tricky dealers have been known to mark a wrong date of maturity on notes, for the purpose of "catching" the bank in this liability. The bank could not escape by showing the wrong date to be that of the dealer, unless it could prove the intent. It is bound to be exact in its own business, and can urge no legal excuse for adopting the errors of others.

After the notes are "timed," they are numbered consecutively on the back and end, and recorded in the Register, from which they are copied into the *Ticklers.*

A *Tickler* is a book which exhibits, when complete, all the notes maturing within the month, each under its proper date of payment. Those which fall due on the first, are transcribed under that date; and those that fall due on the second, under that; and so on, until the book presents a consecutive date record for the month. There are twelve Ticklers for each year, and two sets—one for the collection, and one for the discounted notes. They are designated by the name

FORMS OF NOTE REGISTERS.

DOMESTIC NOTE REGISTER.

When Received.		Owner.	Indorser.	Payer.	Date and Time.	When Due.	Amount. $	c.	
June	18	Peter Scriber......	N. Dixon..........	J. Holly & Co. ...	April 9—4 mo's..	Aug. 12.	1,420	65	
	"	John Adams......	do.	S. Upton.........	Mar. 8—6 mo's..	Sep. 6...	2,504	25	
July	14	William Wilson...	....	Alexander Jones..	Jan. 20—8 mo's..	Sep. 23..	245		

FOREIGN NOTE REGISTER.

When Received.		Owner.	Indorser.	Payer.	Date and Time.	When Due.	Amount. $	c.	Where Payable.	Where Sent.
June	20	Jno. Crane & Co...	H. Wagstaff.......	Hull & Bro........	April 4—4 mo's..	Aug. 7..	1,425	16	Saratoga....	Bank of Albany.
	24	William Wilson...	Jno. Stacy.........	O. Roberts........	Jan. 1—8 mo's..	Sep. 4...	294	28	Lynn, Mass.	Merch'ts' Bank, Bos.
	"	E. Lewis & Co.....	....	Wheeler & Son...	Feb. 6—8 mo's..	Oct. 9...	1,250		Troy	Bank of Albany.
	"	Benj'n Hicks......	Sam'l Snow.......	Frost & Co........	June 5—3 mo's..	July 8..	2,462	50	Albany.....	do.
	"	Gray & Thompson	....	S. Sweet..........	May 4—4 mo's..	Sep. 7...	3,507	20	Salem.......	Merch'ts' Bank, Bos.
July	12	Jno. Crane & Co...	....	Hull & Bro........	May 2—4 mo's..	" 5...	1,240	16	Saratoga....	Bank of Albany.
	"	E. Brown..........	Jno. Jones........	W. Torry..........	June 10—4 mo's..	Oct. 13..	650		New Bedf'd	Merch'ts' Bank, Bos.

of the month—the January Tickler, the February Tickler, and so forth. There is an auxiliary set in the Discount Department, for the foreign notes.

PAGE OF TICKLER.

MONDAY, *June 1st*, 1857.

			$	c.
53	W. Stimson		240	00
62	S. Ackley & Co.		1,650	75
63	T. Watson	Merchants' Bank	1,000	00
110	E. Sickles		500	20
240	Bell & T.		5,240	75
241	Corse & N.	Merchants' Bank	1,320	00
245	T. Thomas		750	00
246	S. Wilson	14 Pearl street	2,250	00
400	O. Jones	Leather Bank	110	16
570	G. Roberts		48	75
860	L. Jackson	Notice to L. J.	10,050	14

One of the chief uses of the Tickler is, to facilitate the drawing of notes from the packages, as the days of maturity come round. The record consists merely of the number of the note, the name of the payer, and the amount. The residence of parties whose names are not in the directory is given, to aid the Runner in serving notices. When notes are made payable at banks, that also is set down in the Tickler, to indicate that notice to the drawers is not necessary.

Application is frequent for notes due at a future day, out of the regular routine of business, either for payment, examination of indorsements, or other purpose. Reference to the Tickler gives the number, and they can be produced in a second.

It is a general rule of banks, that collection-notes should be deposited not later than ten days or a fortnight before their maturity, that there may be ample time to pass them through the various books, and to serve seasonable notice on the payers. But this regulation cannot be strictly enforced, since merchants are in constant receipt of short-time drafts. Their collection-paper is often hypothecated for temporary loans, or attached as collateral to discounted paper; and various other circumstances interfere with their observance of the rule. When notes are deposited too near their maturity to admit of notice being served without unreasonable trespass on the time of the Runner, it is either dispensed with, or the depositor himself serves it.

The Clerk of this department is responsible for the safe keeping and production, at an instant's call, of any note or draft deposited in the bank. If payable in the city, he can exhibit it; if in the country, he can show the course of transmission by which it has passed out of his custody.

The *Foreign* Note Register is a book which differs from the Domestic Register, only in having one additional column for the name of the place where the note is payable, and another for that of the bank, to which it is sent for collection (p. 217).

It is the practice of the banks in New York to make their collections for a district of country through some one bank, which has an established correspondence with all parts of it. For instance, a bank in Albany or Troy will collect notes in all the adjacent counties more promptly and cheaply than it could be done by separate correspondence of the city bank with each town.

On this plan the Clerk opens another book, and records on a page appropriated to the Bank of Albany, all notes that fall within that collection circuit. He writes or stamps on the back of each, below all other indorsements:

PAY BANK OF ALBANY.

Under this the Cashier signs his name; and the letter enclosing the notes, after being copied, is sent to its address by mail.

CHAPTER IX.

THE BOOK-KEEPER.

At first sight, nothing is more simple than the keeping of a bank-ledger of personal accounts. All that is to be done is, to post the deposits of a dealer to his credit, and the checks to his debit. His Bank-book must be "written up" to correspond with the Ledger, and balanced from time to time, as a mutual test between them.

The first requisite of a bank Book-keeper is, a fair style of writing. It is more essential to write plainly than elegantly. To a bank officer, the flourishes and fine hair-strokes of an accomplished penman are like foppery. He wants to see full, strong figures, that can be distinguished from each other at a glance: add to this, that they must be set down in columns—units under units, and tens under tens—and the most important requisitions for bank book-keeping are answered. The Clerk must be ready at addition and subtraction, with a habit of prompt and accurate transcription.

Moderate as these requirements are, our city banks have frequent cause to complain of inefficiency in their book-keepers. Ledgers are not regularly balanced. They gradually fall behind, and it is extremely difficult to bring them up again; for the accumulation of figures never ceases. An account cannot be stopped short, subject to the convenience or tardiness of the Clerk. The whole Ledger, with its five hundred accounts, has hundreds of postings added to it every day. The reason why so many Book-keepers fail, is not for want of capacity, but because of poor system, or no system at all.

The number of Book-keepers in a bank is in proportion with the number of its dealers. Three or four hundred accounts may be kept in a single ledger; but where there are twelve or fifteen hundred, as in the Metropolitan Bank, and others of the same rank, four ledgers are necessary, and a clerk to each. The dealers are classed alphabetically. All names beginning with the letters from A to F are assigned to the first ledger; those from G to L, to the second; those from M to R, to the third, and those from S to Z, to the fourth.

A ledger of the usual size contains twelve hundred pages. On the supposition that four hundred accounts are to be opened in it, it would be very easy to arrange them alphabetically, assigning three pages to each. But the result of this would be, total disorder, after the ledger has been in use a short time. Some accounts will show but one deposit and three or four checks in a week, while others have twice that many for every day—which would soon make it necessary to transfer them from page to page, and so destroy the arrangement. There is another difficulty to be provided against: when a ledger is begun in a new business, the clerk has no prepared list of names in an index to apportion; these will come in the progress of the business. To meet this case, and also the fact that the letters of the alphabet are not equally fruitful in proper names, a complete system of apportionment has been devised, which shows, that in a ledger of 1200 pages, 68 should be appropriated to names beginning with A, 88 to B, 136 to C, 52 to D, only 8 to Q, 6 to Y, and but one to the letter X; that is to say, that the number of proper names beginning with C is about double the number beginning with A, and seventeen times greater than those with Q. This apportionment is based on a careful examination of directories, encyclopedias, dictionaries, library catalogues, gazetteers, and other alphabetical works; and although it embraces the names of objects and places, it may be assumed as correct for all practical uses in book-keeping.

The "vowel order" is generally adopted in the distribution of accounts, and the apportionment under this also has been determined with great accuracy. For example, the 136 pages in C must be appropriated as follows:

To	*Ca,*	*Ce,*	*Ci,*	*Co,*	*Cu,*	*Cy,*	
	48,	12,	12,	48,	12,	4,	pages.

This is the order in which every ledger should be opened, to obtain the full aid of classification to the memory. It gives the following result:

a,	*e,*	*i,*	*o,*	*u,*	*y,*
Charlton,	Cresson,	Chisholm,	Corwin,	Cruden,	Clymer,
Candy,	Crewel,	Crisp,	Crowell,	Church,	Cryder,
Carter,	Creamer,	Clifford,	Corning,	Cludius,	Clyde.

If all the accounts in all the ledgers of a bank are opened in this order, the economy of time must be very sensibly felt in conducting the business; and it is not too much to say, that neglect of such arrangement will inevitably expose it to errors, inaccuracies, and greater expenses.

The continual changes arising from the discontinuance of old, and the accession of new accounts, make it impossible to preserve a stricter alphabetical order than is obtained by following the inflecting vowel.

The number of blank pages to be left for each account depends on the frequency of transactions, and must be left to the judgment of the Book-keeper. The time occupied in laying out his plans, and reducing everything to a regular system, will return to him a thousand-fold in the general economy of his work.

The Certification Check-list, on page 115, being the same in its rulings and forms of entry, may represent equally well the Second Teller's Cash-book, supposing the entries to be deposits instead of checks. The Book-keeper who has the Ledger from S to Z, extends into his column the deposits of Slater & Co., E. West & Co., and Wood & Carpenter; and in like manner, each other Book-keeper makes the extensions which belong to his column, and the amounts are posted to the credit of the depositors in the Ledgers. At the close of the day, the footings of the several columns are brought together, as in the example, and their sum must agree with the addition of the main column. This process of receiving and posting goes on with short intervals until three o'clock, the alternate Cash-book being substituted on the Teller's desk, while the Book-keepers use the other. In the same way precisely the proceeds of collection notes are posted to the Ledger. See page 191.

It appears by their Bank-book, on page 161, that Slater & Co. have deposited at various dates the sums that are attested by the initial of the Teller's name, A. They have received credit also for bills discounted, $22,363.18, and for the notes of Jones, and Brown, from the former of which $12.50 is deducted for exchange or expenses of collection. This is all the variety there is in bank credits. It exemplifies all the entries that are made on every dealer's book to his credit. The checks drawn by Slater & Co., from June 19 to July 16, are charged on the opposite page, and the balance $18,819.84 is carried down as a new starting-point in their dealings, corresponding with the statement of their account in the Ledger.

The transposition of the columns of figures, and of the heading of the Bank-book, so as to read "*Slater & Co. in a/c with the Commercial Bank*," would make an exact copy of the account of Slater & Co., as it appears in the *Ledger*.

All checks paid by the Paying Teller, and all that are received in deposit, or for notes at the desks of the Second and Third Tellers, are cancelled by them, and handed over to the *Check Clerk*, by whom they are recorded in books, called *Check-lists*, from which they are posted to their proper ledger accounts by the Book-keepers. The cancelling of checks consists in passing them on to a wire over a blade, which cuts them, so that if they should be lost and presented a second time, they would be known as old checks already paid. Each Teller has a distinctive cancelling cut, which at any future time indicates the desk at which the check was paid.

Many dealers draw twenty or thirty checks almost every day. These are entered singly on the Check-list in an inner column, extended in one sum into a main column, and posted to the Ledger in one sum, to economize the page. When the Book-keeper "writes up" a dealer's account, he copies the amount of each check *from the list* into his Bank-book, and if no mistake has been made, the book-balance and the ledger-balance will agree. Then he compares the cancelled checks with the record on the dealer's book, and thus arrives at a double test of the accuracy of the account.

Connected with each Book-keeper's desk is a drawer, divided into boxes like the money-drawers, in which the checks are kept distributed, those of each dealer separate from all others. If a dealer should come in at any moment, in the apprehension that a forged check had been paid against his account, the Book-keeper can produce all his checks, instantly, for examination.

It is of the first importance, that the Book-keeper post the deposits and checks (more particularly the latter) as fast as they come in; and keep both sides of every account in the Ledger added up in pencil, that, if he should be absent, either of the Tellers may ascertain at a glance whether a check is good. If present, he can answer from memory as to the condition of the active accounts. It is not necessary that he shall always know the exact balance of an account, to tell whether checks against it may be safely paid or certified. Long familiarity with it enables him to answer on the instant, without interrupting even the additions in which he may be engaged. The Paying Teller asks:

"Is Edward Wilson's account good for ten thousand dollars?"

"Yes—for twenty on top of it."

"Can I certify Peter Smith's check for five hundred dolls?"

"No—not for five hundred cents!"

"How does Robert Taylor's account stand?"

"He has about sixteen hundred dollars here."

The Book-keeper may not have seen either of these accounts for a week; but he knows them by heart.

One of the officers requests him to open the Ledger to John Brown's page.

"What sort of an account does he keep?"

"Very poor—a mere tax on the bank."

"How's that? He seems to make large deposits!"

"Yes, sir; but the Exchange checks consume them every morning, almost to the last dollar."

"Does he ever overdraw?"

"No, sir; but always lean."

John Brown does not succeed in getting the loan he applied for. Neither does he know how completely the Book-keeper has destroyed his chances for the future.

Many accounts appear on the Ledger with a running balance of thousands of dollars, when, in fact, nearly every thing is drawn out by the Exchange checks—a very important point to be watched by the Book-keeper. In stating balances, the Exchange checks are always deducted from the apparent balance at the close of the previous day. Thus, if John Brown had a balance of twelve thousand dollars on the Ledger at night, and his checks for eleven thousand five hundred dollars should come in through the Clearing House on the next morning, his balance of account would be reported at five hundred dollars.

The statement of balances made on the Offering Book is generally an average for the previous month. Heavy deposits, which dealers sometimes borrow to swell their account on the day or two before offering notes for discount, go for nothing.

The freedom of the Book-keeper's accounts from all complexity leaves him without excuse for errors. He has no original entries to make, and there is no variety of transactions, as in mercantile affairs. There are no different currencies, and there is no mixing of work between different ledgers. Each Book-keeper has exclusive control of his own, with such division of labor and susceptibility of proof, at every step, as ought to assure positive correctness. The officers, therefore, hold him to very strict account. Their presumption is, that errors can come about only by inattention—not by want of capacity; and the consequences of inattention may be too serious to admit that as an excuse. For example: the posting of John Brown's deposit of one thousand dollars to the credit of Alexander Jones, would give the latter a chance to draw it out; and Brown may not want to use any money for a month. His check then appears as an overdraft, and the Book-keeper sends him a note:

"COMMERCIAL BANK, June 18th, 1857.

"JOHN BROWN, Esq.:

"Your account appears overdrawn $1,000. Please deposit that amount, and send your book to be written up.

"For the Cashier, W. GREEN,
Book-keeper."

This is a printed form, which the clerk fills up with the name of the delinquent, and the amount.

Mr. Brown very promptly appears, with his Bank-book, to prove that he had the money in bank; and the Book-keeper then discovers his error. The posting is immediately corrected, and the overdraft thrown upon Jones, who is unable to pay, and the bank loses. The rule of revision is, that after the credits have been posted, they shall be checked off between the Ledger and the Cash-Books, either after banking hours on the same day, or before the beginning of business on the next day.

The balancing of the dealers' books is one of the most laborious parts of the Book-keeper's duty. It is the practice to "rule off" the Ledgers on the last day of every month, for the purpose of making the monthly Proof-sheet. The additions of the account, and the balance carried down, are commonly left in pencil, until their accuracy is tested by agreement with the dealer's book. Dealers are requested to leave their books, at the end of every month, for this test.

The monthly Proof-sheet of the Book-keeper is simply a list of all the balances on his Ledger, which, added together, must agree with the amount of deposits posted in gross to the *General Ledger.* A skillful and accurate Book-keeper will generally lay this Proof complete on the Cashier's table, on the first or second day of each month. Otherwise, the Cashier calls on him to know the reason of delay.

The Book-keeper, like every other clerk, has his share of interruptions and annoyances. A dealer, whose own carelessness has led to an overdraft of his account, takes fire at the notice thereof, and throws his book on to the open Ledger, demanding that it shall be immediately balanced. Others want omitted deposits entered, or bills discounted, and collection notes written in at unseasonable times. Many call to know what the balance of their account is; and are surprised to learn that it is less than one hundred dollars, when it ought to be over a thousand. "Hav'n't you made some mistake in the additions? Is that last discount of mine entered? Hav'n't you charged me with a wrong check? Won't you be good enough to get out my checks, and let me examine them," &c.

The Book-keepers have no direct connection with the money department; but they may be accessory to fraud, and successfully conceal it for a long time.

A recent case occurred, in a city bank, of collusion with a dealer, in which, by altering figures on the various books, nearly a hundred and thirty thousand dollars were embezzled. Such a daring act of forgery as this, is fortunately beyond the reach of common hardihood; and therein consists a better security against it, than can result from any degree of vigilance by bank officers. Where one attempt of the kind would succeed, forty would fail from lack of impudence in the guilty person, if not from some weakness of a less disgraceful character. It is, nevertheless, the duty of bank managers to adopt precautions against the most unlikely frauds; and it has been proposed that the Clerks should serve in rotation at the respective desks, so as to increase the chances of detection, or to shorten the term of its possible concealment, if collusion should be attempted between the clerk and the dealer.

The Book-keeper is generally employed about seven or eight hours a day. In that time, with diligence and economy of minutes, he may keep a Ledger of twelve hundred pages and four hundred accounts in perfect order.

For a Ledger of three hundred pages, the following scale is to be divided by 4; for one of six hundred pages, by 2; and so by any number that leaves no remainder.

Scale of Apportionment for a Ledger of 1200 *pages.*
From "GOULD'S *Universal Index.*"

	a,	*e,*	*i,*	*o,*	*u,*	*y.*
A,	1	16	32	52	64	68
B,	72	96	116	124	144	156
C,	160	208	220	232	280	292
D,	296	308	320	328	336	344
E,	348	368	384	396	400	400
F,	404	412	424	436	456	456
G,	460	472	480	488	492	492
H	496	508	516	524	536	540
I,	544	548	556	560	560	560
J,	564	568	568	572	580	580
K,	584	588	596	600	600	600
L,	604	612	620	628	636	636
M,	640	672	676	684	700	704
N,	708	712	720	728	736	736
O,	740	744	752	756	756	756
P,	760	788	808	824	836	844
R,	848	856	868	876	896	900
S,	904	924	956	996	1016	1016
T,	1020	1036	1044	1056	1084	1092
U,	1096	1100	1104	1104	1104	1104
V,	1108	1120	1120	1124	1124	1124
W	1128	1140	1152	1172	1180	1180
X,	1184	1184	1184	1184	1184	1184
Y,	1184	1184	1188	1188	1188	1188
Z,	1192 to	1196	Q,	1196 to	1200.	

CHAPTER X.

THE GENERAL BOOK-KEEPER.

THIS Clerk derives his title from the character of the accounts in his Ledger, which are *general*, in distinction from *individual* or *personal;* and also, from the fact that he brings together the *general results* of the business, which appear in the *Bank Statement.*

In rank, the General Book-keeper stands at the head of the department of accounts. He takes precedence of the Discount Clerk, and is often regarded as equal with the Tellers, rather than below them. The object of describing in advance several of the inferior desks, is to show the origin of all the different entries which are posted to his Ledger.

The books of a bank are kept by double entry, though this is not always apparent in one book, but in the whole, as one set. Thus, the footings of the Discount Books, and of the extension columns of the Cash Books of the Second and Third Tellers, are posted in gross on the General Ledger to the debit of the respective ledgers to which the personal credits are carried, and the footings of the several check-lists are posted in gross to the credit of those ledgers; consequently, the balance must show what amount of deposits there is on the personal ledgers, respectively.

This method furnishes the test of accuracy in the monthly Proof sheets.

When a bank begins business, the General Book-keeper debits Cash to Capital. The cash is transferred to the Paying Teller, and the corresponding entries are then found in the General Ledger and in the Paying Teller's Proof. The entire check-list of the bank continues to be credited daily to the Paying Teller, and all the receipts, including those from the Clearing House, charged to him. It follows that the Teller's daily Proof, if correct, must agree with the balance of the Cash account on the Ledger.

A separate account is kept of the different denominations of circulating bills which are issued by the bank; also of the securities pledged with the Bank Department for their redemption.

The General Book-keeper posts daily the liquidations and the accessions of Bills Discounted to that account, and the balance shows what the addition of the Ticklers should be, and precisely what amount of bills receivable should be on hand. The Certification account shows the balance of outstanding certified checks.

He posts to Expense account all salaries, rents, and expenditures; likewise the debits and credits to Interest, Exchange, and other accounts of this class. These are finally absorbed in Profit and Loss, when the books are made up for a dividend.

He keeps all the accounts with foreign banks, charging them with notes sent for collection, and crediting remittances; and renders to them a monthly account current, or receives one, as the case may be. In some banks this is too heavy a service for one clerk, especially where interest is allowed on balances: the duties are then divided.

From the footings or balances of these various accounts is composed the *Bank Statement* (see pages 236–237), designed to show at a single view the condition of the business. Unimportant details are omitted in the example, as they would serve rather to confuse than to inform the general reader.

Most of the items are sufficiently explained in the record. The "Commercial Bank notes," $102,524, is the unused portion of the circulation, which the Paying Teller retains in his drawer. "Cash items" are unexchangeable funds, such as uncurrent bills, foreign or informal checks, and memoranda which represent money. The item, $1,127,205.33 is the prepared Exchange for the Clearing House. All the sums on this side are actual resources which would be available in liquidating the debts, excepting that set down to Expenses, which stands as an offset to the profits on the other side.

The liabilities are due either to the stockholders, to individuals, or to other banks. To the former belong the capital, and the profits—including the unpaid dividends. The circulating bills, $358,248, are covered by the securities on the other side of the account, $416,490.66. The remainder of the column, amounting to $6,839,396.63, is the debt due to depositors, the certified checks and the certificates of deposit, being substantially a part thereof.

"Profit and loss in reserve," $301,378.20, is the surplus of profits left after declaring the previous

STATEMENT, FEB. 18, 1857,

	$	c.	$	c.
RESOURCES:				
Bills discounted...............	....	..	7,382,812	96
Loans on demand...............	....	..	400,000	00
Expense account...............	....	..	1,640	00
Securities deposited with the Bank Department, consisting of Stocks of the U. S. and of the State of New York.......	....	..	416,490	66
Cash on hand:				
Commercial Bank notes........	102,524	00		
Cash items—1st Teller, 8,423.10				
2d " 14,200.00				
3d " 7,982.23				
	30,605	33		
Bills and checks of city banks...	1,127,205	33		
Specie......................	2,791,499	07		
			4,051,833	73
Real estate..................	....	..	179,916	81
Treasury Notes...............	....	..	181,403	07
			12,614,097	23

dividend. The several items composing the sum of $109,797.90, constitute the profits of the current dividend period up to the date of the statement. These profits will be increased by the end of that period (June 30), and form a fund sufficient to pay the expenses of the bank, and the usual semi-annual dividend, leaving a remainder to be added to the reserved profits. In this way, the reserve is increased every half year, by whatever excess of profits may be realized.

To ascertain the *exact* profits of the bank at any time, interest on the unmatured bills discounted, must be subtracted from the apparent profits in the Statement.

This Statement, for practical purposes, may be

OF THE COMMERCIAL BANK.

	$	c.	$	c.
LIABILITIES:				
Capital	....	..	5,000,000	00
Profit and loss in reserve	....	..	301,378	20
Exchange account	1,250	16		
Interest account	1,500	00		
Discount received	107,047	74		
			109,797	90
Circulation:				
Bills on hand (see opposite)	102,524	00		
Bills in circulation	255,724	00		
			358,248	00
Unpaid dividends	....	..	5,276	50
Due depositors:				
City depositors	3,989,059	23		
Foreign banks	2,262,710	22		
Certified checks outstanding	444,999	71	6,696,769	16
Certificates of deposit	....	..	142,627	47
			12,614,097	23

reduced to fewer terms. The entire debt of the bank is:

To stockholders, the capital and profits	$5,416,452.60
To depositors, including bill-holders	7,197,644.63
	$12,614,097.23

To pay which the bank has:

Bills discounted . . .	$7,782,812.96	
Exchangeable funds .	1,260,334.66	
Specie	3,389,392.80	
Real estate	179,916.81	
Expenses (chargeable against profits) . .	1,640.00	—$12,614,097.23

The point from which the Directors regard the Statement, and which governs the discount of paper, is, the ability of the bank to redeem that portion of its debt which is demandable by the creditors. In this case, it is $7,197,644,63; for the stockholders cannot demand back the capital or profits, until all other debts are paid. They are, corporately, the bank itself. The bank has specie—$3,389,392.80, by which it could reduce its debt to $3,808,251,83; and to provide for this, it has more than twice that amount of bills discounted, in current maturity, to say nothing of its real estate. This would be called *a very strong position*. Allowing that one million of dollars is a sufficient average of specie to hold in reserve with a deposit of seven millions, the bank might safely increase its discount line very materially. The only question then left for the Directors to determine is, whether the deposits of the bank are likely to be maintained; and to judge of this contingency, they have the successive statements of the business, running back for years, showing the average on which they can depend. The general condition of commerce must also be considered.

These are the principal views that govern the councils of bank directors.

The certificates of deposit specified in the Bank Statement are issued to persons who keep no regular account in a bank, and who merely deposit their funds for safe-keeping. This document is frequently used as a bank check in remittance, and is of equal credibility, though subject to a slight discount when negotiated at a distance from the redeeming bank.

The General Book-keeper mostly has the Stock-ledger and Transfer-books in his custody. The former is opened in alphabetical order like other ledgers, and each stockholder is credited with the shares standing in his name. When he sells them, he fills up a form in the book of printed transfers in favor of the buyer, whose credit for the same is balanced by the debit of the seller. No transfer of stock is allowed without the surrender of the old certificate. It is cancelled, and a new one issued in the name of the new holder.

From time to time, the ledger is proved by making out a list of the stockholders with the number of shares held by each, which multiplied by their par value, should give the exact capital of the bank. This proof is necessarily made three times in a year—twice to ascertain who is entitled to receive dividends, and once to know who has a right to vote for directors. The transfer books are closed for a short time previous to the payment of the dividend, to prevent wrong payments by an inaccurate list.

The Officers and Directors of the bank repose much confidence in the General Book-keeper. He is constantly referring to all the different books and desks, to get postings for his own ledger, and is so familiar with their theory, and also with the various methods by which an account may be mystified, that even his casual supervision is regarded as of great value to the institution. He is generally employed about seven or eight hours a day.

CHAPTER XI.

THE ASSISTANT TELLER.

The chief duty of this clerk is to assist the Paying Teller in counting the Exchanges from the Clearing House, and the Deposit Teller in distributing and counting the money received by him. He is also regarded as a pupil in the money department of the bank, and is required to fill the place of the Second or Third Teller, if either should be absent. There would be hazard in employing a clerk in this capacity who is not familiar with bank bills.

When the Exchanges are brought in from the Clearing House, the Assistant Teller immediately begins to examine and count them on a separate table. The items are checked by a pencil-mark, which distinguishes the bank bills from the checks. He marks each check with the number of the sending bank, so that if a question should arise subsequently as to the channel through which it was received, the number would indicate it. Thus all checks received from the Bank of America, would be found to have the figure 6 upon them; and all received from the Irving Bank would be known by the number 34.* Those which are paid at the counter by the Tellers,

* See the Numerical List, on pages 163, 164.

have no number marked on them, but are distinguished by the peculiarity of the cancelling cut. As the Assistant completes the examination of each list, the addition included, he lays the checks and bank bills in separate piles; and every list is thus proved by itself. The bank bills are then counted into packets, and the checks entered on the *Check-list* by another clerk. The sum of the two must agree with the total of the Exchanges.

Before the checks are passed over to the clerk who enters them on the list, they undergo inspection by the Paying Teller, as already described in the duties of his desk.

The Assistant Teller transfers his services to the Deposit Teller about twelve o'clock, and is his aid for the remainder of the day.

An accurate, skillful, and faithful clerk in this place, is sure to be promoted. The officers observe his habits of business, and regard him as a very important aid in the money department. He is frequently obliged to act as Deposit Teller, and gradually acquires all the tact and self-possession necessary to the office. He is the acting Third Teller also, when that clerk is absent, and succeeds him in the scale of promotion.

In some of the larger banks, the examination of the Exchanges from the Clearing House, is kept in its details entirely separate from the Paying Teller's department. A book of printed forms like the following, is used:

CLEARING-HOUSE PROOF.

AMOUNT OF EXCHANGES RECEIVED **$907,658.02**

		$	c.
Composed of			
Checks on Commercial Bank	$823,096.70		
" of country banks	50,109.73		
		873,206	43
Commercial Bank bills		10,210	00
Bills of country banks redeemed		17,016	00
Checks returned for corrections, to 2d Teller	$2,990.89		
" " " 3d "	3,662.73		
" on Commercial Bank returned for correction	571.90		
Error in addition	.07	7,225	59
Proof		907,658	02

SECOND TELLER.	$	c.	THIRD TELLER.	$	c.		$	c.
Crow on Phenix Bank—not good	500	00	Bird on Mec. B'k—wrong sent to Merchants'	1,500	00	Starr on Commercial—returned for correction	571	90
Jones on Republic—no account	240	80	Carroll on America—not due	226	23	Error in addition of Bowery list	....	07
Wilson on City—not indorsed	2,250	09	Smith on Manhattan—no date	1,936	50			
	2,990	89		3,662	73		571	97

By this method the Paying Teller has nothing to do with the details, excepting in examining the checks before they are charged on the ledgers. He adopts the total, $907,658.02, as a receipt, and the amount of checks, $873,206.43, as a voucher for that portion of it. The bank bills, $10,210, are incorporated with his cash, and the foreign bills are sealed up and charged by memorandum checks to the issuing banks. The irregularities of the returned checks are corrected as far as possible and sent back in a subsequent exchange.

CHAPTER XII.

THE CHECK CLERK.

It is the duty of the Check Clerk to make out a separate list of the checks, paid by each Teller, to enable him to make his Cash proof. For this purpose they are assorted alphabetically, and their amounts only, transcribed and added together.

Then, as each Teller has checks to be charged in all the Ledgers, they must be transcribed in the list of each Ledger, for the postings and proof of each. This is a full record, embracing the name of the drawer as well as the amount. It is from these lists, that the checks are posted to the Ledgers, and they are therefore called, also, *Debit Cash Books.*

The agreement of the footings in this different division of the checks, proves the work to be correct.

The Exchange Checks, belonging to the Paying Teller's cash, are the first copied into the Debit Cash Books, and they are added up before any others are entered. These several footings must correspond with the amount of checks in the original list, made up for the Assistant Teller.

It is indispensable that the Check Clerk should be an accurate and rapid copyist, and quick at addition. This is the most of what he has to do. But he acts as a general assistant, when not occupied with his specific duties. This is a course of preparation for the higher desks which he is unwise to neglect; for if well qualified, his chances of promotion are better than if he were nearer the top of the scale. The retirement of any one of the ten or twelve clerks above him will be sure to advance him; whereas, the Note Teller, for example, has but two chances before him, and the Deposit Teller but one.

The Check Clerk is generally a young man, receiving a salary of from five to eight hundred dollars.

Many of the higher Clerks and Tellers, and not a few of the Cashiers of our city banks began their career as Check Clerks. They have advanced step by step, according to their merits, and are among those who possess the best practical knowledge of the banking business.

CHAPTER XIII.

THE RUNNER.

The Runner is so called, because he does the *running* of the bank, to serve notices, collect drafts, and so forth. He is the bank's courier—its local mail; and for the note-paying part of the community, its sergeant-at-arms.

His distinctive office is, to prepare and deliver notices of all payments due at the bank counter. The usual form of the notice is placed at the end of this chapter—the italicized portion being that which he fills up with his pen.

The duties of the Runner are not the same in all the banks. In those of very extensive and active business, he has enough to do to keep up the delivery of his notices, which may average from two to three hundred for every day in the year. In some of the smaller institutions, he "ticklerizes" the notes from the Collection Register, or acts as an assistant to the Tellers. In most of the banks, the collection of the sight drafts which are received by the morning mail is an important part of his service.

The preparation of the bank notices is a work of considerable labor. They are printed in sheets, all on the same sheet with the title of the same month. The Runner takes a sheet for May, and from the

Tickler fills up the blanks with the name of the payer, and the amount, of all notes due on the first day of the month; and so with each subsequent date. They are then cut apart, and arranged alphabetically. By the aid of the directory, he marks on each the residence of the payer. He then assorts them by streets, for the most convenient route of service. After long practice, his memory becomes itself a directory of names and places, and saves him much writing and trouble of reference.

Having arranged his notices for the delivery of the day, the Runner stands ready to receive the drafts, of which there may be from twenty to fifty, to be collected at various points through the city. These are briefly copied in his Memorandum Book, and he sets out on his tour. He returns their proceeds in the course of the day to the Note Teller, who tests their accuracy by comparison with his own record. In an active market, the amount of the sight-drafts collected in a single day often exceeds one hundred thousand dollars. It is very necessary that a bank Runner should possess good judgment and knowledge of men; for he is measurably trusted with the power of credit. The drafts are commonly paid by checks, which, in his discretion, he takes without being certified. But he has often to deal with strangers and new firms, when he insists on certification, or on bank bills. If any refuse to pay in satisfactory funds, he returns the draft to the Note Teller, where it remains till three o'clock, and then, if still unpaid, it is given to the Notary for protest.

The Runner experiences more difficulty when the

market is growing stringent than at other times. He withdraws his credit, and alleging the instruction of the bank officers, declines to take uncertified checks. The payers generally acquiesce in the propriety of the rule, though not always with good grace. Occasionally one refuses to pay except by his check, as usual, which the Runner will not receive. The draft is handed over to the Notary, by whom it is either collected or protested, at a later hour in the day.

The Runner has many short-time drafts, payable after date, or sight, which, if not immediately accepted, are left with the drawee, who agrees to return them to the bank. If declined, they are protested for non-acceptance, and again for non-payment at the due date. Sight drafts must be accepted or protested under the date of presentation, for that is the date on which they are *first seen*, by the drawee. It is *legal* "*sight*," if the presentation is made at the store or domicil of a man, though he may be absent from both; otherwise, a messenger or notary might pursue the drawee for a week or a month, without effecting a proper demand. If the Runner is not satisfied to trust a draft with the drawee, as above stated, he informs him that he can call at the bank in the course of that or the following day, and accept it. One day is allowed, by custom, for examination of the account on which it is drawn.

In the distribution of notices, the Runner has the advantage of not being confined to particular hours. He can serve them while enjoying an evening ramble, and he can walk in no direction that does not give him the opportunity of dropping some by the way.

The Runner at a Loss.

His pockets are always full of them. Every shop, trade, sign, and finally, every man, seems to his imagination to invite a bank notice. A very intelligent Runner once stated to the author, that he seldom met an acquaintance or friend, without being annoyed by an involuntary feeling that his first duty was to serve him with a bank notice.

Frequent complaints are made at the Note Teller's desk that the payer received no notice. Mr. Spitfire flies into a passion, and wants to know "what in the devil a Runner is good for if he can't find where people live, even if their names are not in the directory!" Mr. Short takes some satisfaction in abusing the Runner for not sending him a notice, although there might be a better reason for his not paying promptly. Mr. St. Vitus asks "why that notice was sent to him? He didn't owe it, and wouldn't pay it, and considered it an insult to have other people's debts poked in his face."

The Runner sometimes attempts an explanation. He cannot follow all the removals, nor be advised of the new-comers in a large city. Changes of residence take place from many causes: the pulling down of old stores to rebuild; the destruction of property by fire; the dissolution of old partnerships, and the formation of new firms. Death takes names out of the Directory, though he does not always foil the Runner; for law says that a man shall not die until his notes are paid.

The Runner is embarrassed also by the repetition of names. He may be excused for serving a notice on the wrong John in some families, especially among the Smiths and Browns. These gentlemen, if they are anxious to pay their notes, write their residence as a part of the signature. Again, the number of a store is changed or defaced by accident or design. There are some people who prefer retirement to publicity, and refuse their names to the canvasser. Bankruptcy drives men from the great thoroughfares into alleys and attics. "The Panic" tears down gilt block-letters from plate-glass fronts, and sends the Runner to look after their old owners in upper stories, behind a strip of tin with characters in white paint. One or other of these accidents explains most of his omissions.

The Runner picks up a good deal of information in his jostling intercourse with men, and the bank officers are not above asking him for the results of his observation. He hears the gossip of loungers in stores and along the streets. If a great house is shaking in the wind, he is told of it. He inquires what other great houses are likely to be implicated, or how many smaller are to be drawn into the vortex. He is regarded as an official confidential person, familiar with financial secrets, always answering less than he knows, and therefore subject to many questions. When any extraordinary excitement prevails, he seldom returns from his daily tour without a considerable budget of news.

"Well, Mr. Foote, what do you hear to-day?"—asks the President or Cashier.

"Things look pretty black, sir. Bigg & Co. have failed!"

"What! Bigg & Co?'

"Yes, sir. That's the talk of the street."

"Anything more?"

"Yes, sir. Trouble among the flour men. Sweatem, Sore & Co's paper is offered at three per cent a month."

"You don't say so!"

"It's a fact, sir; and no buyers even at that."

"What else?"

"I heard a good many rumors, but only two names mentioned, besides Bigg and Sweatem.—Hawk & Hawkins, and Blue & Co. There's a rumor about a large shipping-house on South Street, but nothing definite. Sort of apprehension all round."

"Mr. Foote, didn't I hear you say something about Sturgeon, the oil-man, the other day?"

"Yes, sir. I took a sight draft there, and he got mad, because I refused his check without being certified. I took his check once before, and they refused to certify it at bank until his deposit was made."

The Cashier returns to the Directors' room with this information.

Like every other clerk, the Runner is sometimes called in as talesman, to make up a short jury in commercial trials.

IRVING BANK,

CORNER OF GREENWICH AND WARREN STREETS.

Alexander Jones

Your Note for *$5,470.40* Dollars,

is payable *8th* AUGUST.

CHAPTER XIV.

THE PORTER.

The Porter of a bank, though at the lower end of the line, is by no means least among its servants. The authority of the President is exerted from the head to the foot—that of the Porter runs from the foot towards the head; and in this direction it bears considerable analogy to that of his great coadjutor.

His situation is one of high responsibility and trust. Like his associates he gives bonds—generally to the amount of five or ten thousand dollars.

The key of the outer door of the building is placed in his custody. Consequently, he must be at the bank first in the morning, and last at night. In some instances, he takes charge also of the key of the book-vault, that the clerks may have as early and as late access to the account-books as they desire.

It must be an extraordinary and well-authenticated order, that would induce one of the New York City Bank Porters to open the doors of the building, or to surrender the key for a moment, to clerk or officer, during the night-hours, or on Sunday. Yet he might visit it in person, alone, without other authority than his right of office; it is his duty to do so, and to search the premises, if he has any suspicion of danger from burglars, fire, or other cause. Some porters make it a rule to visit the bank once at least on every holiday.

The modern plan of bank building includes under the same roof other apartments for hire; and a Janitor is employed to take charge of the property, which makes the Porter's watch less necessary.

The first work of the Porter in the morning is, to open the bank, and to prepare it for the comfortable possession of the officers and clerks. He unlocks the book-vault, and carries the various account-books to their respective desks. As soon as any of the clerks arrive to relieve his watch, he goes to the Post-office for the letters. He is the only accredited messenger to whom they would be delivered without a special order. Any other would be required, also, to give proof of his identity.

The Porter is regarded as a general assistant to the clerks; but his principal duties are closely connected with the department of the Paying Teller. He counts all the gold that is received, and ties it up in bags, with the bank seal, and a label of the amount affixed, ready to be paid out in quantity on demand. This is done immediately under the eye of the Teller; and the bags are then carried into the vault. The Porter keeps a record, so that he can tell, at any moment, the number of bags on hand, the denomination of the coin, and the total amount.

If two hundred thousand dollars of specie is needed to pay a balance due to the Clearing House, the Paying Teller goes into the vault, and designates the bags which are to be carried out; or if pressed with other duties, he intrusts this service to the Porter, being careful to count the bags before they are taken from the bank.

Every bag is labelled with the name of the sealing bank. Claims for deficiency by miscount, abrasion, or counterfeit pieces, must be made "within a reasonable time," or they lose their validity. The rule of every well-regulated bank is, to count or weigh all coin as soon as possible after receiving it, even if it should be a return of its own bags with unbroken seals. The two hundred thousand dollars paid by the Metropolitan Bank at the Clearing House may be distributed among ten other banks, each of which counts its portion, affixes its own seals and labels, and holds it ready to be paid back through the same channel. The following day may bring some of the same bags again to the Metropolitan, where it is again counted, and sealed as before.

Gold suffers abrasion by long use. It is first counted by hand, and the pieces slip on each other. It is then taken up in iron scoops and poured into bags. These are handled roughly in carriage from place to place, and thrown heavily from the counter to the floor. As often as the bags are opened for counting, the contents are turned out in bulk, and the uneven surfaces grind against each other. It is frequently poured into metallic scales to be tested by weight, or spread out on a table for inspection to detect false pieces. It undergoes no trifling friction in the pocket against other coin. Although this does not for a long time sensibly affect the value of the pieces separately, it is very perceptible when a thousand of them are taken together, especially of the smaller denominations. It is rarely that a bag of five thousand dollars by count, of what is in current use, of the quarter-eagles and of the one-dollar pieces, holds out full value in weight. The deficiency on that sum is very commonly from seven to ten dollars. The ten and twenty dollar pieces of our oldest coinage are not yet sensibly reduced from this cause. The fraudulent process of "sweating" consists in putting the coin into revolving cylinders with sand, after the manner of polishing steel pens, by which it is worn away evenly and imperceptibly. It is also reduced by filing, and by having small holes drilled through it, which are concealed by hammering. The one-dollar pieces are sometimes cut in two with a saw, and the parts are then ingeniously joined together. This last device may be detected by an irregularity in the "milling," or little cross furrows on the edge.

The Porter is watchful against these various processes, and rejects every piece that is impaired by them. It seldom happens that they are brought to the bank for deposit in any quantity, but they slip in singly. When but slightly injured, they are received and paid, over the counter, but are kept out of the bags put up for the Clearing House. If they collect in considerable amount, they are sold by weight to the jewellers, or sent to the mint for recoinage.

The Porter acquires a very delicate skill in the detection of false or light coin. Peculiarities of color attract his eye as it wanders over the table where the pieces are spread out, or as they slide in bulk from the bags. He weighs even the lighter coin with almost unfailing accuracy, on the end of his finger. Both by touch and smell he can distinguish the genuine from the base, of silver or gold—and also by the sense of hearing, as he twirls the piece in the air, or throws it upon the counter to catch its "ring."

Foreign gold is not current in the bank settlements. What is offered on deposit, is received at a fixed rate, a trifle below its value; and when it accumulates, it is sold to the brokers at a small profit.

A very large amount of foreign gold is brought into the United States by emigrants and travellers from Europe. It is mostly taken to the West, either to buy land or to be kept for emergencies. Gradually it finds its way into the shops, and thence either to the banks or private exchange dealers, who ship it to their correspondents in New York. It is quite usual for our city banks to receive from some thriving town beyond the Mississippi River a well-ironed box of fifty pounds' weight, filled with an indiscriminate mixture of half the coinages of Europe, to the value of nearly ten thousand dollars. The Porter assorts the pieces with the interest of a connoisseur in numismatology; and after making a complete invoice, sells them to a specie broker, by whom they are again sold for shipment, generally to France or England.

The amount of coin counted daily by the Porter depends on the activity of the market. It has been much reduced by the adoption of specie certificates for the Clearing House settlements; but still reaches, occasionally, perhaps two hundred thousand dollars, from which it varies to the one-tenth part of that sum. Large amounts are frequently drawn from Philadelphia and Boston to pay balances; and lesser remittances flow in from other places. A Porter in one of our active city banks counts, in the course of a year, from twenty to twenty-five millions of dollars.

The time occupied in counting depends on the denomination of the coin. Twenty bags, or one hundred thousand dollars in Washingtons (twenty-dollar pieces) may be counted within one hour. The ten-dollar pieces require near double the time, and the smaller coin still more in proportion. The one-dollar pieces are put up for counter use in rolls of one hundred dollars each.

Silver is not used in the bank settlements. The immense supply of gold from California and Australia has superseded it in the general exchanges of commerce. As it is not legal tender for sums over five dollars, our banks decline receiving it on deposit in large quantity.

It is impossible for the Paying Teller to satisfy himself, by personal oversight, of the accuracy of the Porter's work in detail, or even to observe him always in the movement of large amounts of coin; and it follows, that there is a divided responsibility between them. This is provided for in their separate relation to the bank. If the Porter should abstract any gold, it would be in his capacity as an assistant; and his bondsmen would be liable. The various expedients by which he could perpetrate a fraud are obvious enough; but his chances of carrying it over from day to day, without detection, are very narrow.

When the Exchanges are fully prepared in the morning, the Porter packs them neatly in his Pouch, in their numerical order, and sets out for the Clearing House, which he reaches a few minutes before ten o'clock. By half past ten, he is back with the return Exchanges.

The Porter's Pouch was formerly made to sling over the shoulder, so that it would rest within the fold of the left arm, leaving the right at liberty. A chain was enclosed within the strap, to foil any attempt that might be made to cut it. Such precautions were regarded as necessary when a large proportion of the Exchanges consisted of bank bills—a single Porter often carrying more than fifty thousand dollars. Several of the banks were in the habit of sending a guard with the Porter—and in one or two instances, he was armed with a loaded pistol; but, happily, no case occurred requiring its use. The route of the Porter was then very long, and through many crowded streets. There has been, however, as the writer is informed, but a solitary instance of personal attack on a bank messenger within the last twenty years, and that was unsuccessful.

The Porter of the present day might readily be mistaken for a traveller, with his valise or carpet-bag in hand; but, more likely still, he may pass along on foot, or in the omnibus, without attracting other than casual notice.

The Porter's Table, with the scales for weighing gold, stands within the enclosure of the desks, near the Paying Teller; and when not occupied with outdoor duties, he sits there awaiting orders. In a busy season, these are not long coming. The Paying Teller requests him to make up a tray of gold pieces—that is, to count them into piles of fifty, twenty, or ten each, as may be required; and, also, to prepare several trays of silver coin—the half-dollars and the quarters, in piles of twenty; the dimes, commonly in paper rolls of two dollars each; and the half-dimes, in rolls of one dollar, with a quantity open for convenient use. This is hardly done, before one of the Book-keepers asks him to "step down to Jones & Brass, and get their bank-book. Those fellows have got credit for a note that belongs to another dealer, and they've drawn against it."

The Deposit Teller requests him, at the same time, to "get that check of Peter Johnson's indorsed by Powell & Company."

The Cashier inquires where Donaldson has gone? "It is *very* singular," he says, "that he is so apt to be out of the way, just when I most want him! Mr. Crook, send him to me as soon as he comes back—will you?"

"Yes, sir."

Donaldson reports himself to the Cashier, and returns from another errand just in time to get fifty thousand dollars out of the vault in exchange for that amount of specie certificates, to accommodate a neighboring bank; and, also, to take part in an altercation between the Receiving Teller and a dealer's clerk, on a claim for ten dollars deficiency in a bag of mixed coin, which the latter had deposited the day before. The clerk is swearing that he counted it himself, and knows that it was correct; and the Teller maintains, with equal obstinacy, that the bank is right. The

Porter affirms that he "counted it three times over, and could not be mistaken." Such differences cannot always be adjusted to mutual satisfaction. They sometimes give rise to petty quarrels, and to suspicions of dishonesty between the disputants; but dealers generally admit that the Porter is the more likely to be correct; and there is little room for doubt, if the accuracy of his reckoning is confirmed by the proof of the Teller's cash at the close of the day. Occasionally, Mr. Donaldson is gratified by an acknowledgment from the depositor:

"You were right in your count of that specie. We discovered the error in our own books."

He is seldom wrong. Old customers, who know how careful he is, what various tests he employs, and how he values his reputation for accuracy, very commonly prefer his count to their own. They do not hesitate to take from him bags of gold without examination, and pay them over at the Custom House for duties.

One of the habitual tests of correctness in counting is, to observe that the tops of piles containing the same number of pieces, of the same coinage, are on an exact level. Each piece being precisely of the same thickness, one more or less in any pile is seen at a glance. The application of a straight-edge to pieces as thin even as the quarter eagle or the silver dime, is an almost infallible test. The Porter has also the test of agreement with the previous count by another person; and finally, that of weight, in scales which sensibly show the difference of a single grain.

The Note Teller seizes the first favorable moment, towards the middle of the day, to dispatch the Porter with notes for certification. There may be thirty, fifty, or a hundred of these, payable at twenty different banks; and at each he is obliged to fall in at the tail of the column that waits at the Paying Teller's counter. This column is always longer and slower in its movements when business is most hurried, and consequently when the Porter's minutes are most precious. If he does not at the same time present the overdrafts and informal checks which have been received through the Exchanges, he must make a second journey for that purpose; and a third to collect from the dealers of his own bank the amount of checks returned from their deposits for similar defects. Within the half hour after one o'clock, he must be at the Clearing house with coin or specie certificates to liquidate the debit to the other banks; or during the subsequent half hour, to receive his credit balance. He is expected to know the earliest moment at which the Southern mail arrives, and to get the letters. The delivery of letters by a foreign steamer may be going on at the same time, and he is subject to the delay of waiting his turn in a long row of applicants. He is the Cashier's authority for the hours at which the departing mails close, and for all changes of rule in the Post-office which may affect the convenience of the bank.

In his various walks and contacts, the Porter gains much knowledge of men and things, which, discretionally, or in answer to questions, he communicates to the bank officers between whom and himself there is free and often confidential intercourse. "What news at the Clearing House to-day, Mr. Donaldson?" asks the President.

"I didn't hear any thing particular, sir. It looks as if things might be a little excited and uncomfortable, that's all."

"Ah! Well, that's a good deal. What makes you think so?"

"A little sort of *snap*, sir. Some of the Porters came in late, as if they'd been holding back for morning checks."

"Did you hear any thing in the street?"

"I heard some talk about a failure among the brokers, but no name."

"No steamer in?"

"Well, yes, sir; but the boys ain't crying an extra yet. They've got a notice on the bulletins—'*Delhi not taken!*'"

The President catches a valuable hint from many a conversation, of which this is an example.

"Delhi not taken! Then, Mr. Cashier, I think you may answer Mr. Borrow that we can't give him any privilege of overdraft, nor re-discount his paper. These country banks must learn to take care of themselves."

An application for a credit of fifty thousand dollars, which had been lying in suspense, is thus decided by the state of things *in India.*

It is not unlikely that the Porter will carry notices to parties within the next half hour, calling in one or two hundred thousand dollars of demand loans, so sensitive are bank officers to imaginary effects that may follow an announcement that some "Delhi" or other is "not yet taken."

During the last half hour before the closing of the bank, the assistance of the Porter becomes indispensable to the Paying Teller. He must replenish the specie trays as they are exhausted of their contents. If large amounts of gold not corresponding with the prepared bags are called for, he counts them up in separate trays to the Teller's hand. He conveys checks to the Book-keepers to see if they are good, before certification. The great brokers, Nimble, Rig & Co. have already obtained advance certifications to the amount of one hundred thousand dollars, and another single check is presented for seventy thousand dollars. The Teller is unwilling to risk certifying such a large additional amount before their deposit is made. He says to the Porter in an undertone: "Ask the Book-keeper if that is good?" and to the customer: "I will answer you in a minute."

The clerk of Nimble, Rig & Co. has just joined the string of depositors outside of the counter, and the holder of the check waits for his certification until the Book-keeper announces that their account is good.

At three o'clock, the Porter carries the letters to the Post Office. He then counts the coin in the trays of the Paying Teller, and makes an exact statement of it. He renders the same service to the other Tellers, if required, and assists them in the carriage of their trunks into the vault.

The Porter's salary ranges from seven to fifteen hundred dollars a year. He enjoys some perquisites for taking charge of the trunks of dealers who are not willing to trust their valuable papers in a common office safe.

The remaining duties of the day consist in seeing that the ledgers and various account-books are conveyed into the book-vault, and that the banking-room is thoroughly swept and cleaned. It is the duty of each clerk to put away his own papers; but the Porter examines the fragments that are scattered about the floor, that nothing of consequence may be destroyed. His last care is to look into all the corners and closets, and under the counters, to see that no thief has made a lodgment for the night. Every window-bar and bolt undergoes his personal inspection; and when he locks the outer door, and puts the key in his pocket, he has more authority over the building than any other person.

"Did I lock that door?" It is not surprising that the habit of twenty years has taught him to do it so mechanically, that he cannot always remember to have heard the bolt shoot when he turned the key. To verify the fact, he returns to try the fastenings, and he may sleep soundly after removing the last doubt of having performed his last duty.

All the services described under this head are generally considered as belonging to the place of Porter. But they are very much varied in different institutions. For instance, in some of the larger banks, an extra hand is employed to do the drudgery, and in some of the smaller, the Porter acts as Runner, or as assistant to the Receiving Teller. He is often competent to discharge the duties of check-clerk or bookkeeper; and with a little practice, might enter some of the higher clerkships.

Matthias.

Many of the principal banks in New York have found it necessary, from the great increase of business, to separate the higher duties of the Porter from the the more laborious, and to institute another office, to which the old and faithful incumbent has fallen heir, under the title of *Specie Clerk*. In truth, the responsibility attached to the counting and partial custody of the coin, the daily contact with confidential affairs, the many grave services rendered, and especially the importance of an intelligent and trustworthy messenger to attend the Clearing House, make altogether a charge that deserves to rank with the higher offices of the bank, both for dignity and compensation. Where the office remains undivided, the Porter, as well as the Specie Clerk, is practically an Assistant Teller; and on many occasions, he has a larger amount of the bank funds within his unsupervised personal control than any other clerk.*

The Bank Porters of the City of New York have singularly maintained their character for integrity and fidelity. But a solitary instance of fraud has occurred amongst them in twenty-five years; and that originated in the bank allowing one of its most important rules to be disregarded. The defaulter was conducting a mercantile business with an extensive correspondence, and numerous agents through the country, while at the same time he was intrusted with an unusual custody of the specie vault. The sum abstracted was small, and repaid by his bondsmen.

* In some instances, the specie vault has been taken from the custody of the Paying Teller, and given to the Specie Clerk, who alone is held responsible for its contents. He makes a daily report of its condition to the officers.

In the mean time, however, Book-keepers, Tellers, Cashiers, Presidents, and Directors, have been implicated in the dishonest use of bank funds, by which successive dividends have been lost to the stockholders, and in a number of cases, the institutions completely wrecked. They have not been able to resist the example and the rage of speculation, which at certain periods has overrun the popular mind, and for a season apparently destroyed the sense of common honesty.

It is no credit to a man that he shall abstain from theft, and that he shall fulfill his solemn engagements —although costly services of plate testify that such an extent of virtue is highly esteemed by some very respectable people; yet there is positive and rare merit in a persistent, faithful discharge of duty, where the desire of personal gain, the strongest and most constant that possesses the human mind, is tempted by the immediate control of the means to gratify it. Contentment with a moderate, but sure income, and resolutely shutting out of view all thoughts of "growing rich" by lucky adventures, has been the safeguard of the Bank Porter in his long and creditable career.

While there are many instances of the Porter advancing by the usual steps of promotion to the higher clerkships, and even of their "jumping over the heads" of Book-keepers into the place of Teller, there are more of their remaining stationary, through a continuous term of years, than in any other grade of bank clerks. This comes from no want of natural ability, but partly from want of cultivation in early life, especially in mercantile practice; partly, because their ambition is satisfied with having secured a more fortunate service than the majority of their class, and partly from a true appreciation of certain advantages of their position over most of the inferior clerkships in the bank. It is less monotonous in its routine, and it imposes less personal confinement. It requires more *character* than the employment of an ordinary book-keeper. It is more in contact with the general history and the extraordinary excitements of the bank. There are many Book-keepers whom the officers would reject as Porter; but there are few Porters who would not be accepted as Book-keepers, so far as substantial character goes. In every valuable quality that constitutes the true man of business, saving the mere practice as clerk, and the cultivation of manner that makes the accomplished officer, the experienced Bank Porter of New York is not second to any class of his associates; and as it relates to knowledge and capacity, it is not extravagant to say, that the interests of the stockholders and the convenience of the dealers, of a proportion no less than one-fifth of our city banks, might be improved by transposition of office between the Porter and the President or Cashier.

The Porter has the same right as any other servant of the bank, and it is equally his duty to exert an independent watchfulness over its interests. It would not excuse him to allege, that it was "none of his business," if he should become acquainted with any abuse of trust in clerk or officer, and fail to report it—if of the former, to the President or Cashier; and if of either of these, then to the other, or to some proper person connected with the institution. A case is known to the writer, in which a Porter, of his own accord, prevented a Cashier entering the vault, when he suspected the honesty of his purpose; and his conduct was warmly approved by the Board of Directors.

The Porter has, comparatively, little direct intercourse with the dealers. The care of the bank checks is commonly assigned to him; and he enjoys, in some cases, a small perquisite in the sale of different varieties of check-books, which are furnished by a stationer. He comes into contact with the specie-shipping houses—receiving and preparing large amounts for disbursement. What is known as a cross-grained disposition, is frequently connected with diligent habits and faithful service. It would be singular, if among the sixty Porters of our city banks, most of whom have had but little chance of education and social refinement, there were not some to adopt the conceit, and to imitate the manners of their superiors.

Of the fifty-three banks now in existence in the city of New York, about one-half have been organized since 1850. Among the older, there have been many instances of Porters holding office from fifteen to twenty-five years; and several have "died in the harness," after faithful service for a longer period.

Mr. James Corkery, at present the Specie Clerk of the Union Bank, is now in the seventy-fourth year of his age. He has served the institution as Porter for thirty years, outliving three Presidents, two Cashiers, and several successive companies of clerks. For the

"Father Cole."

last twenty years, he has been the Receiving Specie Clerk of the New York Savings' Institution (now located in Bleecker street), attending there on the afternoon of two days in the week, in addition to his regular duties at the Union Bank. The specie that he has counted and weighed would be tedious to measure by tons or ship-loads. The amount of money trusted to his charge, in one shape or another, if it could be brought together, would exceed the entire wealth of New York; and of all, he has rendered a true account.

The frontispiece to the volume represents him, surrounded by the implements of his office.

"Father Cole" entered the service of the Ocean Bank, as Porter, when that institution was organized. He was already past the prime of life; but retained his full intellectual vigor, and apparently a good reserve of bodily strength. The faithfulness with which he performed his duty, gained for him a high place in the esteem of officers, clerks, and dealers. He possessed, in a remarkable degree, the qualities that are most valuable in a confidential Porter. But he soon had to contend with failing sight. This mark of age was not acknowledged by the old man, until the clerks, to whom it was apparent, presented him with a pair of gold spectacles, as a proof of the respect and affection with which they regarded him. He unwillingly retired from the service. At a later period, he submitted to a surgical operation for cataract, which was only partially successful. His physical strength gradually declined, and he died on the 8th of March, 1858, in the 74th year of his age.

CHAPTER XV.

PRESENTS.

The strict theory of banking is, "an eye for an eye, and a tooth for a tooth." The bank, at least, gives no favors. If the note offered for discount is not safe, it is rejected. If securities are deficient, they must be increased. And the bank lends only for its own interest. It may be obliged to discount paper for an undeserving dealer who keeps no balance on deposit; but that is to save a running debt, and the motive is still, to serve the bank, and not to gratify the dealer. If ever a loan is granted as *a favor*, it is dishonestly granted. The officers, even with a full Board of Directors acting in concert, have no right to discount a note as a *favor*. The money or the credit which they are dispensing is not their own. It belongs to the stockholders, and they are trustees merely, appointed to invest it. Whenever they have departed from this rule, it has been a violation of duty and integrity which ought justly to involve personal responsibility, if the debtor should fail.

The object of stating the case so fully is, to show that there is no ground for the supposition by merchants, that bank officers confer *favors* when they discount paper for them; or if there is such ground, that it is dishonest. The box of "Black Dragon," or the caddies of "the veritable tears of Confucius," which Mr. Fum sent to the President or Cashier after the discount of his bills receivable last week, therefore, had better been bestowed on the convalescents at a hospital, where the gift would be a thousand times more appreciated, and whence it would never be followed by repentance. The market which cannot be conciliated by a cup of tea, will get into spells of tightness; and if Mr. Fum's balance of account is less, or if his paper is not quite so good as that of Mr. Smith, who never made the officers any present, it will be rejected, as it should be. There is not a market in the world where a merchant is less likely to get two for one, than at the bank counter.

If there is any favor between the dealer and the bank, it is conferred by the former, and by direct solicitation of the latter. The bank seeks deposits. It is dependent on depositors for its ability to declare dividends. The measure of favor that it receives is partly indicated by its willingness to pay interest on balances, where it is demanded. But the mass of personal depositors do not ask interest, and so far as they receive no return in the shape of loans, they confer on the bank a very solid favor, from which great profit is realized. Substantially, deposits are capital—a discounting basis, not subject to dividends, and therein, for the bank, better capital than its own stock.

Nothwithstanding these facts, banks are commonly regarded, with respect to commerce, as the holders and granters of *favor;* and hence comes the habit of dealers making presents in return. Mr. Fum sends choice tea; Mr. Raisin, a sample of new wine from Hungary; and Mr. Plumb, a barrel of fine pippins. It would seem ungracious to refuse such gifts, as they need not draw after them any bad consequences to the bank. But where or how to stop when once begun, is more difficult than to resist the beginning; and the influence of example in the chief officers is not lost on the clerks, who may withhold conveniences, if they cannot grant favors. The notion that banks are superior to commerce, extends to their minor employments. A bank clerk is better than a merchant's clerk. He is treated with more deference; and it is conceded that his position is surrounded with more dignity. In addition to this, he holds some powers which, rightly or not, he may make discretionary. The Book-keeper may not be too strict in reporting occasional overdrafts; or, what is very natural, he may be so impressed with the generous and honorable character of a man as to believe him incapable of taking advantage of his relaxed vigilance. It is, therefore, desirable to conciliate him, and this is done by *presents*. Such is the circumstantial origin of some of the worst frauds in bank history.

The author vouches for the authenticity of the following anecdotes. Most of the incidents related came under his personal observation.

A Cashier asked a Director of the same bank, if he could advise him where to purchase a certain description of tea. The latter engaged to find the article. On the same evening, a "quarter-chest" was left at the Cashier's house without a bill, and the matter was not again alluded to. The director was subsequently indebted to the officer for some favors, which, however, did not keep him solvent.

A dealer in fancy goods asked the same Cashier for his adress, without specifying any object. On going home, the latter found his parlor mantel furnished with some elegant ornaments.

A Bank President inquired of a dealer in foreign porcelain, where he could best get an English dinner-set at a cost not over one hundred dollars. The latter answered that his acquaintance with wholesale importers would enable him to purchase it at a considerable discount, and he did so. The President never asked for the bill, but he discounted his friend's paper liberally "between the Boards."

A Bank Officer said carelessly to a jeweller, after serving him with a loan:

"By the way—where is that gold-headed cane that you promised me?"

The jeweller smiled, but said nothing. In a week, the cane was sent; and when the donor called at the bank subsequently, he was accosted with an expression of great surprise:

"Why, Mr. D., you didn't suppose I was in earnest the other day, did you?"

Another Officer called at the store of a dry-goods merchant, after assisting the latter to a liberal discount of paper. While walking along the aisle, his eye was attracted by some ladies' kid gloves, of superior quality. "Ah!" said he, "you keep these articles, do you? They are really very soft and beautiful!"

"Yes, sir," answered the proprietor, at the same time wrapping up a dozen in some fine tissue-paper—"put those in your pocket. Yes, yes, do!" overcoming the apparent reluctance of his visitor, by unaffected earnestness.

The same scene was acted over again on the next occasion, when the merchant had paper discounted. A third rehearsal taught him to add a dozen of the finest kid gloves to the legal rate of seven per cent, whenever he obtained an accommodation at that bank.

A Clerk took lodgings at a hotel during the absence of his family in the country, which led to the landlord opening an account with the bank. In the "progress of human events," baskets of brown stout were left at the residence of one of the officers, and dining privileges were enjoyed without cost. The result in this case was a loan of over twenty thousand dollars on inferior securities; and although it was finally paid, the process involved transactions of questionable propriety.

A Dealer, who was impatient to rectify his accounts, urged a Book-keeper to balance his bank-book. After waiting several days, the request was repeated, and the clerk promised that it should be done. "But," he added, "you haven't sent me that umbrella yet!" —It was added to his wardrobe.

It was formerly the practice, in some banks, for the clerks to order from the stationers the articles necessary to their convenience, such as pencils, rules, erasers, blotting-paper, and other things. And it was not considered improper for the stationer to distribute small presents among them occasionally. A better system of economy has been established in later years.

Bank clerks receive presents thoughtlessly, and mostly, perhaps, without committing themselves to an improper understanding with dealers. They are not alive to the danger of being made accessory to fraud, and to the consequent destruction of character. The officers have no alternative, but to dismiss immediately a clerk who allows himself, even by accident, to be brought into collusion with a dealer. The collusion of silence only, if a fellow-clerk is in fault, would be fatal to him. In a bank of strict discipline, the discovery that a clerk had received presents from a dealer would lead to the expulsion, both of himself and the donor, from all connection with the institution—so important and critical is the point of this most pernicious practice. Every dealer should know that a bank clerk has no favors to bestow. His duty covers every requisition that can be made of him with respect to the business.

In every case where a bank clerk has been betrayed into collusion, the worst consequences have fallen on himself. Whatever advantages have resulted to others, *he* has reaped none; for, from the first moment, he has been in the power of his betrayer, who takes all the gain, and leaves to him the shame and the disgrace.—Can any trifling gift compensate for such a risk?

Presents from a dealer are always annoying to a high-minded bank officer. They may be interpreted to imply that he can be influenced by them to do what is opposed to his sense of duty or justice. In such case, the donor must sink in his esteem, and their effect be precisely opposite to what is expected.

Mr. George Curtis, the first Cashier of the Bank of Commerce, and late President of the Continental Bank, was occasionally the unwilling recipient of "a present." His well-known high sense of honor and propriety would have protected him against all suspicion of improper influence in the administration of his trust; but so sensitive and scrupulous was he on the subject, that he uniformly placed the article, whatever it was, in the discount-room, and related its history at the next meeting of the Board of Directors.

Mr. Curtis was one of our most accomplished and intelligent bankers. He took an active part in the organization of the Clearing House, and was one of the few persons in New York, connected with finance, who made it a matter of serious study.

CHAPTER XVI.

BANK DISCIPLINE.

THE foregoing chapters contain a description of the different departments of a bank, of the duties of the officers and clerks, and of their daily experience.

It will occur to the reader, that there is one peculiar feature running through the whole system; and that is, *the apprehension of fraud.* It is suggested with every clerk, in the beginning, by the requisition of a bond of indemnity against it; and it is never lost sight of for an instant. The constant purpose of the managers is, to devise a system of accounts to prevent it. Every thing else is easy enough. But that has, hitherto, been the one thing that no vigilance could forestall.

The same idea exists in the public mind. Although there is not an equal amount of any other business in the world transacted with so little fraud, yet the common suspicion is much more alive with respect to it in this business, than in any other. It is certain that there are fifty-three dry-goods, jewellers, and fancy stores in the city of New York from which more money or property is stolen every year than from the fifty-three banks, and the fact is hardly recognized. In this view, the presentment is a very strong testimony to the integrity of bank clerks.

The anxiety of officers is, after all, induced by the *possibility*, rather than the *suspicion* of dishonesty in the clerks. It would be most unfortunate for both parties, if the governing sentiment of the former were not one of thorough confidence. The moment that it ceases to be so, the clerk is dismissed; and dismissal on this ground is very rare, although the number of clerks in the city banks is near one thousand. On the other hand, the cases are also rare, in which a clerk, seeking promotion in another bank, is not cheerfully assisted by the officers with whom he has been employed. It is recognized as his right to refer to them for testimony of capacity and character; and no petty considerations of inconvenience from loss of valuable services are allowed to have influence. The terms of intercourse between them are uniformly and mutually respectful and polite. No insulting superiority is assumed, nor mean servility manifested; but the common feeling is rather that of partners in the same interest.

Neither is the possibility of fraud suggested by reflection on the personal character of the clerk, but by outside circumstances. The embezzlement of bank funds, in most cases, has either had its origin in, or been greatly aggravated by the vice of gambling; and this has generally been brought about by the persuasion, or the acts of persons connected with gambling-houses. The bank clerk or the bank officer is a promising victim, if he can be induced to make a first experiment in this direction; and a single victim will reward many plans. The author will cite but one instance of several that have come to his knowledge within a few years past. A Paying Teller accepted the invitation of a friend to take a ride into the country. The further end of the ride proved to be a house frequented by sporting characters. He believed this to be accidental, until a subsequent proposition, after an interval of several weeks, revealed the true character and design of his polite friend. That plans are deliberately laid to entrap the unwary into the practice of gambling, is well known. It is, unfortunately, a very common vice, and easily concealed. A masonic honor makes one gambler safe with another; but what is more difficult to explain, men who have no interest but to expose a vice which destroys all integrity of character, aid in its concealment. After the development of the fraud described on page 155, several respectable dealers of the bank came forward and said:

"Didn't you know that that fellow was a gambler? —Why, I've known it for more than a year."

"Why didn't you tell us of it?"

"Because it wasn't my business."

The moral of this anecdote might have been appreciated, if the informant's house had been burned down; and a friend had called at the ruins on the next morning to say: "I saw a man in the act of setting fire to it."

The knowledge of such facts as these is the root of the bank officer's anxiety on behalf of his clerks. It induces a more attentive study of their character, and a desire to know something of their habits and associations. Their hours of leisure are many, compared with those of commercial clerks, affording time either for idle dissipation or mental improvement; and the manifestation of these opposite dispositions cannot be concealed, nor fail to command respect, or to excite distrust. However uncultivated may be the officer himself, he appreciates the fact that the mental habit is a better safeguard against embezzlement than can be put into a legal instrument. The author is acquainted with a Paying Teller whose healthful rambles before and after bank hours have made him an accomplished botanist; with another, who is a diligent student in political economy; and with a third, who is devoted to natural philosophy. It is almost needless to say, that these gentlemen enjoy, in an unusual degree, the respect and confidence of their superiors, and that their chances of promotion are greatly improved by their habits.

Finally, however, the real safeguard of a bank against collusion and fraud from without, as well as from embezzlement within, is to be found in the general organization of its accounts, and in its discipline.

Nothing short of daily personal supervision of all the postings, additions, and transfers in the work of ten or fifteen desks, could give to the bank officers a positive assurance that there is no error or fraud concealed in the accounts. This being impossible, the next best thing is to prove the accuracy of *results.* When a dealer's book is balanced, and the balance agrees with his own cash-book, the presumption is, that the account is correct in its details, because the same result is attained by two persons, each independently of the other, and by different processes. On this theory, one of our city banks has adopted a system of *daily reports* of the reciprocal departments, the separate entries of which are checked off against each other. The following are the principal of these reports for one day:

PAYING TELLER'S DAILY REPORT.

Balance of cash from previous day........	4	000	000	1			
Received from the other Tellers..........	1	500	000	2			
					5	500	000
" " Clearing House...........	..	...	...	3	1	700	000
Added to Exchanges..................	..	...	...	4		200	000
				5	7	400	000
Paid Clearing House (Exchanges).........	..	...	...	6	1	300	000
" " balance, in specie.....	..	400	000	7			
" Checks at counter in specie.....10,000							
" " " bills.......50,000							
" " in Exchanges........1,600,000	1	660	000	8			
					2	060	000
" Receiving Teller..................	..	...	...	9		25	000
" Note Teller.......................	..	...	...	10		10	000
" Uncurrent Teller..................	..	...	...	11		15	000
				12	3	410	000
Balance of cash carried to next day.......	..	...	...	13	3	990	000
				14	7	400	000

Completed, 3½ o'clock. Difference in cash, 0.

RECEIVING TELLER'S DAILY REPORT.

Number of deposits, 275—amount.........	1	000	000	15			
Received from Paying Teller.............	..	25	000	16	1	025	000
Deduct checks on this bank, charged.....	..	...	...	17		120	000
Balance of cash.........................	..	...	...	..	..	905	000
Consisting of:							
Specie..................................	..	5	000	18			
Clearing House matter...................	..	875	000	19			
Office matter...........................	..	5	600	20			
Foreign checks..........................	..	19	400	21			
						905	000

Completed, 4 o'clock. Difference in cash, 0.

NOTE TELLER'S DAILY REPORT.

Amount credited......................		900	000	22			
" received from Paying Teller.....		10	000	23			
" " " Uncurrent Teller..		50	000	24			
						960	000
Deduct checks on this bank charged.....		150	000	25			
" am't added to morning Exchanges		200	000	26			
						350	000
Balance................................	..	......	...	..	..	610	000
Consisting of:							
Specie................................		40	500	27			
Clearing House matter................		560	000	28			
Office matter..........................		9	500	29			
						610	000

Completed 3.40 o'clock. Difference in cash, 0.
Number of notes paid, 350—protested, 12—of discounted, none.

EXCHANGES SENT TO CLEARING HOUSE.

Receiving Teller's footing..............		750	000				
Note Teller's footing....................		350	000				
					1	100	000
Added by Note Teller....................	..	....	...	..	..	200	000
Total....................................	..	....	...	30	1	300	000

EXCHANGES RECEIVED FROM CLEARING HOUSE.

Number of checks, 2,500.							
Am't of checks on Commercial Bank.....	1	450	000				
Bills of " " "		45	000				
					1	495	000
Redemptions for other banks in bills		65	000				
" " in checks...		124	000				
						189	000
Sundries..........................	..	....	...			16	000
Total....................................	..	....	...	31	1	700	000

Completed —— o'clock. Difference in cash, 0.

UNCURRENT NOTE TELLER'S DAILY REPORT.

Received from Paying Teller	..	...	...	32	..	15	000
" " Correspondents	..	...	...	..	..	30	000
" " City depositors	..	...	...	..	..	15	000
" " other banks, redemptions	..	...	...	..	..	50	000
				33		160	000
Deduct redemptions charged	..	...	...	34	..	35	000
						75	000
Paid Note Teller	..	50	000	35			
Office matter	..	25	000	36			
						75	000
Amount rec'd for credit on the following day	..	...	...	..	..	25	000

Completed, —— o'clock. Difference in cash, 0.

CHECK CLERK'S DAILY REPORT.

Amount of Paying Teller's checks:							
In Exchanges—domestic	1	400	000				
foreign	..	200	000				
Checks paid at counter	..	60	000				
				37	1	660	000
Receiving Teller's checks—domestic	..	...	...	38	..	120	000
" foreign	..	...	...	39	..	19	400
Note Teller's checks—domestic	..	...	...	40	..	150	000
General Ledger checks, redemptions charged	..	...	...	41	..	35	000

Completed, —— o'clock.

PORTER'S DAILY REPORT.

Specie received by Receiving Teller	..	...	...	42	..	5	000
" " Note Teller	..	...	...	43	..	40	500

GENERAL BOOK-KEEPER'S DAILY REPORT.

Balance of cash	..	...	...	44	3	990	000
Amount of Receiving Teller's credits	..	...	...	45	1	000	000
" Note Teller's credits	..	...	...	46	..	900	000
" certifications	..	...	...	47	..	700	000

CERTIFICATION CLERK'S DAILY REPORT.

..........................185

Number of checks certified, 250.
Amount.........................|48|....$700,000

Completed, 3½ o'clock.

COMMERCIAL BANK.

No. Letters received from Post Office, A. M.....225
" " " P. M..... 75
— 300

No. Letters sent, 295.
185 Amount of Postage, $11.50.

COLLECTION CLERK'S DAILY REPORT.

..........................185

No. of Sight Drafts sent out for payment.........150
" Time Drafts sent out for acceptance......... 50
" City Notes and Acceptances registered......270
" Drafts protested.......................... 3
" Foreign Notes and Drafts registered.........150

Time completed, 3½ o'clock.

These reports are laid on the Cashier's desk every day, after the close of business, by the respective clerks. For brevity of explanation, the items will be designated by the number opposite to each.

Number 1 is the balance of cash brought forward from the previous day. It is verified by the report of the General Book-keeper for that date. Number 2 is the sum of the several Tellers' receipts, also for the previous day, including the exchanges, the office matter, and the specie. Number 3 is verified by number 31; 4, by 26; 5 is the entire amount of cash from which the payments are to be made. Number 6 is verified by 30; 7, by subtracting the amount sent to the Clearing House (6) from that received (3); 8, by 37; 9, by 16; 10, by 23; 11, by 32; 12, by addition; 13, by the balance test and by 44; 14, by 5; 15, by 45; 17, by 38; 18, by 42; 19, 20, 28, and 29, by the reports of the succeeding day; 21, by 39; 22, by 46; 24, by 35; 25, by 40; 27, by 43; 34, by 41; 36, by the Paying Teller's report of the next day; and 47, by 48.

The report of every clerk is thus proved by the report of another clerk; and mostly the proof of one is established by comparison with the items of several others, each distinct. The Cashier is enabled by this system to check off the results of each day's business in all the departments, in the space of fifteen minutes.

When a report shows extraordinary results, an explanation is required on the back of the ticket. For example, if the Paying Teller should pay out an unusual amount of coin, a memorandum on the back of the report would give the names of the drawers, and for what purpose it was required—perhaps to pay duties, or for shipment. If any discounted notes are protested, the Note Teller writes on the back of his reports the amounts, with the names of the indorsers and drawers. The *Certification Clerk* commonly notes the names of the dealers who have obtained the largest certifications.

The protection gained by these reports is measurably secured by other methods of supervision in many of our city banks. It cannot be said that they preclude the possibility of fraud; but they make an incredible extent of collusion necessary to carry it on continuously and successfully.

In the same institution, the record of certified checks has been given to a separate clerk; which, in connection with the separate counting of the Exchanges, is an effectual bar to abuse by the Paying Teller, of the power of certification. The check is first recorded by the Certification Clerk, who writes his initials upon it, and it is then certified by the Paying Teller. When it returns through the Clearing House for redemption, it comes to the Assistant or Exchange Teller, by whom it is checked off on the Certification List, before it passes into the hands of the Paying Teller.

Under this plan, a fraudulent certification, to be carried over a single day, must have the collusion of at least four persons—three clerks in the bank, and a confederate outside. If this is not guard enough against the dishonest issue of certified checks, it is hardly to be secured by human vigilance.

CHAPTER XVII.

HOW TO TRANSACT BUSINESS WITH A BANK.

If you are a stranger to the officers, and wish to open an account, get some respectable person who is known to them to introduce you, either to the President or Cashier. Do not ask him to vouch for anything beyond your integrity and fairness in dealing. Tell your own story about capital, business, property, and other matters which pertain to your commercial prospects — and exaggerate nothing. There is no humbug that will recoil upon yourself so surely as an attempt to palm off big tales on a bank officer. Your deposit-tickets, your checks, your bills receivable, your indorsements, and your ledger account, make together a history that dispels all shams, and leaves little to say. A man who begins with an exaggerated account of himself is measured by it afterwards, and appears relatively small.

Borrow no money of your neighbors to swell your first deposits. This is a common practice, with the idea that it will make a favorable impression on the officers. They see through it at once, and take it as a proof of weakness.

Never try to bargain for special indulgences, such as the certification of your checks before your deposit is made or the discount of your paper by the officers without its submission to the Board of Directors. The character of your account will settle these matters much more satisfactorily to all parties.

Let your intercourse with the officers be candid and respectful, and be sparing in your personal solicitation for discounts. Choose the earlier hours of the day for your interviews, and especially avoid the last hour before three o'clock.

Write your signature with the same freedom that you do in your own office, and never vary the style of it.

Teach your clerks to use always the deposit-tickets furnished by the bank, to examine the date and indorsement of every check, and also to see that the writing of the amount corresponds with the figures. Instruct them to learn and to follow the rules of the bank with respect to getting checks certified before deposit.

Make your deposit as early in the day as possible. If you are accustomed to have many checks, or large packages of bank bills, it is better to make two deposits—one at an early hour—than to hand in all at once just at three o'clock. Never change checks with other people merely to make larger figures. It causes needless labor to the bank clerks, makes you responsible for the debts of others, and is a real prejudice to your credit.

Never try to put in your deposit before those in advance of you, but take your place in the line, and wait your turn patiently. Never make deposits without your bank-book, if you can help it. Avoid all unnecessary conversation with the clerks, especially with the tellers.

Never get angry if the Paying Teller examines your account before certifying your check; nor if he keeps you waiting a few seconds before he can pay it.

Make it an invariable rule to give checks only out of your own check-book, and at your own office; and never write a check payable to *order*, when you can as well do it to "*the bearer*." When you want the indorsement of the person to whom you give it, let him indorse it in your presence, and write your own name below, to assure the Teller that it is right.

Never give out checks dated ahead. When you have need to cut checks out of the end of your check-book, mark in the margin what they are for — to supply duplicates, or otherwise. Keep your check-books out of sight and reach of strangers. Never give a stranger a check unless you have some evidence that he is not seeking it for fraudulent purposes. Never draw checks against your account, on the ground that you have sent some abroad that will not return immediately. Always consider a check paid when you give it out.

Never attempt to pay a note with an uncertified check, at a bank where you keep no account. If you make your promissory notes payable at bank, give the Paying Teller a list of them on Monday morning for the current week, or send him your bank-notices on the day of their maturity.

When you want notes discounted, offer them on the regular days, and in good season for the clerk's convenience. Never call on bank officers to discount notes between the Board meetings, if you can wait until the following discount day. Do not put off the offering of notes for discount until the last day of your need. It is better to keep from ten days to a fortnight ahead, and to let your balances remain in the bank until you require them. The loss of interest is very trifling at best. You lose more by anxiety and unfitness for business.

When you want your bank-book balanced, or entries made in it, apply to the Book-keeper early in the day. Never ask a service of him later than one o'clock if you can wait till the next morning. Do not allow your book to run too long without being balanced, and when balanced, examine your cancelled checks without delay.

If the bank ledger shows a larger balance in your favor at any time, than your own check-book, acquaint the Book-keeper with it immediately. As you value your credit with the bank, never take advantage of deposits wrongly entered to your account, but let your dealings be strictly honorable.

If you have any cause of complaint against the clerks, state it directly to the officers. The clerks act under their instructions, which they dare not disobey.

The Book-keeper is the proper person to apply to, to know if collection notes are passed to your credit.

The Note Clerk will inform you of the maturity of notes for a future time. In the case of discounted notes apply to the Discount Clerk. The Discount Clerk, or the Note Clerk, will commonly tell the exchange or charges for collecting foreign paper.

When you have notes to send abroad for collection,

deposit them in ample time for deliberate record and transmission by the bank.

If the drawers of any notes lodged as collateral to loans or discounts should fail, do not wait for the bank officers to discover it, but substitute good notes for them without delay.

The observance of these rules, and such others as may be suggested by your own observation, will be a great economy of time to yourself as well as to the bank clerks, and promote your real credit with the institution.

Dealers should always instruct inexperienced clerks not to transact business with strangers outside of the counter. If they want advice how to proceed, let them ask any clerk who is not too busy to answer, or go direct to the officers. There are often well-dressed persons in the lobby, or about the counters, watching for those who appear at a loss, and ready to assist them very politely. An old merchant sent his carman to draw a check for two hundred dollars. It was his first message to a bank. A *gentleman*, observing him to be a little gawky, said very kindly: "You want the money for that check—this is the place!" and took him to the proper teller, who paid him in large bills. "Now," he added, "you want some of this in small notes. Come with me." He took him into a broker's office in the same building, changed the bills, and managed to retain thirty dollars in his own possession. The teller and broker supposed the two to be friends, and the carman thought that the bank was very accommodating, to keep a clerk only to help strangers!

CHAPTER XVIII.

THE NEW YORK CLEARING HOUSE.

An account of the Clearing House may very properly be introduced by a sketch of the old plan of exchange and settlement between the banks.

During the few years following 1849, the number of banks in New York was increased from twenty-four to sixty. To make the daily exchange, one-half of them must necessarily send to the other half. But this plain division of the service was not convenient or economical. It was found better for all of them to do a part of the distribution, and thus the whole sixty Porters were in motion at the same time. Each carried a book of entry, and the money, for every bank on which he called. The Paying Teller of the receiving bank took the exchange and entered it on the credit side of the book; then he entered on the debit side the return exchange, and gave it with the book to the Porter, who hastened to the next bank in his circuit. The Porters crossed and recrossed each others' footsteps constantly; they often met in companies of five or six at the same counter, and retarded each other; and they were fortunate to reach their respective banks at the end of one or two hours. This threw the counting of the exchanges into the middle and after part of the day, when the other business of the bank was becoming urgent.

Instead of attempting a daily adjustment of accounts, which would have consumed several hours, and caused much annoyance, it became a tacit agreement, that a weekly settlement of balances should be made after the exchange of Friday morning, and that intermediate draft-drawing should be suspended. The weaker and more speculative banks took advantage of this by borrowing money on Thursday, which restored their accounts for Friday; and its return on Saturday threw them again into the debit column. In this way, the banks distant from Wall street managed to carry an inflated line of discounts, based on debts due to other institutions. It became an affair of cunning management by some to run a small credit of two or three thousand dollars each with thirty or more banks, making a total of one hundred thousand dollars, on which they discounted bills. Consequently, the Friday settlements proved to be no settlements at all, but a prodigious annoyance. As soon as the Paying Teller or his Assistant completed the Exchange Balance List, the Cashier of each bank would draw checks for every debt due to him by other banks, and send out the Porters to collect them. A draft on one in favor of another might settle two accounts at once, but there was no understanding that made it possible to secure that small economy; or if there was, it was disregarded. The sixty Porters were out all at once, with an aggregate of two or three hundred bank-drafts in their pockets, balking each other, drawing specie at some places, and depositing it in others; and the whole process was one of confusion, disputes, and unavoidable blunders, of which no description could give an exact impression.

After all the draft-drawing was over, came the settlement of the Wall street Porters among themselves. A *Porters' Exchange* was held on the steps of one of the Wall street banks, at which they accounted to each other for what had been done during the day. Thomas had left a bag of specie at John's bank to settle a balance, which was due from William's bank to Robert's; but Robert's bank owed twice as much to John's. What had become of *that!* Then Alexander owed Robert also, and William was indebted to Alexander. Peter then said, that he had paid Robert by a draft from James, which he, James, had received from Alfred on Alexander's account. That, however, had settled only half the debt. A quarter of the remainder was cancelled by a bag of coin, which Samuel had handed over to Joseph, and he had transferred to David. It is entirely safe to say, that the Presidents and Cashiers of the banks themselves could not have untangled this medley. Each Porter had his tally, and by checking off and liberating, first one whose account was least complicated, and then another, they finally achieved a settlement.

This scene was re-enacted on every Friday. In consequence of the Porters being withdrawn from their regular service in the bank, extra labor was imposed on others, responsibilities became mingled together, and the officers were kept for the whole day

The Old Fashion of Settlement on Friday.

in a state of distraction and anxiety. The Paying Tellers were subject to frequent interruption, as they were obliged to receive and deliver all specie.

Not the least irritating feature of the case was, that a single small draft by any one bank on any other induced a general drawing, and all became involved in commotion, and "war" upon each other. If time were allowed, the debtor banks would finally be obliged to pay the liquidating balance; but three o'clock arrested the process, and the banks where the demand was then in force were obliged to disburse the coin. It was not unusual for a debtor bank to add fifty thousand dollars to its specie at the close of the day, with its debt doubled, while a creditor bank to half a million in the general account, would find itself, at three o'clock, depleted of one or two hundred thousand dollars in coin.

The question had been occasionally discussed whether these difficulties might not be obviated by some other mode of exchange; but without approaching a practical issue. It began now to be more seriously entertained.

The subject was discussed in all its bearings, at informal meetings of bank officers, and steps were taken to obtain general co-operation in some partial and experimental plans. Such, however, was the diversity of opinions, even among those who were most anxious to promote the object, that nearly a year passed before it was thought expedient to issue notices for a meeting to take decisive action upon it. Then, it encountered much silent and determined opposition. Those banks which had profited most by enforced credit balances, feared the restraint and domination of the others; and these had prejudices to overcome, and a long score of annoyances to forget; but it was manifest that the subject could be deferred no longer. A plan was finally adopted, and went into effect on the first of October, 1853. Its complete success soon banished all feelings but those of gratification and common interest.

The operations of the Clearing House were carried on for nearly one year without a Constitution. Some opposition was manifested, on the ground that it was not needed, and might favor a dangerous concentration of power in the hands of a few managers; but the necessity of fixed rules soon became apparent, and the following Constitution, prepared by GEORGE CURTIS, Esq., was adopted on 6th of June, 1854:

CONSTITUTION.

§ 1. THE name of this Association shall be, "THE NEW YORK CLEARING HOUSE ASSOCIATION."

§ 2. The objects of the Association shall be, the effecting at one place of the daily exchanges between the several Associated Banks, and the payment at the same place of the balances resulting from such exchanges. But the Association shall be in nowise responsible in regard to such exchanges, nor in regard to the balances resulting therefrom, except so far as such balances shall be actually paid into the hands of the Manager. The responsibility of the Association is strictly limited to the faithful distribution by the Manager among the Creditor Banks, for the time being, of the sums actually received by him; and should any loss occur whilst the said balances are in the custody of the Manager, they shall be borne and paid by the Associated Banks, in the same proportion as the other expenses of the Clearing House, as hereinafter provided for.

§ 3. The Association at present consists of the following Members: [The same as the Proof-lists.]

§ 4. Each Bank belonging to the Association shall be represented at all meetings thereof, by one or more of its principal officers, and shall be entitled to one vote.

§ 5. A general meeting of the Association shall be holden at the Clearing House, on the first Tuesday in October, in each year, at 12 o'clock, M. At every annual meeting, a Chairman shall be elected, by ballot, to preside at that meeting, and all subsequent meetings during the year. Whenever he shall be absent, a Chairman *pro tem.* shall be appointed. At the same meeting, a Secretary shall also be elected by ballot.

§ 6. Special meetings shall be called by the Clearing House Committee whenever they may deem it expedient, or whenever they shall be thereto requested by any seven of the Associated Banks.

§ 7. At all meetings of the Association, a quorum for the transaction of business shall consist of a majority of the whole number of Associated Banks.

§ 8. At every annual meeting, a Standing Committee of Five Bank Officers shall be elected by the majority and by ballot, to be called the Clearing House Committee, whose duty it shall be to procure, from time to time, a suitable room or rooms for the Clearing House; to provide proper books, stationery, furniture, fuel, and whatever else may be necessary for the convenient transaction of business thereat; to appoint a Manager annually, and such Clerks as may be necessary; to establish rules and regulations to be observed at the Clearing House in cases not provided for in this Constitution, subject to the approval of the Association; and generally to supervise the Clearing House affairs. This Committee shall have charge of the funds belonging to the Association; shall draw on each Bank for its quota of the expenses; and shall also, at the first meeting of the Association after their election, submit detailed estimates of the expenditures that will be required for the Clearing House during the current year.

§ 9. The salary of the Manager shall always be fixed by the Association. The salaries of the Clerks shall be fixed by the Clearing House Committee. The Manager shall give a bond, with sureties in the sum of ten thousand dollars, and each Clerk in the sum of five thousand dollars, to be approved by said Committee.

§ 10. The Manager, under control of the Clearing House Committee, shall have immediate charge of all business at the Clearing House, so far as relates to the manner in which it shall be transacted; and the Clerks of the establishment, as well as the Settling Clerks and Porters of the several Associated Banks, while at the Clearing House, shall be under his direction.

§ 11. The Clearing House Committee shall have power to remove the Manager, or any of the Clerks, whenever, in the opinion of the Committee, the interest of the Association shall require.

§ 12. The hour for making exchanges at the Clearing House shall be 10 o'clock A. M., precisely. At one o'clock P. M., the Debtor Banks shall pay to the Manager, at the Clearing House, the balances against them, either in actual coin, or in the certificates hereinafter mentioned, except fractional amounts. At 1½ o'clock P. M., the Creditor Banks shall receive from the Manager, at the same place, the respective balances due to them, provided the balances due from the Debtor Banks shall then have been paid.

§ 13. Should any one of the Associated Banks fail to appear at the Clearing House at the proper hour, prepared to pay the balance against it, the amount of that balance shall be immediately furnished to the

Clearing House by the several Banks exchanging at that establishment with the defaulting Bank, in proportion to their respective balances against that Bank resulting from the exchanges of the day; and the Manager shall make requisitions accordingly, so that the general settlement may be accomplished with as little delay as possible. The respective amounts so furnished the Clearing House, on account of the defaulting Bank, will, of course, constitute claims on the part of the several responding Banks against that Bank: but, as before stated, the Association shall in nowise be responsible therefor.

§ 14. Errors in the exchanges, and claims arising from the return of checks, or from any other cause, are to be adjusted directly between the Banks who are parties to them, and not through the Clearing House, the Association being in no way responsible in respect to them.

§ 15. Reclamations for errors and deficiencies in specie received at the Clearing House, contained in bags or other packages, sealed and marked in conformity with any rules established upon that subject by the Clearing House Committee, should be made within a reasonable time by the receiving Bank directly against the Bank whose mark the sealed bag or package bears, the Association not being responsible for the contents of such sealed bags or other packages.

§ 16. The Associated Banks shall, from time to time, appoint one of their own number to be a Depository to receive, in special trust, such coin as any of the Associated Banks may choose to send to it for safe keeping. The Depository shall issue certificates in exchange for such coin, in proper form, and for convenient amounts. Such certificates shall be negotiable only among the Associated Banks, and shall be received by them in payment of balances at the Clearing House. Such special deposits of coin are to be entirely voluntary, each Bank being left perfectly free to make them or not, at its own discretion. The coin thus placed in special deposit is to be the absolute property of such of the Associated Banks as shall, from time to time, be the holders of the certificates, and is to be held by the Depository, subject to withdrawal, on the presentation of the proper certificates, at any time during banking hours.

§ 17. New members may be admitted into the Association at any meeting thereof. Such new members shall pay an admission fee of one thousand dollars, and shall signify their assent to this Constitution, in the same manner as the original members. But no new member shall be admitted except by a vote of three-fourths of those present.

§ 18. A Standing Committee of Five Bank Officers shall be appointed at every annual meeting, to whom all applications for admission into the Association shall be referred for examination.

§ 19. For cause deemed sufficient by the Associated Banks, at any meeting thereof, any Bank may be expelled from the Association, and debarred from all the privileges of the Clearing House, provided a majority of the whole number of Associated Banks vote in favor thereof.

§ 20. A Standing Committee of Five Officers of Banks shall be elected at every annual meeting, who, acting in concurrence with the Clearing House Committee, shall have power, in case of extreme emergency, to suspend any Bank from the privileges of the Clearing House until the pleasure of the Association thereupon shall be ascertained. But no such suspension shall take place, unless a majority, at least, of each of these two Committees, shall be present at the ordering thereof, nor unless the vote be unanimous. In case of such suspension, the Clearing House Committee shall forthwith call a general meeting of the Association, to take the matter into consideration.

§ 21. Any member of the Association may withdraw therefrom at pleasure, first paying its due proportion of all expenses incurred, and signifying its intention to withdraw, to the Clearing House Committee.

§ 22. The expenses of the Clearing House, not including the expense of printing for the several Banks (which last-mentioned expense shall be apportioned equally), shall be borne and paid by the several Banks belonging to the Association, according to their respective capitals, as follows:

Banks having capitals of less than $500,000, shall pay $100 each, annually.

Banks having capitals of less than $1,000,000, and not less than $500,000, shall pay $200 each, annually.

Banks having capitals of $1,000,000, and over, shall shall pay $300 each, annually.

And in the same proportion, if more funds become necessary.

§ 23. This Constitution, when agreed to by the Association, at any general meeting thereof, by a majority of votes, shall be submitted to the respective Boards of Directors of the several Banks herein named as members of the Association, for their adoption. When adopted by a majority of the whole number of Banks, it shall be deemed and taken to be in full force and operation. Adoption shall be signified by the signature of the proper officer of the Bank to two copies hereof—one to be kept by the Chairman of the Clearing House Committee, and the other by the Secretary of the Association. A copy of the vote or resolution of the Board, authorizing such signature, shall be deposited with the Secretary. Such Banks as shall not adopt this Constitution within two months from the time it is agreed to in general meeting, as above mentioned, shall, at the expiration of such two months, cease to be members of the Association, provided the Constitution shall then be in operation.

§ 24. Amendments of this Constitution may be

made at any meeting of the Association, by the vote of a majority of all the members thereof, notice of the proposed amendments having been given at a previous meeting.

The following amendments, proposed by George Curtis, Esq., January 11, 1855, were subsequently adopted:

§ At every annual meeting, a Standing Committee of Five Bank Officers shall be appointed, to be called the Committee of Arbitration, whose duty it shall be, to hear and determine all disputes that may be submitted to them by both parties thereto; any member of the Association being one: such Committee shall record a brief abstract of each case referred to them, together with their decision therein, in a book to be provided for that purpose, which book shall be kept at the Clearing House, open to the inspection of all members of the Association. The first Committee shall be appointed immediately upon the adoption of this amendment, and shall serve until the next annual meeting.

§ Whenever exchanges shall have been made at the Clearing House, by previous arrangement between members of the Association through one of their own number, and Banks in the city and vicinity who are not members, the Receiving Bank at the Clearing House shall in no case discontinue the arrangement without giving previous notice, which notice shall not take effect until the exchanges of the morning following the receipt of such notice shall have been completed.

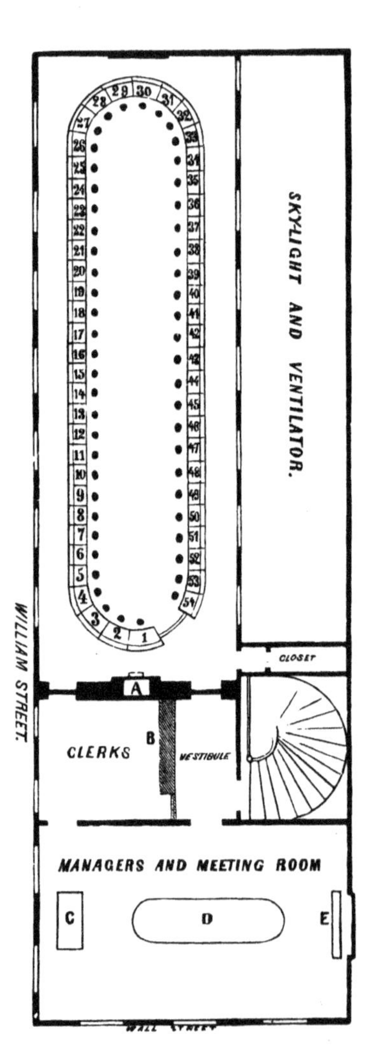

SKY-LIGHT AND VENTILATOR.
CLOSET
WILLIAM STREET.
A
B
CLERKS
VESTIBULE
MANAGERS AND MEETING ROOM
C
D
E

THE CLEARING HOUSE ROOMS.

The opposite diagram represents the ground plan of the rooms of the Clearing House Association. They occupy the fourth floor of the new building recently erected by the Bank of New York on the north-east corner of Wall and William streets.

The Manager's Room has a front of thirty-six feet on Wall street, and is twenty-four feet in depth. It has a slightly raised platform at E, with a desk and chair, suited for the occupancy of the President in the meetings of the Association.

D is a solid centre table, on which are usually kept files of the daily papers and financial periodicals. The Ledgers are laid upon it for examination by the members.

C is the Manager's desk, facing the middle of the room. A book-case with the nucleus of a financial library stands against the northern wall. The apartment is carpeted, and every arrangement speaks of taste, order and discipline.

A door near William street communicates with the Clerks' Room, twenty-four feet by seventeen feet in size, neatly furnished with desks and drawers for the books and papers. B, in this room, is the settling counter at which the Bank messengers transact their business. On one end of it is placed the Specie Clerks' Receipt Book for balances paid to them. An iron railing and wire net-work protects the other part from intrusion by visitors. The vestibule on the outside, at the head of the stairway, communicates with the Manager's Room on one side, and the *Exchange Room* on the other.

The Exchange Room is eighty feet long by twenty-four feet wide. It is well lighted on both sides; that opposite to the street looking out into a spacious area with a glass roof, which ventilates the building. The black spots inside of the counter, on which the desks are placed, represent stools for the use of the Settling Clerks. The desks are numbered from one to fifty-four, beginning at the left hand of the entrance. The name, also, of each bank is engraved on a plate on the outside.

A is the Manager's pulpit, in a raised doorway which opens from the Clerks' apartment, and overlooks the Exchange Room. The floor of this room is covered with a stout rug, to deaden the noise of feet while the Clerks are in movement.

The desks on the counter are separated by a light iron railing, and each one is furnished with pigeon-holes and drawers for the necessary papers and implements of writing. Closets under the counter afford convenience for hats, coats, &c.

THE DAILY ROUTINE.

EACH bank sends to the Clearing House a messenger or *Specie Clerk*, and a *Settling Clerk;* the former to distribute the packets of money of which his exchange is composed, and the latter to receive the return packets from the other messengers. They begin to arrive about fifteen minutes before ten o'clock, A. M., that being the hour at which the Manager gives the signal for the distribution to begin.

Each Specie Clerk leaves at the settling-desk B, as he passes into the long room, a printed form, the blank of which is filled with the gross amount of money that he has brought to exchange. For example, the Clerk of the Bank of New York leaves the following:

NEW YORK CLEARING HOUSE.	*No.* 1.] NEW YORK CLEARING HOUSE, *March 20th*, 1857. *Credit* BANK OF NEW YORK, *$842,539.19* ....*Settling Clerk.*

The Assistant Manager is thus furnished with the amounts composing the right-hand main column of the *Clearing House Proof* (page 310), which he transcribes under the head of "Banks Cr.," and adds together, making in the example $40,515,703.66. This is the total sum sent in by all the banks, and it is called *the Credit Exchange.* If each Messenger has a packet of money for every bank in the House (excepting his own), there are of course twenty-five hundred and fifty packets to be distributed. The manner of effecting this distribution is the distinctive feature of the Clearing House system, as compared with the old plan of separate exchange.

The Manager appears on his stand under the door way (A) at two or three minutes before ten o'clock, and giving a stroke on his bell, calls out: "Take your places."

The Settling Clerks immediately occupy their respective desks on the inside of the counter, and the Specie Clerks, standing, on the outside. Each of the latter carries on his left arm an open box of some light material, containing his packets of money arranged in the consecutive desk-order for delivery as he passes round the counter. He has also a Receipt List,* called "The Specie Clerks' Statement," with the amount designed for each bank, set down in the same order.

A fine is imposed for absence or late attendance.

There are now in the room one hundred and two Clerks, besides those who are attached to the House, and the scene is not always free from confusion by loud conversation, which the Manager corrects by a call:

"Order, gentlemen, order!"

Occasionally there are notices to be given of change of rules, or other matter relating to the business. The Manager calls the attention of the Clerks to any violation of rules that may have come to his knowledge, and perhaps enforces in a few words the necessity of strict discipline. Some one bank may have a communication on a subject of common interest. A discrepancy in the cash of any one, on a previous date,

---

* This is a copy of the Receiving Teller's Proof List, with a blank column for the Settling Clerks to sign their initials as a receipt.

The Manager in his Pulpit.

Making the Exchange in Six Minutes, at the Clearing House.

is notified, and perhaps discovered by a corresponding error in some other. New counterfeits or altered bills may be reported.

When the minute-hand of the clock reaches the stroke of ten, a second ring of the Manager's bell gives the signal for the distribution of the exchanges to begin.

Each Specie Clerk advances one step forward, and is brought opposite to the first desk, at which his delivery is to be made. He hands over the packet of money designed for it, and also the "Statement," on which the Settling Clerk writes his initials against the amount as a receipt, being careful to observe that the record is correct. The Statement is then returned to the Specie Clerk, who goes through the delivery at each desk in like manner. The whole line advances at the same time, resembling in its movement a military company in lock-step. While this is going on, the Manager walks round the interior of the desks, and silently identifies every Specie Clerk with the bank which he represents. It is rarely that a substitute is employed in this service; and if not already known to the Manager, he must be officially introduced.

In about six minutes the circuit is made, bringing each Messenger round to the starting-point, opposite his own desk. His Statement, signed by every Settling Clerk, is the voucher to his bank that he has delivered all the money intrusted to his care.

There is no part of the Clearing House routine that exhibits such striking results in economy and safety, compared with the old plan of exchange, as this movement of six minutes. Two thousand five hundred and fifty packages of money have been distributed and receipted for in this short space of time, by a method that excludes almost the last possibility of loss or error. The same work, on the old plan, occupied each messenger an average of not less than two hours, and was attended by great exposure in passing through jostling streets from one bank to another. Supposing the whole service to be performed by one person, the relative time occupied would be as five hours is to eight days of twelve hours each, or a clean saving of ninety-seven out of one hundred and two hours!

Each Settling Clerk has now on his desk the packets of money which constitute his *Debit Exchange.* He copies them in his Statement,* under the head of "Banks Cr.," and the accuracy of the copy is tested by the Specie Clerks calling back the amounts from the packets. The footing of this column furnishes the debit of his bank in the Clearing House Proof.

The Specie Clerks are now at liberty to leave the House with their return exchanges, which they do generally within fifteen minutes of the time that the distribution begins; and although not able to state the precise balance of their banks with the House, they can report it in round numbers. The Settling Clerks are obliged to remain until the Manager announces an exact proof.

---

* "The Settling Clerks' Statement" is the original of the "Specie Clerks' Statement," with a blank column in which to copy the return exchange; and when complete, the difference between the two columns is the debit or credit balance for the day.

The rapidity and accuracy with which the more skillful of the Settling Clerks accomplish their work, is almost incredible. The distribution occupies six minutes. At the end of two minutes more, they have copied and footed their column. But they must then make a deliberate revision of it, to be assured against errors.

The two footings of the Settling Clerks' Statement, and their difference, *debit* or *credit*, are written in the following form, which is sent to the Assistant Manager, to make up "the Clearing House Proof" (page 310).

The examples given will enable the reader to trace the figures in the course of their transfer.

NEW YORK CLEARING HOUSE.

No. 1.] NEW YORK CLEARING HOUSE.

March 20th, 1857.

Debit BANK OF NEW YORK, Am't received, $780,070.76
Credit " " " " " brought, $842,539.19

$..................Debit balance due Clearing House,
Credit balance due BANK OF NEW YORK.... $62,468.43

..................*Settling Clerk.*

While the Proof is in preparation from these forms, the Settling Clerk of each bank fills up a set of blanks with the amount credited on his list from every other. For example, the Clerk of the Bank of New York sends to the Clerk of the Manhattan Bank the following:

CLEARING HOUSE PROOF.

March 20th, 1857.

No.	Banks.	Balances due to Clearing House.	Banks Dr.	Banks Cr.	Balances due to Banks.	
1	Bank of New York		780 070 76	842 539 19	62 468 43	1
2	Manhattan Company		1 198 412 96	1 377 768 55	179 355 59	2
3	Merchants'		3 484 091 94	3 732 778 77	248 686 83	3
4	Mechanics'	179 476 36	1 592 992 22	1 413 515 86		4
5	Union	12 929 43	2 813 023 77	2 800 094 34		5
6	Bank of America	285 304 33	2 600 723 63	2 315 419 30		6
7	Phenix		1 115 098 42	1 133 515 35	18 416 93	7
8	City	35 502 19	580 666 56	545 164 37		8
9	North River		172 720 94	196 283 59	23 562 65	9
10	Tradesmen's		104 139 73	107 791 84	3 652 11	10
11	Fulton		241 717 85	254 445 12	12 727 27	11
12	Chemical		197 007 27	197 816 47	809 20	12
13	Merchants' Exchange		410 632 22	526 873 22	116 241	13
14	National	39 217 96	452 994 22	413 776 26		14
15	Butchers' & Drovers'		129 719 75	131 771 66	2 051 91	15
16	Mechanics' & Traders'	11 587 23	41 182 48	29 595 25		16
17	Greenwich		35 404 ..	37 882 56	2 478 56	17
18	Leather Manufacturers'		991 464 07	1 053 650 08	62 186 01	18
19	Seventh Ward		180 572 37	248 770 ..	68 197 63	19
20	Bk. of the State of N. Y.		3 893 899 27	4 035 962 93	142 063 66	20
21	American Exchange		3 076 473 27	3 109 168 27	32 695 ..	21
22	Mech. Banking Assoc'n		247 589 06	254 257 05	6 667 99	22
23	Bank of Commerce	294 626 99	3 272 050 33	2 977 423 34		23
24	Bowery		72 330 36	77 006 08	4 675 72	24
25	Broadway	4 858 02	218 402 41	213 549 39		25
26	Ocean		334 539 77	358 516 63	23 976 86	26
27	Mercantile		446 973 09	579 107 92	132 134 83	27
28	Pacific	1 951 43	92 845 83	90 894 40		28
29	Bank of the Republic	164 525 52	2 352 505 03	2 187 979 51		29
30	Chatham		79 367 82	80 167 13	799 31	30
31	People's		94 507 05	96 111 76	1 604 71	31
32	Bank of North America		686 922 86	724 620 78	37 697 92	32
33	Hanover		352 352 64	420 800 52	68 447 88	33
34	Irving	2 205 25	117 442 73	115 237 48		34
35	Metropolitan	97 302 91	1 760 562 96	1 663 260 05		35
36	Citizens'		88 984 55	101 304 17	12 319 62	36
38	Grocers'		112 690 88	112 692 58	1 70	38
40	Nassau	17 019 11	331 872 15	314 853 04		40
41	East River		52 996 92	57 328 88	4 331 96	41
42	Market	8 451 80	207 143 25	198 691 45		42
43	Saint Nicholas		295 366 85	345 923 39	50 556 54	43
44	Shoe and Leather	103 597 02	366 901 55	263 304 58		44
45	Corn Exchange	2 498 35	1 038 323 69	1 035 825 34		45
47	Continental	63 020 44	1 390 183 83	1 327 163 39		47
48	Bank of Commonwealth	50 721 86	847 108 34	796 386 48		48
49	Oriental		33 732 03	40 745 32	7 013 29	49
50	Marine	21 788 70	390 693 54	368 904 84		50
52	Atlantic	47 839 89	247 831 91	199 992 02		52
53	Importers' & Traders'		310 624 45	360 601 47	49 977 02	53
54	Park		579 850 08	658 471 74	78 621 66	54
55	Artisans'					55
		1444 419 79	40 515 703 66	40 515 703 66	1444 419 79	

No. 2.

MANHATTAN COMPANY

From No. 1,

BANK OF NEW YORK.

$65,733.40..................

The words: "From No. 1, Bank of New York," run through the whole set; and in like manner, the number and name of each bank runs through the set belonging to it. The other number and name is the address of the particular bank to which the ticket is sent.

This ticket ought to correct all errors of transcription, although the money has been carried away. It is to be remembered that the Specie Clerks' Statement is a transcript of the "total debit" column in the Settling Clerks' Statement. If any Settling Clerk copies a wrong amount from his list in one of these tickets, the Clerk, to whom it is sent, discovers the mistake by comparison with the original Statement in his hands. So perfect is this plan of direct and alternate revision, that the Clearing House Exchanges have been made for nearly five years without the error of a single cent.

If no mistake is made, the Assistant Manager announces a proof in thirty minutes from the beginning of the movement. But the first trial is rarely so fortunate. Fifty-one clerks make over twenty thousand figures in less than ten minutes, and a single one faulty or obscure vitiates the result.

The accuracy of the General Proof consists in the agreement of the debit and credit columns with each other, and in that of the balance columns. Such is the regularity and discipline of the House, that the Assistant Manager seldom varies a minute from the half-hour in announcing his first trial.

"The difference is $7,643.22"—or it may be but a few cents.

The writing and distribution of the small tickets has been going on in the meantime, and it frequently happens that the error is discovered almost simultaneously with its announcement. At other times, the whole corps of Settling Clerks may be detained an hour or more by further revision.

If the tickets fail to expose an error promptly, the Manager requires the Clerk at either end to pass down the line with his Statement, whilst the others call back, each the amount charged as delivered by the Specie Clerk. The second Clerk follows the track of the first, and the third that of the second, as they successively pass. This is the final method of revision; and if the additions are correct, it must make the proof.

Errors discovered within forty-five minutes from the beginning of the distribution incur no penalty; but after that, they are chargeable with a fine, payable by the bank in whose figures they occur. The banks are therefore careful to send accurate and skillful clerks. It is, moreover, a matter of pride and economy with themselves to avoid errors, as they involve detention from home duties.

SCALE OF FINES.

For all errors remaining uncorrected at the expiration of one hour and a quarter from commencing, the Fines in this list will be doubled—and at the expiration of two hours, the Fines will be quadrupled.

1st—All errors on the Credit side of the Settling Clerk's Statement (*i. e.* in the amount brought) whether of footing or entry, and all errors causing disagreement between the credit entries, the check tickets, and the exchange slips—each	$3.00
2d—Errors in making the Debit (*i. e.* amount received) entries—each	2 00
3d—Errors in the Tickets reported to the Clearing House, causing disagreement between the balances and aggregates—each	2.00
4th—All other errors—	1.00
5th—Disorderly conduct of Clerk or Porter at the Clearing House; or disregard of the Manager's instructions—each offence .	1.00
6th—Clerk or Porter, failing to attend punctually at the morning exchanges—each	2.00
7th—Debtor Banks, failing to appear to pay their balances by 1½ o'clock, P. M. . .	3.00

The Clearing House Proof exhibits in one view the total amount of the exchange, the amount received from each bank, the amount taken away again by each, and the balance due to or from each; also the total balance of the Clearings.

Up to this point, the Clearing House has nothing to do with the money. None of its employés touch it, and neither does the Manager. It has been during the whole process entirely within the custody of the Clerks and Messengers—the representatives of their respective banks; and every package has been receipted for, immediately on delivery. The exchange is effected independently of the House, the authority of the Manager being limited to the preservation of order, and to the enforcement of the rules of the Association.

The column on the left hand of the Clearing House Proof shows the balance due from each debtor bank to the House, which here stands for all the other banks; and that on the right, the amount due to each creditor bank from all the others—both in the aggregate. This is another remarkable economy over the old system, by which settlement was effected only by the drawing of as many different drafts as there are banks. For example: the balance of $179,476.36, due by the Mechanics' Bank to the House, can now be paid in one sum, and by coin certificates, in the time necessary for a single messenger to walk over the ground between the two places; whereas, formerly, it involved the drawing of a separate draft by the Mechanics' Bank for every debit balance, and the liquidation of another for every credit balance; besides, the frequent carriage of gold by hand or in carts, and the time of one or more messengers for the entire day—to say nothing of the interdrawing and confusion growing out of cross-errands and disarrangement of original balances.

At one o'clock, the debtor banks begin to send in their balances, for which the Manager's receipt is returned:

Paying out a Ton of Gold in the old Clearing House on Broadway.

No. 4.] NEW YORK CLEARING HOUSE.

March 20*th*, 1857.

Received from the MECHANICS' BANK *One hundred and seventy-nine thousand four hundred and seventy-six* $\frac{36}{100}$ *Dollars, in full for balance due the Associated Banks.*

$179,476.36........[Signed by the Manager.]

Each bank keeps a current ledger-account with the House, charging it with all money sent, and crediting it with all that is returned; and this receipt is charged, as a voucher, on the books of the paying bank.

The Specie Clerks of the creditor banks come in from half-past one to two o'clock, to get the balances due to them, for which they give receipts in a book prepared with suitable forms for that purpose. The settlement is completed by two o'clock. It is for this period of one hour only, that the Clearing House has any money in actual possession, and then simply as trustee—receiving from one to pay to another.

Default in payment, on the part of any bank, leads to its immediate suspension from the Exchange. The balance due from it to the House is assessed on the other banks in the proportion of their respective claims against the defaulting member, and the settlement is not deranged, so far as the House is concerned. In effect, the several claims revert to the condition in which they stood before the exchange was made, and become open accounts between the banks and the defaulting member, with which the Clearing House has thereafter nothing to do. [See section 13 of the Constitution, page 298.]

The amount of coin required in the settlement of March 20th, 1857, when the exchanges were heavier than on any other day since the establishment of the Clearing House, was $1,444,419.79—equal in gross weight to about three tons avoirdupois, or six thousand five hundred pounds, which would make nearly three hundred bags of gold of five thousand pounds each. The daily movement of such a weight, first from the debtor banks to the House, and thence to the respective creditor banks, would be attended with considerable expense and risk. To avoid this, the Association constituted the Bank of America a common-coin depository, to hold in trust, and to issue certificates, for such sums of gold as the other banks might place therein. The form of the Certificate is as follows:

No. 246.] NEW YORK, *May* 4*th*, 1858.

BANK OF AMERICA. [$5,000.

This certifies that the Bank of New York has deposited in this bank Five Thousand Dollars, in coin, to be held in trust as a special deposit, payable in coin, on demand, to any bank member of the New York Clearing House Association, only on presentation of this Certificate, indorsed by the bank demanding payment of the same.

[Signed by the Cashier and Receiving Teller of the Bank.]

The New-Fashioned Way of Bank Settlement. The Specie Clerk has $500,000 of Co n Certificates in his pocket.

These certificates are issued for the several amounts of $1,000, $5,000, and $10,000, in the option of the depositing bank. They are numbered, registered, and countersigned on the back, by the General Book-keeper of the Bank of America. When paid in at the House, they are indorsed by the paying bank—and when paid out, charged to the receiving bank; so that they can always be traced by the records. They are valid only in the Clearing House settlements, or directly between the banks.

Any of the Associated Banks that may have these certificates on hand, and a deficiency of ready coin, can obtain the latter in exchange with any other that has an excess.

The bills of the several banks are admitted in settlement of balances under one thousand dollars.

The Clearing House is not responsible for any mistakes, overdrafts, or other irregularities that may occur in the exchanges. These are corrected by the banks between themselves.

Reclamations for differences, resulting from the miscount of money, or the omission of entries on the exchange slips, have always furnished cause for dispute between the banks. The open exchange is in the exclusive personal charge of the messenger, between the bank and the Clearing House, either way. He might abstract bills without being discovered. Claims for deficiency have frequently been resisted on this ground. To remove it, some of the banks seal up their exchanges in large envelopes, and thus relieve the transit of all suspicion. For reasons not apparent, the practice is far from general.

The economy of time and labor effected by the Clearing House system is stated by the Manager, Mr. GEORGE D. LYMAN, in an appendix to "CLEVELAND'S Banking Laws of New York," as follows:

"On the day when the Clearing House began business, about twenty-seven hundred open, active accounts on the ledgers of the associated banks were balanced—the most of them for the first time,* and all of them finally. The business which had rendered necessary this large number of accounts was thenceforth accomplished more quickly, with less annoyance to bank officers, and with greater safety to all concerned. The results may be briefly enumerated as follows:

"*First*—The condensation for each bank of forty-eight balances into one, and the settlement of that balance without a movement of specie.

"*Secondly*—The avoidance of numerous accounts, entries, and postings.

"*Thirdly*—Great saving of time to the Porters, and of risk in making exchanges and settlements from bank to bank.

"*Fourthly*—Relief from a vast amount of labor and annoyance to which the great army of Cashiers, Tellers, and Book-keepers were subjected under the old system.

"*Fifthly*—The liberation of the Associated Banks from all injurious dependence on each other.

"*Sixthly*—The absolute facility afforded by the books of the Clearing House for knowing at all times the management and standing of every bank in the Association."

---

* The practice of the banks had been to draw settlement-checks on each other for even thousands of dollars near the balance due, and the account was never settled to a point. The accuracy thereof was frequently tested by comparison of the books.

OF THE CLEARING HOUSE RECORDS.

The daily footings of the General Proof are posted to the Ledger, exhibiting a continuous history of the aggregate dealings of the banks.

In like manner, the daily debit and credit exchange of each bank is posted to its account, and shows not only the *extent* of its business, but measurably its *character* also. This is the most essential of all the records. It is that which brings the banks separately within the supervision and control of the Clearing House—a necessary complement of the joint responsibility created by the organization.

The twentieth section of the Constitution empowers a Committee to suspend any bank from the privileges of the Clearing House, "in case of extreme emergency." This emergency is indicated by the daily course of the exchanges; and there is no possibility of concealing it. For example: The sworn weekly statements of a bank may show that it held up to a certain date an average reserve of coin of three hundred thousand dollars. The records show that its debit balances of the three following days reach that sum. It must then be entirely exhausted of its coin. If, on the fourth day, it is again brought into debt sixty thousand dollars, it must either borrow or buy coin to pay it—both extreme resorts, and hurtful to the character of the institution. With the knowledge of these facts, the Committee visit the bank, and investigate its affairs. If they are found to be hopelessly involved, it is suspended from the exchange at the

Clearing House—a last blow to its credit. If, on the the other hand, the embarrassment is temporary, and does not impair the solvency of the bank, it receives assistance, and is preserved in line. This action of the House has been exemplified in several instances, with most satisfactory results. If the restrictive power has brought unwisely-expanded, but otherwise well-conducted banks to the bar of examination, the preservative power has given relief, and saved them from public discredit. If the insolvency of a badly-conducted bank has been hastened by the requirement of prompt and full daily liquidation, no mischief or injustice has been done thereby; and the general credit of our banking system has been improved by the excision of a bad member.

A bank which receives frequent remittances of specie from abroad is an exception to the supposed case. With such an explanation, its debit balances at the House may exceed its credit, without injury to its standing.

A Summary-book is made up from the daily postings, showing the total receipts and payments of specie by each bank for the week, and also for the month and year. The adverse balances of one period may be compensated by the favorable balances of the succeeding period; and thus the specie history of each, and of the whole, is followed up with unfailing precision. If, at the end of a month, it appears that a bank has paid in to the House one million of dollars more than it has received, and if it has no foreign sources of replenishment, the conclusion is, that it has supplied itself by purchase. If the same result should be shown at the end of another month, without signs of recuperation, and so on continuously, it becomes evident that the institution is carrying a forced average of loans, and it will receive a call from the Committee, under the twentieth section of the Constitution. But this extreme case is most unlikely to happen. The credit that every member derives from the Association is too valuable to be cast off or treated with lightness. The action of the Association is too impartial and just to give offence, or to admit excuse for disregarding its advice.

A positive principle, or rule of financial government, has been demonstrated by this action of the Clearing House on the city banks—that is, the restriction of loans, by the necessity of maintaining a certain average of coin *from resources within the bank.* Borrowing from day to day will no longer do. It cannot be concealed. The records will show conclusively whether the average is kept up by a healthy business, or by a forcing process.

The limitation imposed does not stop at the bank loans, but passes through them into the commercial system. The loans rest on the coin average, this rests on the deposits, and the deposits rest on the means of trade. The Clearing House has not created any new dependence of this kind, but it has brought the facts into a manageable shape, and established something like an axiom in the banking business. It is not a mere arbitrary requirement that a specific average of coin must be maintained, but it is in the constitution of that average as a *result*, and the control of it by an organization which permits no escape, and works no injustice,—and what that organization is for the city of New York, the city is for the country; a restrictive power over the general currency of trade must be exerted through this channel to its remotest sections.

Each bank in the city of New York is required by law to publish, "on the morning of every Tuesday, in a newspaper printed in the said city, a statement under the oath of the President or Cashier, showing the average amount of loans and discounts, specie, deposits, and circulation, for the next preceding week." The object of this law, which went into effect on the 1st of August 1853 (two months before the organization of the Clearing House), was to check the tendency to a dangerous expansion of bank loans. While it answered the purpose measurably, it proved the inadequacy of legislative action of itself to correct the evil. The law was satisfied with the *publication*, merely, of the statement. It neither imposed penalties nor indicated any relation to be preserved between the amount of loans and that of specie. It did not compel banks to liquidate between themselves. A bank might show a creditable average of coin, whilst carrying a discreditable average of debt—enough, if paid, to exhaust the last dime in its vaults. In reality, nearly all the force and value of the Weekly Statement is due to its incorporation with the records of the Clearing House. These have given it the stamp ot truth, which it had not before. There is no longer a possibility of "fixing it up" so as to give a false show of the condition of a bank. It must tell "the truth, the whole truth, and nothing but the truth."

Every bank in the State of New York is required by law to publish, in a local newspaper, under the oath of the President and Cashier, a quarterly statement of its condition, and to transmit a manuscript and a printed copy thereof to the Bank Department at Albany, where a synopsis of the whole is prepared and published by the General Superintendent, for presentation to the Legislature. The original law specified a certain day near the end of each quarter, on which this statement should be made up. It was supposed that this would be sufficient to restrict the business of the banks within safe limits; but it proved wholly ineffective. To show how the purpose of the law was defeated, the form of a Quarterly Statement is given on page 324.

The date on which the Statement was to be called for, being known, nothing was easier than to prepare for it. Some of the new banks especially, whose loans were generally stretched beyond prudence, found it difficult to make a creditable show by the side of the older institutions. Deposits were borrowed for a single day. The loans to directors were reduced for a few hours, or jumped over by transit checks through other banks. Any desirable changes, to make a good show out of bad facts, could be carried long enough for a commissioner to administer the oath; and the purpose of the law was so effectually defeated, in the very spots where it was chiefly intended to apply that the Legislature amended it by authorizing the Superintendent to specify, after the expiration of the quarter, an antecedent date, under which the Statement should be made. But even this

QUARTERLY REPORT OF — BANK.

RESOURCES.

Loans and discounts		$1,225,419 42
Overdrafts		663 86
Due from Banks		70,867 78
Due from the Directors of the Bank	$56,500	
Real estate		178,074 16
Specie		154,862 22
Cash Items, viz: Checks and sight drafts on solvent Banks, taken in the course of the day previous		109,001 93
Stocks		146,398 90
Bills of solvent Banks		19,544 00
Loss and expense account		3,931 42
		$1,908,763 69

LIABILITIES.

Capital		$979,200 00
Circulation registered	$125,802 00	
Less notes on hand	28,080 00	97,722 00
Profits		41,042 91
Due to Banks		175,080 77
Due to Individuals and Corporations other than Banks		16,780 87
Due Depositors on demand		597,749 14
Amount due, not included under either of the above heads, for dividends unclaimed		1,188 00
		$1,908,763 69

STATE OF NEW YORK, COUNTY OF NEW YORK, ss.: ——— ———, President, and ——— ———, Cashier of the —— Bank, an Associated Bank, located and doing business at New York City, in said county, being duly and severally sworn, each for himself, saith, that the foregoing is, in all respects, a true statement of the condition of the said Bank, before the transaction of any business, on the morning of Saturday, the 26th day of September, in the year one thousand eight hundred and fifty-seven, in respect to each and every of the items and particulars above specified, according to the best of his knowledge and belief; and that the business of the said Bank has been and is transacted at the location aforesaid.

(Signed) ——— ———, President.
——— ———, Cashier.

Severally subscribed and sworn by both deponents, the 10th day of October, 1857.

(Signed) J. VAN NAME, Commissioner of Deeds.

was not beyond the constructive ingenuity of dishonest bankers. The accounts coûld be so kept as to justify, technically, a different analysis from that contemplated by the law, and the result could be shaped accordingly.

It was not until the Clearing House was organized that the Quarterly Statements of our city banks could be depended on for general accuracy. It was only when the Clearing House *records* were brought to such perfection as to give the means of analysis and test beyond dispute, that the positive integrity of those statements could be guaranteed to the public. That concealment can yet be practiced, in some details, is true; but the main fact of truth is assured to the public.

It has been shown, that the moment a bank increases its loans imprudently, it begins to feel the check of depletion in its specie; and if it does not return immediately within the common average, it is subject to discipline, from which there is no escape. But what is to prevent a bank from making *bad* loans, and becoming gradually insolvent? What is to prevent the absorption of the funds by a few persons—by the directors, and a "startling development" some day when it is least expected? This question brings into view a cause of jealousy that was manifested by opposition to a Constitution, on the first organization of the Clearing House. It was feared that an inquisitorial power might grow up, and find pretexts for arbitrary supervision; and even for inspection into personal accounts. While the practical action of the House has developed no such tendency, it has wrought a healthful change in the business of each bank, enforced better judgment over its internal affairs, improved the character of its loans, and started anew the subject of bank discipline; so that, not only is all jealousy dispelled, but every member of the Association has come to regard it as a necessary auxiliary to his own prosperity!

The improvement in the character of its loans is consequent upon the fact, that if a bank becomes embarrassed by their imprudent extension, it can get *a good class* of paper rediscounted, and thus obtain immediate relief; whereas, if its discounted paper is of a low grade, or if the assistance required is to help the directors only, and not its dealers generally, it loses sympathy and reputation. The *character* of its discounted bills is, therefore, its sheet-anchor in a storm. In fact, the credit of the Clearing House Association would itself be impaired, if it should allow one of its members to fail from inability to convert good assets into cash funds.

Before the establishment of the Clearing House, a bank might have maintained specie payments with the other banks almost to the entire exhaustion of its means of liquidation with the public. It could have borrowed or bought specie continuously for a long period, without exposure. It cannot now *borrow or buy a dollar*, without the knowledge of the House. It is arrested immediately, in the first steps towards insolvency.

There is one fact stated in the foregoing description which deserves repetition, for the testimony that it bears to the admirable working of the system in its practical details. It is, that *the exchanges have been made, and the liquidations effected, for five years, without an error or loss of one cent.*

The whole amount of bank funds that passed through the House, up to August 31, 1858—was *thirty thousand six hundred and seventy-five* MILLIONS, *nine hundred and thirty-three thousand, five hundred and fifty-six dollars, and fifty-six cents*—$30,675,933,556.56.

The amount of specie or its representative certificates received and paid out, during the same period, was *fifteen hundred and seventy-four* MILLIONS, *four hundred and thirty thousand, three hundred and thirty dollars and forty-six cents*—$1,574,430,330.46.

The specie is counted four times, twice when received, and twice when paid.

To avoid carrying bags of coin up to the rooms, a clerk is stationed in the Bank of New York on the first floor, who gives receipts for it, which receipts are presented at the settling desk. A speaking-tube enables the Manager to communicate with the Clerk below, and thus to verify such transactions.

The expense of conducting this vast amount of business does not exceed eight thousand dollars a year. This covers salaries, clerk hire, and the pay of a detective police officer, who is always in attendance while the rooms are open. Stationery bills and rent amount to about eight thousand dollars a year; but these are not strictly chargeable to the conduct of the business. In fact, the stationery bills of the several banks are much less for being executed under one order, and the House acts merely as an agent to get the printing done. Instead of the old paper labels to bags of coin, it furnishes strips of leather, printed with the several amounts that are sealed up.

In this account of the Clearing House, the author has, doubtless, overlooked some of its bearings. The original idea of its founders was, simply to facilitate the exchanges between the banks. It has already added to this many other advantages and uses which were not contemplated; and more are suggested. It has put an end to speculative banking in New York. It has exerted a powerful influence to arrest speculative commerce. It has set the example of *positive liquidation*, which henceforth must spread and increase. Especially, in the organization of accounts, it has gained results which were before thought to be out of reach. There is probability, at least, that the New York Clearing House leads the way, in a practical use of statistics and commercial facts, far beyond our present attainments, and for which there has long been great need.

To Mr. George D. Lyman, the Manager of the Clearing House, belongs chiefly the credit of systematizing its details, planning its records, and bringing them to their present state of efficiency and perfection. His practical acquaintance with the banking business, gained as Clerk and Teller in several institutions of high standing, have well qualified him to discharge the duties of his responsible office; while the intelligence, zeal, and perseverance with which he follows up every suggestion that occurs in the working of the system, is a guarantee for any improvements that may be required, or of which it is susceptible.

To Mr. WILLIAM A. CAMP, the Assistant Manager, to whom is intrusted the principal labor of details, is due the merit of unusual accuracy and promptness in the daily proofs, on which directly depends the convenience of fifty settling clerks, and of hundreds, if not thousands of bank dealers.

The following tables, copied from the Clearing House records, exhibit the rise and fall of bank credits, in the City of New York, from the first of August 1853, to the 31st of August 1858.

The accompanying diagram illustrates these tables in fluctuations from week to week of the loans, specie, and deposits. The scale is constructed on the actual averages of the year ending on the 29th of July 1855, which were ninety millions of loans, fifty-five millions of deposits, and fourteen millions of specie.

Each line across the diagram represents one million of dollars in the loans and the deposits; and half a million in the specie. The lines up and down represent the weeks. The scale for loans is on the left hand; that for deposits, on the right; and that for specie, in the middle. By following the line for any week of the year to its intersection with the other lines, and thence referring to the respective scales, the relative amount of loans, deposits, and specie, is ascertained.

WEEKLY AVERAGES OF THE NEW YORK CITY BANKS,

FROM AUGUST, 1853, TO AUGUST, 1858.

1854.		Loans.	Specie.	Circulation.	Deposits.
Aug.	6	97,889,617	9,746,452	9,510,465	39,410,756
	13	95,562,277	10,654,618	9,451,945	39,166,712
	20	93,866,970	11,092,552	9,414,696	39,817,718
	27	92,386,954	11,319,049	9,427,191	38,431,808
Sept.	3	91,741,338	11,268,049	9,554,294	38,502,970
	10	91,108,347	11,380,693	9,597,336	38,545,164
	17	90,190,589	11,860,235	9,566,723	38,612,301
	24	90,092,765	11,340,925	9,477,541	39,312,334
Oct.	1	90,149,540	11,231,912	9,521,665	38,968,661
	8	89,128,998	10,266,602	9,673,458	38,985,760
	15	87,837,273	11,330,172	9,464,714	37,435,499
	22	85,367,981	10,303,254	9,388,543	36,186,864
	29	83,400,321	10,866,672	9,300,350	35,731,038
Nov.	5	83,092,630	11,771,880	9,492,158	36,241,623
	12	82,882,409	12,823,575	9,287,629	37,970,796
	19	83,717,622	13,691,324	9,151,443	39,047,016
	26	84,802,530	13,343,196	9,032,769	42,099,942
Dec.	3	85,824,756	12,830,772	9,133,586	39,121,739
	10	86,708,028	12,493,760	9,075,704	39,600,092
	17	87,865,073	12,166,020	8,939,830	39,243,501
	24	88,760,623	11,981,270	8,867,261	40,262,979
	31	90,162,106	11,058,478	8,927,013	41,372,382
1854.					
Jan.	7	90,133,887	11,506,124	9,075,926	38,551,290
	14	90,010,012	11,894,453	8,668,344	40,516,717
	21	90,068,738	11,455,156	8,605,235	41,311,989
	28	89,759,465	11,117,958	8,642,677	41,405,422
Feb.	4	90 549,577	11,634,653	8,996,675	41,476,160
	11	91,434,022	11,872,126	8,994,083	42,983,138
	18	92,698,085	11,742,384	8,954,464	43,257,792
	25	93,529,716	11,212,693	8,929,314	42,965,270
March	4	94,558,421	10,560,400	9,209,830	41,655,792
	11	94,279,994	9,832,483	9,137,555	40,955,635
	18	93,418,929	10,018,456	9,255,781	40,278,250
	25	92,972,711	10,132,246	9,209,406	40,124,736
April	1	92,825,024	10,264,009	9,395,820	39,861,920

1854.		Loans.	Specie.	Circulation.	Deposits.
April	8	92,551,808	10,188,141	9,713,215	38,993,744
	15	91,636,274	11,044,044	9,533,998	39,729,730
	22	90,376,340	10,526,976	9,353,854	39,153,964
	29	90,245,049	10,951,153	9,377,687	40,270,391
May	6	90,739,721	11,437,040	9,823,008	40,625,252
	13	90,245,928	12,382,068	9,507,797	42,212,552
	20	90,886,728	12,118,043	9,480,018	42,591,851
	27	90,981,974	10,981,531	9,284,807	41,114,763
June	3	91,916,710	10,281,969	9,381,714	50,775,744
	10	91,015,171	9,617,180	9,307,889	51,871,900
	17	90,063,573	10,013,157	9,144,284	51,243,245
	24	88,751,952	9,628,375	9,009,726	49,938,638
July	1	88,608,591	11,130,800	9,068,253	51,865,928
	8	88,347,281	12,267,318	9,195,757	54,803,679
	15	90,437,004	15,074,093	8,837,681	56,549,703
	22	92,011,870	15,720,309	8,768,289	58,871,544
	29	92,588,579	15,386,864	8,756,777	58,925,151
Aug.	5	93,723,141	14,468,981	9,124,648	58,271,954
	12	93,435,057	13,522,023	8,917,179	57,582,455
	19	92,880,103	14,253,972	8,855,523	57,037,727
	26	91,447,075	14,395,072	8,811,369	57,055,505
Sept.	2	91,391,188	14,714,618	8,934,632	58,114,408
	9	91,528,244	14,446,317	8,968,707	56,080,400
	16	91,639,782	14,484,259	8,820,609	56,439,110
	23	92,095,911	12,932,386	8,802,623	55,221,762
	30	92,102,013	12,042,244	8,712,136	54,308,512
Oct.	7	91,380,525	10,630,517	8,918,492	51,480,375
	14	88,618,936	11,130,377	8,534,188	50,352,306
	21	87,092,810	10,320,163	8,497,556	47,781,224
	28	84,709,236	9,826,763	8,131,933	45,058,781
Nov.	4	83,369,101	10,004,686	8,238,126	43,504,964
	11	82,717,052	10,472,538	8,197,444	43,619,326
	18	82,191,994	10,801,532	7,877,604	44,100,821
	25	81,699,705	10,200,983	7,718,158	43,409,843
Dec.	2	81,678,423	10,488,383	7,849,289	43,491,999
	9	80,593,636	10,484,501	7,480,833	43,118,595
	16	80,946,663	11,471,841	7,261,111	44,334,684
	23	80,721,224	11,490,495	6,914,866	44,877,723
	30	81,653,637	12,076,147	7,075,880	45,402,377
1855.					
Jan.	6	82,244,706	13,596,963	7,049,982	47,740,767
	13	83,976,081	15,488,525	6,686,461	50,614,846
	20	85,447,998	16,372,127	6,681,355	53,290,317

1855.	Loans.	Specie.	Circulation.	Deposits.
Jan. 27	86,654,657	16,697,260	6,639,823	55,127,932
Feb. 3	88,145,697	17,439,196	7,000,766	56,712,546
10	89,862,170	17,124,391	6,969,111	58,124,415
17	90,850,031	17,339,086	6,941,606	59,186,888
24	91,590,505	16,370,875	6,963,562	58,992,863
March 3	92,386,125	16,531,279	7,106,710	59,100,643
10	92,331,789	16,870,669	7,131,998	59,543,221
17	92,447,345	16,933,933	7,061,018	59,688,105
24	93,050,773	16,602,729	7,452,231	59,620,122
31	93,634,041	16,018,105	7,337,633	59,948,549
April 7	94,499,394	14,968,004	7,771,534	59,283,096
14	94,140,399	14,890,979	7,523,528	59,478,598
21	93,632,893	14,355,041	7,510,124	59,025,615
28	92,505,951	14,282,424	7,610,985	58,345,546
May 5	93,093,243	14,325,050	8,087,609	58,403,227
12	91,642,498	14,585,626	7,804,977	58,365,766
19	91,675,500	15,225,056	7,638,630	58,999,522
26	91,160,518	15,314,531	7,489,637	58,687,274
June 2	91,197,652	15,397,674	7,555,609	59,034,612
9	92,109,097	15,005,155	7,502,568	59,042,817
16	93,100,385	14,978,559	7,452,161	60,092,058
23	94,029,425	14,705,629	7,335,653	60,661,862
30	95,586,424	15,640,146	7,396,119	63,553,440
July 7	97,852,491	15,381,093	7,743,069	68,459,591
14	98,521,002	16,576,506	7,515,724	67,770,124
21	99,029,147	15,918,999	7,407,086	66,006,131
28	99,083,799	15,920,976	7,409,498	66,070,296
Aug. 4	100,118,569	15,298,358	7,642,903	65,846,924
11	100,774,209	15,280,669	7,714,401	64,583,266
18	101,154,060	14,649,245	7,610,106	66,128,237
25	100,604,604	13,326,378	7,582,095	64,009,067
Sept. 1	100,436,970	12,852,823	7,620,178	63,900,757
8	100,273,733	12.006,625	7,861,153	62,340,942
15	99,397,009	12,213,240	7,721,825	61,963,872
22	98,581,734	11,655,391	7,717,860	60,729,518
29	97,385,225	9,919,124	7,724,970	57,908,647
Oct. 6	95,515,021	11,110,687	7,853,217	56,527,490
13	95,059,420	11,138,878	7,840,114	56,632,069
20	95,103,376	12,461,723	7,888,164	57,372,644
27	94,216,373	11,163,521	7,828,489	56,038,975
Nov. 3	93,369,079	11,106,298	8,071,508	54,785,463
10	92,454,290	10,855,526	8,088,608	53,538,966
17	92,029,920	11,302,917	7,941,579	53,617,740

1855.		Loans.	Specie.	Circulation.	Deposits.
Nov.	24	92,312,408	11,715,239	7,779,567	54,612,212
Dec.	1	92,526,921	11,227,134	7,841,654	58,663,668
	8	93,189,803	11,844,625	7,861,741	55,474,116
	15	93,800,138	11,584,075	7,701,052	56,111,334
	22	94,380,487	12,088,359	7,778,893	56,555,999
	29	95,114,060	10,788,098	7,841,946	56,736,775
1856.					
Jan.	5	95,863,390	11,687,209	7,903,656	58,320,328
	12	96,145,408	11,777,711	7,612,507	58,575,652
	19	96,382,968	13,385,260	7,462,706	60,161,127
	26	96,887,221	12,733,059	7,406,986	60,430,978
Feb.	2	97,970,611	13,640,437	7,622,826	61,622,874
	9	98,344,077	14,233,329	7,819,122	62,128,682
	16	99,401,315	15,678,736	7,693,441	64,341,903
	23	100,745,448	15,835,874	7,664,688	66,329,670
March	1	102,632,235	15,640,687	7,754,392	67,237,728
	8	103,909,688	15,170,946	7,888,176	67,881,084
	15	104,528,298	14,045,024	7,863,148	67,020,460
	22	104,533,576	14,369,556	7,912,581	67,153,493
	29	104,745,307	14,216,841	7,943,253	67,661,944
April	5	106,962,618	13,381,455	8,347,498	67,985,678
	12	107,840,435	12,626,094	8,281,525	68,300,783
	19	106,765,085	12,958,132	8,221,518	66,839,625
	26	105,538,864	13,102,858	8,246,121	66,285,880
May	3	105,325,962	12,850,228	8,715,163	65,025,870
	10	103,803,793	13,317,365	8,662,485	64,854,416
	17	103,002,320	12,796,541	8,488,152	63,905,512
	24	102,207,767	13,850,333	8,335,097	63,874,195
	31	102,451,275	14,021,289	8,269,151	64,527,837
June	7	103,474,921	16,166,180	8,430,252	67,033,708
	14	104,168,881	17,414,680	8,360,735	69,586,695
	21	105,626,995	17,871,955	8,278,002	70,381,210
	28	107,087,525	17,069,688	8,250,289	71,349,933
July	5	109,267,583	16,829,236	8,637,471	77,318,825
	12	109,748,042	14,793,409	8,405,576	71,522,716
	19	110,873,494	15,326,131	8,346,243	72,744,569
	26	111,346,589	13,910,848	8,386,285	72,381,621
Aug.	2	112,221,563	14,328,253	8,646,043	73,075,328
	9	112,192,322	13,270,602	8,676,759	71,377,871
	16	111,406,755	12,806,673	8,584,499	70,357,736
	23	110,188,004	12,914,732	8,588,413	69,022,934
	30	109,373,911	12,965,237	8,589,745	67,606,118
Sept.	6	109,560,943	13,098,876	8,887,860	67,225,342

1856.		Loans.	Specie.	Circulation.	Deposits.
Sept.	13	109,579,775	12,281,387	8,741,064	66,049,411
	20	109,715,435	12,270,685	8,760,383	65,866,422
	27	108,992,205	10,873,220	8,665,194	63,661,171
Oct.	4	107,931,707	11,015,184	8,830,628	62,052,545
	11	107,147,392	10,382,751	8,748,930	60,978,200
	18	105,929,265	10,846,857	8,696,736	60,319,718
	25	104,156,483	10,580,795	8,649,802	58,696,456
Nov.	1	103,142,093	11,057,675	8,686,835	58,024,128
	8	102,508,639	11,516,420	8,946,721	56,933,387
	15	103,554,450	12,253,737	8,856,977	58,942,049
	22	104,504,919	12,971,868	8,818,323	65,362,520
	29	105,483,053	12,123,887	8,608,228	61,570,260
Dec.	6	106,898,534	12,278,347	8,671,758	62,923,969
	13	108,336,586	10,832,543	8,516,854	62,854,773
	20	108,334,593	11,151,317	8,397,440	62,265,155
	27	108,527,429	10,392,428	8,387,167	62,259,390
1857.					
Jan.	3	109,149,153	11,172,244	8,602,113	63,677,829
	10	110,150,234	11,090,109	8,328,394	64,316,552
	17	110,860,401	11,955,054	8,047,065	66,076,987
	24	111,094,415	11,633,924	7,879,026	66,877,981
	31	111,785,332	12,191,825	8,024,948	67,241,670
Feb.	7	112,876,712	11,143,894	8,426,817	65,997,161
	14	112,722,799	10,497,382	8,151,799	65,943,495
	21	111,773,571	10,432,158	8,106,074	65,098,896
	28	111,137,717	10,645,254	8,159,275	64,627,068
March	7	111,899,649	11,707,346	8,465,697	64,894,959
	14	113,250,988	11,077,732	8,452,540	66,694,524
	21	113,448,692	11,291,373	8,494,238	65,975,949
	28	112,884,024	11,325,733	8,473,829	66,228,415
April	4	114,833,902	11,538,732	8,812,328	66,884,088
	11	115,374,717	10,884,490	8,787,344	67,042,866
	18	114,398,174	12,061,372	8,770,828	67,547,241
	25	113,391,910	11,827,862	8,736,768	67,068,424
May	2	114,409,275	12,009,910	9,006,566	68,078,676
	9	115,068,322	12,011,491	9,182,783	67,954,460
	16	114,620,042	12,543,693	8,935,297	68,595,168
	23	114,049,102	13,126,735	8,738,025	68,517,240
	30	114,049,633	12,815,515	8,696,693	68,565,909
June	6	115,338,592	13,134,714	8,838,575	69,233,090
	13	115,412,541	11,974,879	8,696,893	68,111,324
	20	115,114,765	12,790,701	8,590,132	68,791,049
	27	115,015,504	10,901,091	8,505,065	67,212,278

1857.		Loans.	Specie.	Circulation.	Deposits.
July	4	115,044,303	12,837,346	8,901,590	65,391,582
	11	116,028,617	12,666,146	8,693,578	65,702,597
	18	117,365,321	13,594,606	8,448,833	67,005,588
	25	118,848,131	12,956,855	8,528,814	67,377,056
Aug.	1	120,597,050	12,918,014	8,665,422	68,682,088
	8	122,077,252	11,737,367	8,981,740	67,372,941
	15	121,241,472	11,360,645	8,780,012	66,814,929
	22	120,139,582	10,097,178	8,694,011	64,241,471
	29	116,588,919	9,241,376	8,671,060	60,860,801
Sept.	5	112,221,365	10,227,964	8,673,192	57,260,609
	12	109,985,573	12,181,857	8,322,316	57,334,121
	19	108,777,421	13,556,186	8,073,801	57,851,965
	26	107,791,433	13,327,095	7,838,308	56,918,863
Oct.	3	105,935,499	11,400,413	7,916,102	52,798,365
	10	101,917,570	11,476,294	7,523,599	49,745,176
	17	97,245,826	7,843,231	8,087,441	42,696,012
	24	95,593,518	10,411,643	6,884,739	47,873,901
	31	95,317,754	12,883,441	6,334,748	51,853,159
Nov.	7	95,866,241	16,492,153	6,434,312	56,424,807
	14	95,239,247	19,451,967	6,258,652	60,601,556
	21	95,375,432	23,167,980	6,283,417	64,917,932
	28	94,963,130	24,303,144	6,520,783	64,307,380
Dec.	5	96,333,687	26,069,833	6,555,000	64,444,375
	12	96,526,037	26,058,877	6,348,494	62,907,999
	19	97,211,690	27,957,326	6,309,466	63,710,106
	26	97,902,035	27,142,098	6,352,187	65,239,374
1858.					
Jan.	2	98,549,983	28,561,946	6,490,403	67,300,760
	9	98,792,758	29,176,838	6,615,464	65,942,282
	16	99,473,762	30,211,266	6,349,325	67,723,909
	23	101,172,642	30,829,151	6,336,042	69,523,586
	30	102,180,089	31,273,022	6,369,678	70,467,784
Feb.	6	103,602,932	30,652,948	6,873,931	70,544,737
	13	103,783,306	30,226,274	6,607,270	70,425,906
	20	103,706,735	31,416,077	6,542,618	72,003,657
	27	103,769,127	31,658,694	6,530,759	71,728,972
March	6	105,021,863	32,739,731	6,854,624	72,379,748
	13	105,293,631	32,691,076	6,755,958	73,552,929
	20	107,440,350	31,902,656	6,853,852	74,173,918
	27	109,095,412	30,929,472	6,892,231	73,606,709
April	3	110,588,354	31,530,000	7,232,332	76,023,176
	10	110,847,617	32,036,436	7,245,809	76,790,864
	17	111,344,891	33,196,449	7,190,170	78,121,025

1858.		Loans.	Specie.	Circulation.	Deposits.
April	24	111,003,476	34,113,891	7,140,851	79,198,893
May	1	111,868,456	35,064,214	7,431,814	80,563,303
	8	112,741,955	35,453,146	7,735,056	81,727,146
	15	114,119,288	34,730,728	7,502,975	83,599,295
	22	115,658,082	34,047,446	7,307,445	84,297,738
	29	116,650,943	31,496,144	7,252,616	83,152,244
June	5	116,424,597	32,790,332	7,548,830	83,506,886
	12	116,022,152	33,367,253	7,367,725	84,283,194
	19	117,797,047	32,396,456	7,297,631	85,280,949
	24	118,823,401	31,948,089	7,215,689	85,950,307
July	3	119,812,407	33,830,232	7,458,190	88,337,184
	10	118,863,937	34,705,593	7,571,373	92,337,042
	17	119,165,731	35,329,988	7,346,213	90,064,144
	24	118,940,482	35,515,243	7,351,045	90,105,690
	31	119,850,456	35,712,107	7,408,365	91,145,874
Aug.	7	120,892,857	35,145,844	7,784,415	90,339,478
	14	123,374,459	31,150,473	7,588,939	89,826,080
	21	126,341,827	28,343,998	7,484,306	89,159,341
	28	126,084,424	27,817,006	7,466,846	87,719,139

Totals and Averages of the foregoing Tables, for the Years ending at the given Dates:

		Loans.	Specie.	Deposits.
July 31, 1854—	Total,	4,690,181,881	596,813,662	3,199,800,399
	Average,	90,195,805	11,477,185	42,287,491
July 31, 1855—	Total,	4,683,097,192	735,515,384	3,775,339,284
	Average,	90,059,561	14,144,526	55,377,224
July 31, 1856—	Total,	5,225,378,400	696,290,025	4,400,980,965
	Average,	100,488,046	13,390,192	63,208,919
July 31, 1857—	Total,	5,781,082,592	618,053,639	4,809,971,107
	Average,	111,174,665	11,885,646	65,195,290
July 31, 1858—	Total,	5,607,403,139	1,323,396,873	4,496,592,884
	Average,	107,834,676	25,449,940	71,898,419

The average of circulation was, for the year ending July 31:

1854	$9,228,388
1855	7,738,839
1856	7,975,405
1857	8,604,582
1858	7,226,475

The diagram exhibits a remarkable coincidence, or parallelism of movement, in the several years. The loans reach their highest point on the first week of August in 1853, 1854, and 1856; on the third week of August in 1855, and on the second week of August in 1857. They begin to fall at these dates, and reach their lowest point on the second week of November, in 1853, 1856, and 1857; on the third week of November in 1855, and on the second week of December in 1854—the year uniformly going out with an ascending average. Another decline takes place from the early part of March or April, previous to the uniform ascent to August. There is a general concurrence of movement with the loans, in the deposits and specie. The year 1857 is exceptional only in the violence of fluctuation after August.

The adoption of some scale of relation between the several movements which compose the volume of bank transactions, will be a great help in forming a judgment of its condition within itself, at any given period. The averages of the year, ending with July 1855, are more "conservative" for this purpose than those of any other year in the record. They exhibit a remarkable correspondence of movement, perfect agreement with the periodical currents, which are demonstrated in the commercial system, and the full amount of depression in the autumn, which is always our most important and critical season. The average line in the chart represents this scale. When the other lines recede from it above, proportionate expansion is indicated; when they recede below, proportionate contraction or depression. When the lines recede from each other, and from the scale also, there is a proportionate destruction of the equilibrium. Beginning with August 1854, it is apparent that the relation of the loans, specie, and deposits, is not materially changed with respect to the scale, or to each other, up to August 1855. The lines are in close contact, and mingle with each other. But an extraordinary fact is developed after that date. The proportion of specie with the loans and deposits, on the adopted scale, is lost. It separates from them in the second week of June; in the third week of August, it falls below the scale, and instead of returning again to cross and recross the other lines, it continues permanently below them; and only for two short periods, about February and June, does it re-ascend above the scale, until the chasm is closed on the first of November 1857. The gradual widening of the gulf between the specie and the liabilities after June 1855 is shown with singular clearness and force. There is not a more significant demonstration in the whole record than at this precise point. It does not appear that the specie line sinks even so far *below the scale* as it had done at former periods; but the *deposits and loans ascend rapidly above the scale.* In July, 1856, the loans separated from the deposits in a gradual rise, and did not return to the scale of 1854 until the panic of 1857. As it will be necessary to refer again to the chart, in the history of that event, a further illustration of it here would be superfluous.

The first proposition to establish a Clearing House in New York, was made by the late ALBERT GALLATIN. In a pamphlet of 124 pages, entitled: "Suggestions on the Banks and Currency of the several United States, in reference principally to the suspension of specie payments," published by WILEY & PUTNAM, in the year 1841, occur the following paragraphs, on pp. 63 and 64:

"There is a measure which, though belonging to the administration of banks, rather than to legal enactments, is suggested on account of its great importance. Few regulations would be more useful in preventing dangerous expansions of discounts and issues on the part of the city banks, than a regular exchange of notes and checks, and an actual daily or semi-weekly payment of the balances. It must be recollected, that it is by this process alone that a Bank of the United States has ever acted or been supposed to act as a regulator of the currency. Its action would not in that respect be wanted in any city, the banks of which would, by adopting the process, regulate themselves. It is one of the principal ingredients of the system of the banks of Scotland. The bankers of London, by the daily exchange of drafts at the Clearing House, reduce the ultimate balance to a very small sum; and that balance is immediately paid in notes of the Bank of England. The want of a similar arrangement among the banks of this city, produces relaxation, favors improper expansions, and is attended with serious inconveniences. The principal difficulty in the way of an arrangement for that purpose, is the want of a common medium other than specie for effecting the payment of balances. These are daily fluctuating; and a perpetual drawing and re-drawing of specie from and into the banks is unpopular and inconvenient.

"In order to remedy this, it has been suggested, that a general *Cash office* might be established, in which each bank should place a sum in specie, proportionate to its capital, which would be carried to its credit in the books of the office. Each bank would be daily debited or credited in those books for the balance of its account with all the other banks. Each bank might at any time draw for specie on the office for the excess of its credit beyond its quota; and each bank should be obliged to replenish its quota, whenever it was diminished one-half, or in any other proportion agreed on.

"It may be that some similar arrangement might be made in every other county, or larger convenient district of the State. It would not be necessary to establish there a general cash office. Each of the banks of Scotland has an agent at Edinburgh, and the balances are there settled twice a week, and paid generally by drafts on London. In the same manner, the balances due by the banks in each district might be paid by drafts on New York, or any other place agreed on."

These extracts contain the whole germ of the Clearing House system. They comprehend, essentially, the manner of its action, by the establishment of a "cash office" (the coin depository); and also, the effect—-to prevent "relaxation and improper expansions;" and they even suggest, negatively, the *coin certificates*, in the "commom medium other than specie, for effecting the payment of balances," the want of which was "the principal difficulty in the way" of a Clearing House at that time. The merit of removing this difficulty belongs to Mr. FRANCIS W. EDMONDS, late Cashier of the Mechanics' Bank. A year before the organization of the Clearing House, he induced the Bank of America, the Merchants', the American Exchange, and the Metropolitan Banks to join with the Mechanics' Bank, and to make up an aggregate sum of one million of dollars in coin, for which the last named institution issued its certificates. These were received by the other banks in payment of balances, and when the depositing banks were creditors, they were entitled to a preference in their payment back, and were thus saved the trouble of counting, and the risk and burden of carrying coin. These certificates were held as more desirable than coin, on account of the greater facility, expedition, and safety of their transfer.

Mr. EDMONDS was chairman of the committee, under whose directions the Clearing House was organized, his associates being Mr. JAMES PUNNETT, Cashier of the Bank of America, and Mr. AUGUSTUS E. SILLIMAN, Cashier of the Merchants' Bank—now Presidents of those institutions. The names of these gentlemen, and also that of Mr. LYMAN, the Manager, are inseparably connected with the origin and early history of the New York Clearing House. But to Mr. GEORGE CURTIS, the author of its Constitution, was conceded by the common voice of his associates, the precedence, as it regards intelligence and ability, in regulating and administering its powers. Though not publicly connected with the first movements in favor of its establishment, he made it the subject of attentive study, and prepared a plan for its organization at a very early period. His personal influence was particularly exerted in removing objections, and in bringing the discordant elements of the Association into harmony with its general purpose. Like Mr. GALLATIN, he appreciated from the outset all the advantages that would accrue from it to our financial system; and he was unanimously chosen as Chairman of the Committee on Suspensions, which made it his duty to take cognizance of all short-comings on the part of the different banks. This was at the same time, the least popular, most important, and critical post in the Association. It exposed him to the jealousy of the weaker members on one hand, and to censures for a dangerous indulgence on the other; but he exercised his powers with such strict justice and impartiality, that no instance of appeal from his judgment is on record.

CHAPTER XIX.

THE PANIC.

Up to August 1857, our commercial affairs were generally prosperous. The local journals throughout the country represented business as in a wholesome condition. High prices were said to have enriched the farmer, the stockgrower, and the planter. Trade and mechanical industry flourished with corresponding success.

In estimating probabilities for the future, great stress was laid on the fact, that the madness of railroad building was arrested. The bond market, and with it improvement securities generally, had fallen into disrepute. Stock companies could no longer send an agent to Europe with five millions of credit tokens, and receive the money for them within sixty days from the engraver's press. Heavy financial negotiations in this direction were suspended; and although the country had several hundred millions of foreign capital in use, there was no danger of any considerable portion of it being recalled, since our home market would reject the bonds which represent it, at half the par cost. We might, therefore, continue to enjoy the use of this large capital, and avoid the disaster consequent on a further accumulation of foreign debt. The common sentiment was, that we had passed the dangerous point in railway credits, and with the immense productions of the year at our doors, there was little probability of serious financial disturbance. The most sagacious of our city bank officers saw no indications of an unusual storm in the commercial skies. When the loans reached the unprecedented height of one hundred and twenty-two millions of dollars, on the eighth of August, they pointed to the annual reduction of ten or twelve millions in the autumn months, as one of the regular ebbs to which the market is subject; but they had no foresight of extraordinary pressure, and no dreams of panic. Credit was extended, but "the country never was so rich."

The banks began to contract their loans about the eighth of August. Securities immediately fell in price at the Stock Board. The failure of a heavy produce house was explained by the depression of that particular interest in the market. A report of dishonest jobbing, and of the misuse of funds in a leading Railway Company, caused partial excitement, without seriously disturbing confidence in mercantile credit.

On the twenty-fourth of August, the suspension of the Ohio Life Insurance and Trust Company was announced. It struck on the public mind like a cannon shot. An intense excitement was manifested in all financial circles, in which bank officers participated with unusual sensitiveness and want of self-possession. Flying rumors were exaggerated at every corner. The holders of stock and of commercial paper hurried to the broker, and were eager to make, what a week before they would have shunned as a ruinous sacrifice.

Several stock and money dealers failed, and the daily meetings of the Board of Brokers were characterized by intense excitement.

Every individual misfortune was announced on the news bulletins in large letters, and attracted a curious crowd, which was constantly fed from the passing throng.

The Clearing House report for the twenty-ninth of August—the first after the suspension of the Ohio Life Insurance and Trust Company—showed a reduction of four millions of dollars in the bank loans during the previous week.

The most substantial securities of the market fell rapidly in price at public sale.

The safety of bank notes in circulation was suspected or denied. The publishers of counterfeit detectors spread alarm among the shopkeepers and laborers, by selling handbills with lists of broken banks, which were cried about the streets by boys, at "a penny a piece."

One of the Associated Banks fell into default at the end of August, and a fraud of seventy thousand dollars by the Paying Teller, roused suspicion of similar misconduct in other institutions.

The regular discount of bills by the banks had mostly been suspended, and the street rates for money, even on unquestionable securities, rose to three, four and five per cent a month. On the ordinary securities of merchants, such as promissory notes and bills of exchange, money was not to be had at any rate.

House after house of high commercial repute succumbed to the panic, and several heavy banking firms were added to the list of failures.

The settlements of the Clearing House were watched with the expectation of new defaults; and their successful accomplishment, each day, was a subject of mutual congratulation among bank officers.

The statement of the city banks for the week ending September 5th, showed a further reduction in the loans of more than four millions of dollars.

Commercial embarrassments and suspension became the chief staple of news in all the papers of town and country. The purchase and transportation of produce almost entirely ceased.

From this period, there was nothing wanting to aggravate the common distress for money. The failure of the Bank of Pennsylvania, in Philadelphia, was followed by that of the other banks of that city, and by those of Baltimore, and of the Southern Atlantic States generally. Commercial business was everywhere suspended. The avalanche of discredit swept down merchants, bankers, moneyed corporations, and manufacturing companies, without distinction. Old houses, of accumulated capital, which had withstood the violence of all former panics, were prostrated in a day; and when they believed themselves to be perfectly safe against misfortune.

The bank suspension of New York and New England, in the middle of October, was the climax of this commercial hurricane.

Such is the outline of the most extraordinary, violent, and destructive financial panic ever experi-

Wall Street on Suspension Day. Oct. 14, 1857.

enced in this country. What caused it? To what source or sources can it be traced? Where lies the responsibility of it? What lessons does it teach? What preventives are indicated against the recurrence of similar disaster? These are questions which agitate the public mind, and which ought to be answered, if possible, for our instruction and future guidance.

A financial panic has been likened to a malignant epidemic, which kills more by terror than by real disease. If its exact causes could be ascertained, they would doubtless be found in minor proportion with the imaginary and the accidental; but so many terms enter into the case, which, from their character, are beyond our grasp, and equally beyond estimate, that a clear, practical analysis is impossible. For example: Who can tell how much gold is hoarded—how much of what has been supposed to be real capital, is nominal or mortgaged—how much insolvency has been buoyed up for years on the general tides of credit—and to what extent dishonest people take advantage of the common distress, to repudiate debts which they are able to pay? Who can tell what frauds are carried along in stock companies, or what speculations in land, mines, and railways are mixed up in the mass of trade? On these points, the sharpest scrutiny is wholly at a loss. In truth, the egg of the crisis of 1857 was buried where it could not be seen—in the private and household accounts of individuals. The relation of the exports and imports of a country is comparatively of little consequence, so long as its home trade and labor is in a sound condition. It signally failed in this instance, to give warning of the approaching storm, if it did not sadly mislead those who most relied on it for instruction.

A state of crisis, or severe financial pressure, is not necessarily destructive of all confidence. We have been accustomed to its frequent recurrence, and found it to be manageable without excessive straining of our financial means. The loans have uniformly declined from the highest point, in August, to their lowest, in November or December, and the stringency has then gradually relaxed. This annual pressure may be compared to a high Spring wind, which breaks the superfluous growth of vegetation, and gives stronger development to the uninjured mass. The following table shows that stringency in the market, more or less severe, is not inconsistent with a prosperous state of commerce.

	No. of Days.	Reduction of			Increase of Specie.
		Loans.	Deposits & Circulation.	Specie.	
1853, Aug. 6 to Nov. 12,	84	15,000,000	1,600,000		3,000,000
1854, " 5 " Dec. 9,	100	13,000,000	16,800,000	4,000,000	....
1855, " 18 " Nov. 17,	78	9,000,000	12,200,000	3,300,000	....
1856, " 2 " Nov. 8,	84	9,700,000	15,800,000	2,800,000	....

The rate of reduction in loans was very gradual in each of the four years preceding 1857. The greatest fall for any week during the entire period was $2,800,000, from October 7 to October 14, 1854, and for the several previous weeks it was hardly appreciable. The characteristic feature of this annual contraction was an almost insensible ebb; and this was frequently relaxed to suit the convenience oı dealers, as is manifest from an examination of the weekly tables.

It is clearly shown that a reduction of loans of from ten to fifteen millions of dollars may take place in an average term of ninety days without serious injury to commerce.

Is there sufficient reason for assuming that this scale of contraction might not have been as successfully applied in 1857, as it was in 1853—or that it might not have been extended several millions of dollars beyond that of the latter year, if the emergency had required it? This is the point about which opinions clash. The best evidence bearing upon it is to be found in the same tables.

The bank contraction began on the eighth of August, and continued for two weeks on the gradual scale of former years. This brings us to the twenty-third of the month, on which day the commercial interest was undisturbed by any extraordinary accidents or apprehensions.

On the twenty-fourth of August, the Ohio Life Insurance and Trust Company—a chartered institution with banking privileges—closed the doors of its branch office in New York. It was not a bank of issue, nor, to any considerable extent, of deposit, in this city. Its principal business was to receive remittances from the home office in Cincinnati, and numerous correspondents in the West, and to hold them subject to draft. It was not a discounter of bills receivable; but on the contrary, a large borrower from other institutions. The consequences of its stoppage, therefore, did not fall directly on our merchants, as in the case of a bank on which they are depending for continuous loans. The capital of the company was two millions of dollars.

The general circumstances of this failure, so far as they were published, were not in themselves very alarming. The home office was reported, by telegraph, to have its doors open as usual, with its affairs apparently unembarrassed, notwithstanding the stoppage of the New York branch. It was soon known, however, that the entire capital of the institution had been virtually embezzled, and serious alarm was immediately manifested in banking circles.

On the day after the failure, our merchants found that the terms of business between them and the banks were changed. The discounting of commercial paper was stopped. The certification of checks was imposed with unaccustomed rigor. It suddenly dawned on financial managers, that the city loans were ten millions of dollars higher than ever before—a very gratifying fact during their accession, but now inspiring only fear and distrust, which in a few hours, comparatively, ripened into symptoms of alarm.

The Weekly Statement of August 29th showed a reduction in the loans of four millions of dollars, and that of September 5th as much more. This unmistakable indication of the course of bank policy was every where accepted as evidence of existing panic. Who should know better than bank managers how much consequence to give to the failure of the Ohio Life and Trust Company? They were terrified by the stupendous fraud. They saw no safety, but in compelling the payment of their loans at maturity, and denying all indulgence. The gradual scale of reduction was abandoned at once. Instead of ten millions of dollars in eighty-four days, it was ten millions in fourteen days. Whether this was forced on the banks by the withdrawal of deposits, or whether it was the result of a common understanding, or of the want of such understanding on the part of bank officers, is of little importance, so far as relates to its effect on the public mind. Its immediate sequence to the collapse of the Trust Company gave to that event the distinction of the first act in the panic of 1857. The institution had stood high in the public esteem for a number of years. It was regarded as the more safe, because it was not a bank of issue, and because its affairs were supposed to be conducted on the conservative plan of our Trust Companies, avoiding the active and changeable risks of commerce, or touching them only with extreme caution. The bankers and exchange dealers of Ohio bought its drafts for remittance very extensively; and the immediate injuries caused by its failure arose from these being dishonored at New York, where, for several successive days, they accumulated in the hands of many parties, to the extent of several hundred thousand dollars. There was not a bank in the city, with a Western correspondence, that had not these drafts sent to them in payment for collections, or for deposit, to be drawn against by the remitters. The sensible consequences of the failure were, therefore, widely distributed, especially among the city banks, several of which were large lenders to the Company. The Company had borrowed, also, of individual bankers, exchange dealers, and stock brokers, hypothecating not only its own collaterals, but the property of its dealers, for whom it was merely a collecting agent. Most persons who held claims against it were persuaded that they would be lessened in value by an untimely exposure of its affairs, and a curtain of mystery was thus drawn before them.

The quick apprehension, by bank managers, of the dangers to which our financial system is exposed by the loss of public confidence, their knowledge of the facility with which frauds may be concealed and propagated in large institntions, and the immediate reflection of the consequences upon the banks, explain why they so promptly take the alarm when any material part of the fabric of credit gives way. They were the first to seize and to act upon the suggestions which were provoked by the sudden collapse of the Ohio Trust Company. If its entire capital of two millions of dollars could be dissipated—if its means could be employed in desperate stock-gambling in the public market, with all the usual hypothecation of securities, and transfers, and extensive bank loans, of which the records of the Company must have given *some* evidence—all this without discovery, and even without exciting suspicion in the minds of the trustees—why might not similar transactions be concealed in other institutions of which the trustees are equally well accomplished and esteemed? Under the fears instigated by such thoughts, the manifestations of distrust were more open from day to day. The notes of houses in high standing were rejected when presented for payment in the usual manner, unless the deposit to cover them was already made. The most trivial accommodations were denied, with a positiveness that sent the applicant away dissatisfied and indignant. All the forms of suspicion were thrust out into a prominence that was not unfrequently insulting. The honor of the best dealers, who had never committed an impropriety in their accounts, was totally ignored. Good faith and confidence disappeared from the bank counters, under the rigid instruction of the officers; and personal intercourse with them became difficult, without such delays and exposures as were offensive to high-minded and honorable men. Stocks held as collateral security were marked down in value from ten to thirty per cent; and successive instalments on loans were required to restore the continuous depreciation caused by this process. All these hard points were pushed out with such disregard of the trying necessities of the dealer, that a common feeling of indifference to obligations began to spring up as their counterpart.

It is remarkable that there was no interval of pressure between the plentiful money-market, which lasted until the twenty-second of August, and the panic with which the month closed. There was no treaty between commerce and money as to the common interest. The panic was an explosion without notice or premonition. It was not, as in former cases, the result of gradually increasing embarrassment after vain struggles to prevent it. This is demonstrated by the following figures:

Weekly Fluctuation of Loans, Deposits, Circulation, and Specie, from Aug. 22d to Sept. 26th, 1857.

	Loans.	Deposits.	Circulation.	Specie.
Aug. 29	dec. $3,550,663	dec. 3,380,670	dec. 22,951	dec. 855,802
Sept. 5	dec. 4,367,554	dec. 3,600,192	inc. 2,132	inc. 986,588
" 12	dec. 2,235,792	inc. 73,512	dec. 350,876	inc. 1,953,893
" 19	dec. 1,208,152	inc. 517,844	dec. 248,515	inc. 1,374,329
" 26	dec. 985,988	dec. 933,102	dec. 235,493	dec. 229,091
	dec. 12,348,149	dec. 7,322,608	dec. 855,703	inc. 3,229,917

The deposits and circulation are the basis of the loans and specie.

The exact loss of basis, during this term, was $8,178,311, while the loans were reduced $12,348,149. The increase of specie reserved from the liquidations makes the true relative decrease $15,578,066. The most violent action was between September 5th and September 19th, when the loans were reduced $3,443,944, in the face of an *increase* of deposits of nearly six hundred thousand dollars. In the latter period, the true relative change is represented by a reduction of $6,172,775 in the loans, while the deposits actually increased $591,356.

There can be no escape from these figures. They show, beyond cavil, that the *banks*, not the depositors, took the lead in forcing liquidation. In the twenty days prior to the 26th of September, the depósits fell off but $341,746, while the resources of the banks were increased $6,694,179.

An important fact must be stated in connection with the fall of deposits between August 22d and

September 26th, viz., that of the $7,322,608, full three-fourths was drawn out by the country banks; so that the amount withdrawn by the individual dealers was, at most, not above two millions of dollars. Thus, the consequences of holding a treacherous country fund *on interest*, and treating it as bank capital, fell ultimately on our city merchants.

When dealers are denied the usual facilities by discount, they have no recourse for their payments but to their deposits; but they did not use these to the full extent of their loan reduction in any single week from the 22d of August to the 19th of September.

The fluctuating part of the basis of bank loans is composed of deposits and circulation—the capital being a permanent investment by the stockholders. The force of reduction is, therefore, measurable by the proportion between this fluctuating basis, and the amount of loans above the capital. It is this proportion which constitutes, at the same time, the profit and the danger of our banking system. For example: the capital of the banks was $65,000,000 on the 22d of August. Deducting this from the loans of that date, $120,139,582, gives $60,139,582 as the proportion resting on the deposits and circulation, which then amounted to $72,935,482. The proportion of loans on this fluctuating, or pure credit basis, was eighty per cent. The same percentage on the deposits and circulation of September 26th, would have given the dealers an aggregate loan of $51,805,737; whereas, they had but $42,791,433—a deficiency of $9,014,304, relatively, with the resources of the banks. The loss of basis, by the decrease of circulation and the diminution of deposits, was but eleven per cent, while the reduction of loans was twenty-nine per cent.

This method of estimating the force of a financial contraction, by taking into view the fluctuating basis only, exposes the real danger of extending loans on that basis beyond the point which experience has determined as safe. It is the true scale of measurement for the guidance of the Bank Board.

"The sudden withdrawal of country balances" has been assumed as the chief cause of the panic, by some of our principal bank officers. The Clearing House tables give no support to this assumption. No feature of our financial system is more remarkable than the stability of its deposit line. The monthly average for 1857 is directly to the point. It is as follows:

January	$65,638,204
February	65,416,635
March	65,948,462
April	67,135,655
May	68,342,291
June	68,336,935
July	66,369,206
August 1st to August 22d	66,777,857

This brings us to the exact date of the panic, with so little fluctuation of deposits, that the loans were not more affected, from week to week, than is usual in the best condition of our market.

But we have direct testimony, on this part of the subject, in the Report of the Clearing House Committee, to whom was referred the proposition to abolish the payment of interest on deposits.

They say, on page 17: "During the week of financial excitement, in October last, the exaggerated reports of which were carried with the speed of lightning to every part of the land, this new medium of communication (the telegraph) filled our banks with imperative orders for the immediate return of their deposits, in specie."

It was not, then, until October, that *the withdrawal of deposits* operated so fatally!

The point implied by the Committee is, that the panic occurred in October; and the purpose of the implication is, to shift the responsibility of having caused it, from the banks to the depositors. There is no evidence to sustain this presumption. The Bank Superintendent says, in his report to the Legislature, "that about the first of October, a list of more than thirty failed banks, in the State of New York, was to be seen daily in our newspapers." He says, also, that the interior banks began to return their circulation, and to withdraw their securities, for sale, about the 20th of September—an extremity of action that does not characterize a state of ordinary pressure. The weaker banks began to fail near the first of September; and the commercial failures of the early part of that month, were largely of a class that had withstood all former panics.

A comparison of the stock sales from August 22d to September 30th, with those of the "week of financial excitement in October," further refutes the theory of the panic set up by the Clearing House Committee.

RELATIVE DECLINE IN BONDS AND STOCKS.

	From Aug. 22 to Oct. 1.		From Oct. 1 to Oct. 13.	
Virginia State Sixes	13½	per cent	10	per cent.
Missouri State Sixes	11	do.	8	do.
Illinois Central Railroad Bonds	32	do.	16	do.
New York Central Railroad Sixes	18	do.	4	do.
do. do. Stock	19¼	do.	5	do.
Delaware & Hudson Canal Company	16	do.	24	do.
Bank of America	15	do.	19	do.
Bank of Commerce	22¼	do.	13	do.
American Exchange Bank	40¼	do.	15½	do.
Metropolitan Bank	33	do.	17	do.
Park Bank	26	do.	18	do.
Panama Railroad	20	do.	10	do.
Reading Railroad	36½	do.	3½	do.
Michigan Central Railroad	37	do.	6	do.
Michigan Preferred Railroad	21⅝	do.	0	do.
Illinois Central Railroad	32½	do.	9½	do.
New York & Erie Railroad	17	do.	3	do.
Galena & Chicago Railroad	25	do.	9	do.
Chicago & Rock Island Railroad	31½	do.	3¼	do.
Cleveland & Toledo Railroad	15¼	do.	7¼	do.
Milwaukie & Mississippi Railroad	36	do.	0	do.
Cleveland & Pittsburgh Railroad	20¾	do.	1	do.
Pennsylvania Coal	11¾	do.	15¼	do.

The foregoing list includes a wide range of securities, from the best, down to what are called "fancy." The general decline of the market was from three to thirty-six per cent more between August 22d and October 1st, than it was during "the week of financial excitement in October." It is apparent that the latter period was but the sequence of the former —the breaking away of the dykes, when the pressure of the flood became irresistible. The ball had been set in motion, and it was impossible to stop it on the side of a hill.

Although the assumption that the panic was caused by the sudden withdrawal of country balances is not borne out by the tables, it is true that those balances constituted a bad element in the market, and that they contributed to the common wreck. The presence in our financial system of a borrowed fund, payable on demand, of fifteen millions of dollars, on which loans were predicated, was a disturbing fact, even with the probability that it was not likely to be withdrawn suddenly, or all at a time. But the conditions on which it was held prohibited that state of preparation, which alone could protect the market from the injuries of a requisition for immediate payment. It carried interest; it was reloaned on interest, and doubtless re-reloaned to various parties, who had invested it, perhaps mostly in the hazardous speculations of the stock market. If the country banks, which were borrowers No. 1, were called on by their depositors, they called on the city banks, which were borrowers No. 2; and these called on the large broker, who was borrower No. 3; and he again on the small brokers, who were borrowers No. 4, in whose hands the money spread out into various channels of fluctuating investment, if it was not further loaned to a fifth series of borrowers. The difficulty of collecting loans is in proportion to the number of borrowers between the first and the last. The city banks do not commonly "call in," until they have paid drafts against the fund, and they are likely to be left a day or two in the lurch before they can restore themselves — meanwhile falling behind at the Clearing House, or denying usual accommodation to their commercial dealers. This is the literal history of the "call loans" of the city banks, and the only management by which they can reimburse themselves for the interest which they pay on borrowed money. The committee justly denounce the practice as "a departure from sound principles." They show that it reflects injury on the whole community, while the profit is confined to a few banks, and is inconsiderable at best; also that it accumulates balances beyond the necessities of a healthy exchange, and withdraws capital from productive employment in the country.

It is not to be doubted, that the "imperative orders" from the country banks, together with the action of the home depositors, did cause, directly, the suspension of specie payments. It is impossible to ascertain how much they contributed, separately, to the final result, though appearances indicate that country depositors had less to do with it than the resident dealers.

The balances of the foreign bankers had accumulated, in consequence of the stoppage of specie shipments, and the non-sale of bills of exchange. These were understood to be specialized by agreement with the bank officers. That is, they were either to be reserved in coin, or the owners were to be advised in season, that they might withdraw them before the suspension of specie payments. The tables show that seven millions were withdrawn between the tenth and the seventeenth of October—the greater part of it, probably, on the morning of the suspension. The

A Run on a Bank.

next week brought it all back again. The restoration of the specie line was even more remarkable than its depletion. A single glance at the diagram will excite astonishment at the resources that were found immediately available; and still more astonishment, that suspension could have occurred while they were within such speedy grasp.

The relative decline in loans and deposits, from September 26th to October 17th, covering the period referred to by the Committee, was as follows:

	Loans.	*Deposits.*
Oct. 3 . . .	$1,855,934	$4,120,498
" 10 . . .	4,017,929	3,053,189
" 17 . . .	4,671,744	7,049,164
	$10,545,607	$14,222,851

Besides this loss in deposits, the banks suffered depletion in coin to the amount of $5,483,864. They could not withstand such an onslaught. In twenty-one days, the deposits fell twenty-five per cent, while the loans were reduced but eleven per cent—a complete transposition of the movement following the 22d of August, when they fell but eleven, while the loans decreased twenty-nine per cent.

The history of the panic is clearly divisible into these two periods: the former, when the banks took the initiative in forcing down their loans; and the latter, in which the depositors seized it and brought on the closing act of suspension.

The depositors were not alarmed, up to the 26th of September. For five successive weeks, preceding, they withdrew less from the banks each week than the banks withdrew from them by the depression of loans. So far from exhibiting distrust, there is every appearance of striving against it on their part, with the hope that the storm might pass its crisis, and subside. The united community will testify to the anxiety with which the Clearing House Reports were watched, for signs of relaxation in the forced contraction; but no such signs were given. At length, the third of October exhibits a sudden and marked change. Over four millions of deposits are withdrawn during a single week, and in twenty days, over fourteen millions. It is probable that a much larger amount was withdrawn up to the fourteenth (the day of suspension) than is indicated by the statements; for these do not show the restoration which began on the fifteenth, and which materially lessened the average of withdrawal for the week ending on the seventeenth. The report of the Clearing House Committee confirms the fact that the depositors did not become alarmed before this period.

The gradual expansion of bank credits through the several previous years, not only on a fictitious home basis, but on country deposits which had been allured by competing rates of interest, made sufficient ground for an extraordinary pressure, when a reduction was to be effected; and thus the banks were doubly responsible for the pending issue. There is no evidence, however, in the records of the Clearing House, nor in the experience of past years, nor in any events which have transpired since the suspension, to prove that a panic was inevitable. The foregoing facts indicate that it was directly caused by *the violent contraction of bank loans immediately after the twenty-fourth of August.*

The beginning of the contraction on the twenty-fifth of August, marks the precise point at which the panic was started on its destructive course. From that date, distrust grew rapidly. The telegraph spread it throughout the country. Every latent cause of embarrassment sprung into activity. Trifling causes were a thousand-fold magnified. False alarms were created, and public apprehension kept up by successive disasters. Unusual accidents were added to excite the popular mind. For the first time since the establishment of regular intercourse with California, the steamers were delayed with their remittances of gold; and one of them was lost.

In this state of things, the Clearing House daily settlements in coin exerted a crushing influence on the commercial interest, and became a new source of terror. What in ordinary times was a safe-guard against the unwise expansion of bank-credits, was now a remorseless power compelling the smaller banks—the majority of the whole—to a violent contraction of their loans to dealers, forcing them into the sacrifice of property, and finally into bankruptcy; thus sending out through a thousand channels daily, new streams of misfortune. *Default at the Clearing House*, was the presiding spectre at every Bank Board of the smaller institutions. It was forgotten that the whole of a thing is composed of its parts—that public credit is made up of the credit of individuals—that if the parts of a thing are broken and scattered, there is no longer a whole.*

It did not occur to the managing committees of the Clearing House to relax its destructive energy, whilst there was yet a chance of preserving the last stronghold and pledge of commercial integrity—specie payments. They thought of it afterwards, and found in it a wholesome alleviation for themselves; but the time had passed for it to be of any material service to our merchants. The admission of the State debt of New York, and of the debt of the United States, represented by the bank currency, as a substitute for coin in the daily settlements, was of great service in preventing further depreciation, and in repairing the mischief that had been done.

It is often the case, that things good in themselves become hurtful by a change of circumstances which destroys their fitness. This may be said of the Clearing House, without detracting from its real value to our financial interests.

There are always operating causes in commercial and financial affairs, of which any violent disturbance may be made to appear as the consequence, after the issue is over; but which, nevertheless, may have had no actual share in its production. Thus, the advocates of a protective tariff see in low duties on foreign

---

* "All community of interest, all concert of action, as the crisis approached, was apparently, if not actually abandoned."—*Report of Bank Superintendent*, p. 7.

"The suspension was preceded by a desperate struggle between all the banks themselves; and distrust and fear of currency was more apparent among them than with the public generally."—*Ibid.*, p. 17.

merchandise a primary and sufficient cause for the panic of 1857; and the "hard currency" theorists find its explanation in the use of paper money. Fortunately, the figures of the Clearing House afford such a palpable demonstration of a direct and simple cause in this instance, that all complicated questions of political economy may be left out of view. Yet, it is often important as well as interesting to look back over the history of things, and to discover, if possible, the exact point where judgment was lacking, and where a slight turn of the rudder would have saved the vessel from destruction. The chart constructed from the Weekly Statements is instructive on this point.

In August, 1853, commenced the publication of the Weekly Statements; and in October following, the Clearing House was organized. The lines of the chart of that year begin in a straggling, and apparently dubious manner, as if engaged in an uncertain experiment; but they are brought into complete harmony in July, 1854, when the influence of the Clearing House is perfectly established; and from this point they rise and fall together. During the year ending with July, 1855, the specie was kept at twenty-five per cent of the deposits. The evil of *disproportionate* expansion by the banks separately, which was so grievous before the organization of the House, was effectually cured; but afterwards came the evil of *harmonious* expansion, which was something quite new, and not contemplated. The balance-wheel was perfect so far as to prevent individual members going astray; but for want of a *fixed scale*, it did not prevent the whole from going astray together. In August, 1855, the specie line fell below the scale, and did not again ascend to it before the suspension in October, 1857. The transient recovery in February, and in June, 1856, was extraneous from the market, being caused by the payment of a State loan at the former, and of a city-loan at the latter date. The average of specie with respect to the deposits, sunk from twenty-five per cent in 1854–5, to twenty-one per cent in 1855–6, and to eighteen per cent in 1856–7, while the loans were steadily on the increase.

It is held that a fair proportion of the resources of a bank should be reserved in coin, to meet immediate liabilities. The market is uneasy with high loans and low specie. Tried by this measurement, the force of our bank expansion after August, 1855, is exhibited in a most striking manner. The proportion of coin with the whole resources for the year, ending July 31, 1855, being preserved in the subsequent years, would have given but eighty-five millions of loans on the actual coin of 1855–6, whereas they were $100,488,046; and it would have admitted but seventy-six millions of loans on the actual coin of 1856–7, whereas they were $111,174,665. That is to say, that the loans of 1855–6 were fifteen millions of dollars in excess of the scale, and the loans of 1856–7 were *thirty-five millions* in excess! These results are astounding. If such a departure from equilibrium does not foreshadow the suspension of specie payments as inevitable, it lessens our surprise that it should have occurred (to borrow the words of the Bank-Superintendent)—"with overflowing granaries,

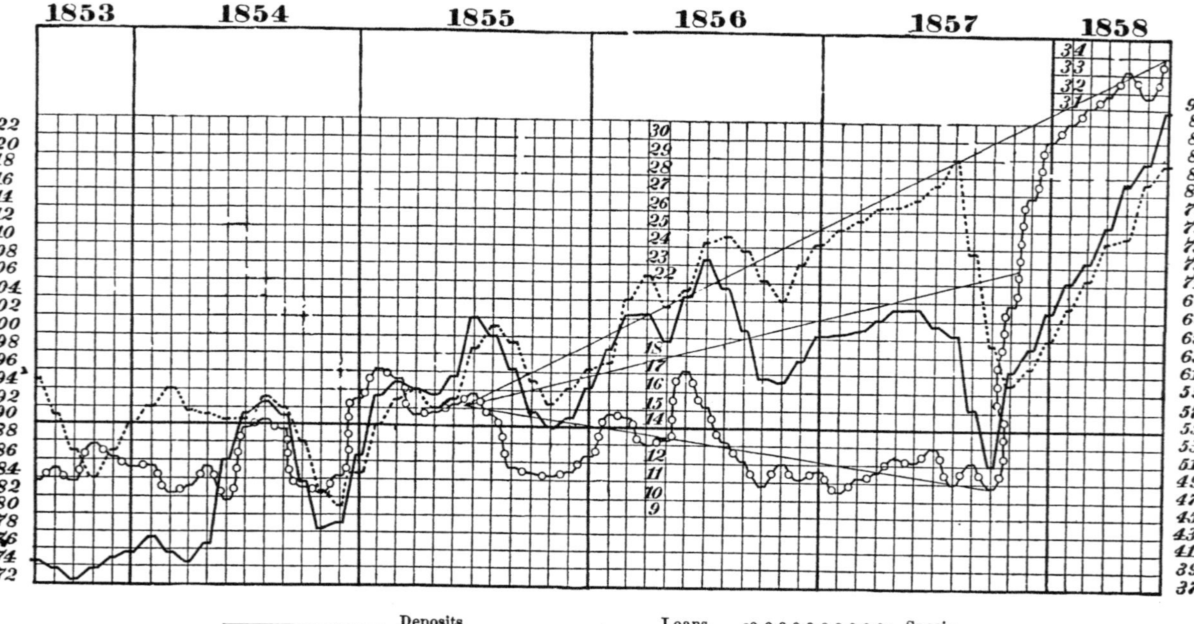
1853
1854
1855
1856
1857
1858
122
120
118
116
114
112
110
108
106
104
102
100
98
96
94
92
90
88
86
84
82
80
78
76
74
72
91
89
87
85
83
81
79
77
75
73
71
69
67
65
63
61
59
57
55
53
51
49
47
45
43
41
39
37
34
33
32
31
30
29
28
27
26
25
24
23
22
18
17
16
15
14
12
11
10
9
Deposits.
Loans.
Specie.

exemption from pestilence, neither internal insurrection nor foreign invasion, and our country at peace with every nation of the earth."*

The chart shows that, in July 1856, a new gap was opened between the loans and their basis. The *deposits* receded, but *bank expansion* went on, in defiance of this significant change of current, and the continued depression of specie; until on the 8th of August, 1857, it reached its highest point. The loans, then, with respect to the specie reserve, were in excess *forty-five millions* of dollars!

All these movements are shown on the reduced diagram, on which the point of departure from the scale is indicated by straight lines. It is manifest that the rules of sound discretion in our bank management were lost sight of as far back as July, 1855; and since the expansion was not arrested at any subsequent period, when it was possible, but one result could follow. In fact, it appears that the escape from panic in the two previous years was remarkable, since the excess of loans, with respect to the specie, reached, on the 29th of September, 1855, *thirty-three millions* of dollars, and on the 27th of September, 1856, *thirty-eight millions* of dollars!

The relative condition of our city banks at the different periods named, with their condition on the 31st of July, 1858, is strikingly shown by the amount of loans that their average reserve of specie would have admitted, in the same proportion, viz.: *two hundred and thirty-five millions of dollars!*

---

* Report of 1857, page 4.

It is, doubtless, the examination of the whole ground here set forth, that has induced a majority of our bank officers to name arbitrarily a proportion of specie, as proper to be kept in reserve from the resources.* The Bank Superintendent, also, has recommended to the Legislature, that the banks be obliged to maintain an average of twenty per cent of their deposits in coin; though for want of a more practical acquaintance with bank figures, he quotes their deposits in gross at $72,602,678, instead of $55,377,224, omitting to deduct the clearings. It may rather be doubted whether the proportion of twenty per cent is sufficient to assure a steady equilibrium. That of the years ending with July in 1854 and 1855, was over twenty-five per cent of the net deposits, while that of 1856 was but little below twenty, and that of 1857, eighteen per cent.

The circulating bills may safely be left out of view in this provision, as their independent security has been abundantly tested.

AN EXCEPTION.

A very important exception remains to be noticed, as to a portion of our city banks, in connection with

* At a meeting, March 16th, 1858, where forty-two banks were represented, the following resolution was adopted:

Resolved, That in furtherance of the end proposed by our agreement, to discontinue the payment of interest on deposits, and in accordance with the recommendations of the Report of the Committee on that subject, we also agree, each to keep on hand, at all times, an amount of coin equivalent to not less than twenty per cent of our net deposits of every kind, which shall be made to include certified checks and all other liabilities (except circulating notes), deducting the daily exchanges received from the Clearing House.

the expansion of credit which prepared the conditions of the panic.

From 1839 to 1850, our banking capital was increased but little over three hundred thousand dollars; and during these eleven years, more than thirty per cent had been added to our commerce and population. Unquestionably, there was room for some additional banks. Several were organized, and soon acquired such a prosperous business, that bank stock became a favorite investment. It was so easy to "get up" a bank, and its offices were so respectable, that Tellers and Clerks, who were ambitious to become Cashiers, called their friends together, and began subscription-lists. A retired capitalist was flattered with an offer of the Presidency; mechanics and merchants were pleased at the idea of becoming Bank Directors, with the enjoyment of unrestricted "facilities;" lawyers and notaries were flattered with the hope of counsel and protest fees; and all joined together to get stock taken. Scores, if not hundreds, of small subscription-books were in circulation at the same time, in all trades and professions. Under-clerks in old banks, who were desirous of promotion, aimed at tellerships in the new institutions, and sought to make claims by soliciting stock; subscribers became solicitors, on condition of having their friends appointed to clerkships; brokers became solicitors, in view of large commissions for the purchase of securities; stationers were actively engaged, under a promise of furnishing the ledgers and account-books; engravers were set to work, by the promise of employment in their art; and people in particular sections were stimulated by the prospect of increased value to their real estate, by the near location of a bank. In 1851, a new bank was started for every month in the year; in 1852, one for every two months; nine were added for 1853—making twenty-seven in three years, with an aggregate capital of over sixteen millions of dollars. If this had been *real* capital, the case had been better; but it was mostly fictitious—merely paper capital—nothing, in fact, but the creation of a book debt, with hypothecated stock certificates as collateral security. More than half of it was of this character—and at least another fourth was in excess of the commercial want; but it was legally organized, and it attracted, or *hired* deposits, and so created a larger basis for more credit in the shape of loans, which, in August, 1857, were extended to over forty millions of dollars. It is safe to say, that two-thirds of this prodigious debt was a grievous burden, super-imposed on the legitimate debt of the community; and that, instead of benefit, it brought embarrassment and injury to the trade and labor of the city.

This was the expansion that prepared the crisis of 1857. It was an overgrowth of banks, and an overtoppling of credit on the overgrowth. It does not alter the case, that many of the new institutions have since become entirely successful and well managed; but it furnishes the ground of an important exception in favor of the older banks, as to exact responsibility for the panic. These, almost without an exception, *maintained their discount lines nearly unchanged*, while the panic was created by other institutions.

The affairs of some of the new banks, also, had been so judiciously managed as to rank them with the exceptional part of the system.

The author does not pretend to find a complete apology for the older banks, in the fact here stated. If their managers were more experienced, they might have furnished counsel, and ability, to guard the system against the calamity which the figures of the Clearing House prognosticated as far back as August 1855.

Bank government, as it relates to the whole system in the City of New York, is made difficult by the composition of its management. The twenty old banks, with their established machinery, worked together with comparatively little difficulty; but when forty others were added, making an aggregate Board, of directors and bank officers, of over eight hundred persons, without any representative body to deliberate upon common interests, the whole system was out of control. To this fact, must be added another, before the difficulties of the case can be fairly appreciated. A very large proportion of the new bank managers were without experience in the business. Presidents were chosen with no reference whatever to their knowledge or capacity. One had acquired wealth by selling dry-goods, and therefore he was fit for a bank president; another had been equally successful in making shoes; another had been a ship-chandler, and fortunate in the schooner coasting-trade; another had been a stage-driver: not a few were men of the narrowest minds, wholly lacking in mercantile education, and without the ability to conduct the simplest commercial correspondence. It is due to some of these gentlemen to say, that if they were ignorant in the beginning, they have improved by close attention to practical duties, and that for general intelligence they are not far below the average of their cotemporaries in office. They have yet to learn, however, that it is one thing to be a bill broker and a shrewd calculator of balances, and quite another to understand the principles of true economy in finance.

The natural consequences of placing incompetent men in the responsible office of bank president, could not in all cases be averted. Several instances of gross mismanagement occurred, in which institutions were saved from insolvency, either by a change of officers, or by the help of the Associated Banks. Several others maintained a feeble existence for a short time, and sunk into final discredit; and in five or six cases, at least, there were such serious deficiencies, as to justify suspicions of dishonesty and collusion among the Directors. How the legal weekly and quarterly statements could be sworn to, up to the time when the entire stock of a bank was lost or squandered, is a question for the parties concerned to settle with themselves.

It is not necessary to clog this sketch with the numerous accidents that were added from day to day, to increase the popular excitement, and to multiply its terrors. The embarrassment of the exchanges between different parts of the country, and the consequent stoppage of remittances; the depreciation of the bank currency, which the farmer refused to take in payment for produce; the failure of individuals and corporations, including the Illinois Central Railroad Company; the run on the Savings' Banks—all these were but the gathering wrecks that fell in as the torrent rushed on.

There was one cause of aggravation, however, that cannot be called an accident. The weekly publication of failures, in *The Independent*, a religious paper of wide circulation, spread dismay over the country. This frightful record was copied by all the principal journals, from Boston to New Orleans. It sharpened and fed the common appetite for calamities. It cut off remittances from debtors who were too ready to adopt the plea, that "money would be of no use to broken merchants," and to follow it up by assuming that "all were as good as broken"—a pretext that found some color of support, in a record that embraced, by the middle of October, more than twelve hundred merchants of all classes, incorporated stock companies, and banks. It became a reproducing cause of embarrassment, and one of the chief agencies in propagating that moral insolvency which constituted a prominent feature of the panic. The sanctity of engagements was openly repudiated, under the pretext of universal bankruptcy. The authors of this commercial necrology could urge nothing in its defence, but *the improved sale of a newspaper!* Their excuse might be thoughtlessness, or incapacity to see that any rule of decency is broken by holding up the misfortunes of individuals to gratify a morbid public curiosity.

The disclosures of the panic show, measurably what was the state of things before it commenced. Notwithstanding the appearances of prosperity, there existed all the conditions of extraordinary financial disturbance.

A prodigious weight of insolvency had been carried along for years in the volume of trade. Extravagance of living had already sapped the foundations of commercial success, in hundreds of instances where credit supplied the place of lost capital. Mismanagement and fraud had gained footing in public companies to an incredible degree. Hundreds of millions of bonds were issued with little regard to the validity of their basis, and pressed upon the market by dishonest agents, at any price, from sixty down to thirty cents on the dollar. False quotations were obtained by sham auction sales. The Press, in particular instances, was bribed into silence, or became a partner in the profits to be derived from the various schemes which it commended to general confidence. The land grants by Congress to railway companies gave renewed activity to speculation, and State Legislatures were bribed to locate roads to serve individual interests. Public, as well as private credit, was compromised. The example of corruption in Government commissions and contracts, and of bad faith with neighboring nations, was an extreme, but a faithful expression of the tone of popular feeling with respect to the sacredness of trusts and obligations.

The general mass of credit in the United States rested on these facts; and the strictly commercial part of it was involved in the common risk. There were few merchants whose secret drawers did not contain sore evidences of capital sunk or withdrawn from legitimate use, to be invested in some dazzling speculation. The deficiency of means to carry on business could be supplied only by an increase of the *personal credit.*

It is this personal credit that prepares all the extreme fluctuations of our commercial or financial system. The bills payable of the merchant represent not only his merchandise debt, but his debt for sunken capital, his debt for railway bonds, his debt for extravagant living, for real estate, and for fancy stocks. The one hundred and twenty-two millions of bills payable that constituted the bank loans in August, was probably less than one-fourth of the personal debt then current in the city of New York. Three times that amount besides, floated in other channels, in the hands of private capitalists, in trust and insurance companies, in open book account, and in foreign banks. Immediately on the accession of a financial pressure, this entire mass of debt starts into new activity. It presses on every bank, and through every channel, for negotiation, renewal, or compromise. That which is least entitled to consideration—the extra-commercial portion—is most pressing, and leads the market in paying high interest; while that which represents real trade, is reluctant to go above the bank rates. Speculative rates are thus imposed on the whole market.

There are no positive limitations to the expansion of individual credit. A pernicious practice* prevails

* This practice originated with the commission merchants.

of making promissory notes payable to the order of the drawer, and thus negotiable without indorsement. When the seller finds that his customer has reached the line of credit that he is willing to allow, instead of refusing to sell more, and thus offering a prudential restriction to the extent of his business, he goes on selling, and disposes of the accumulating excess of the buyer's paper in "the street." In this way he overstocks the market with goods, and gives a credit of thirty thousand dollars to a man whom he considers it unsafe to trust for more than three thousand; and the risk of twenty-seven thousand is scattered broadcast in the community! The buyer knows that his creditor gets rid of his notes, and what does he care if strangers lose by him? This should be regarded as a commercial offence of the gravest character. It is impossible to have an honest money-market while it is tolerated. What better is it, than a trick of the manufacturer and wholesale merchant to reap the profits of trade while throwing off his risks upon innocent people? It corrupts credit, and turns commerce into mere headlong chances.

OF BANK CURRENCY.

Of all theories intended to explain our financial fluctuations, that which attributes them to the *bank currency* has least foundation in fact. A confusion of terms is probably the chief source of the misunderstanding that prevails on this point.

In common parlance, *bank currency* means *circulating bank notes*—"paper money." Yet, it would seem that some writers include under the same head, checks and *promissory notes*, if not also loans and deposits; considering them all to belong to the volume of the business, and to be subject to expansion or contraction at the will of bank managers. Thence comes the general idea, that whatever is not specie, in bank transactions, is *bank currency*.

WEBSTER defines currency to be that which "continually passes from hand to hand, as coin or bills of credit; circulation, as the *currency* of cents, or of English crowns; the *currency* of bank bills or Treasury notes."

That which "continually passes from hand to hand," in buying or selling, is the primary idea of currency. *Bank currency* can properly refer only to that which emanates from banks; and circulating notes, or "paper money," is the only form of credit which they are authorized by law to issue, or which practically answers the function of currency in their transactions.

Again, *bank currency* is something that it is in the power of the banks to control—to increase, or to diminish; and above all, which they are bound to redeem on presentation.

If this definition is correct, it cannot include checks and promissory notes; because, in the first place, these are not issued by the banks; in the second, they do not continually pass from hand to hand; and thirdly, they are not redeemable by the banks.

In reality, the several terms employed represent but one thing. Checks, promissory notes, and loans are mere accessories of the *deposit.* The first are issued by the individual dealer in his discretion, and the bank pays them out of his deposit; promissory notes are a dormant security during the continuance of the loan, which itself is made available to the dealer in the character of a *deposit.* The only question to be answered is, therefore, whether deposits can be called *bank currency.* The only approach to circulation by any document which represents the deposit, is in the check, when it is certified and sent abroad to pay a debt, or when it is deposited in another bank and redeemed through the exchanges. The "certificate of deposit" is the same thing in another form. The promissory note, when it is discounted, is filed away in the vault, and is rather withdrawn from, than put into circulation.

Banks cannot govern the amount of deposit by the dealers, otherwise than by discounting paper, and giving them credit in account for the proceeds. They cannot govern the issue of promissory notes in the market, this being the act of individuals. It would be a solecism, to apply the term *bank currency* to documents which are issued by every merchant in the community without the knowledge of bank managers.

Finally: banks do not send out, for circulation, a single document in any shape, excepting the bank note—"paper money."

Whatever terms may be employed to distinguish the different evidences of debt which are circulated in the market—whether *individual currency* or *commercial currency*—it seems proper to confine the application of *bank currency* to bank notes. It is certain that this is what the advocates of "hard currency" aim at, when they urge their theory as the only preventive of excessive financial fluctuations.

The following table shows the relative movement of loans and circulation in our city banks, from August, 1853, to September, 1858, excepting periods which exhibit no remarkable fluctuation:

1853.......	From Aug. 6 to Nov. 5,	dec.	$14,796,987	dec.	18,307
1853-4.....	" Nov. 12 to Mar. 4,	inc.	11,676,012	dec.	77,799
1854.......	" March 4 to July 8,	dec.	6,211,140	dec.	14,073
1854.......	" July 8 to Aug. 5,	inc.	5,373,860	dec.	71,109
1854.......	" Aug. 5 to Dec. 9,	dec.	13,129,505	dec.	1,643,815
1854-5.....	" Dec. 9 to April 7,	inc.	13,905,758	inc.	290,701
1855.......	" June 2 to July 28,	inc.	7,886,147	dec.	146,111
1855.......	" Aug. 25 to Nov. 10,	dec.	8,150,314	inc.	506,513
1855-6.....	" Dec. 8 to Mar. 15,	inc.	11,338,495	inc.	1,407
1856.......	" April 12 to May 31,	dec.	5,389,160	dec.	12,374
1856.......	" May 10 to Aug. 2,	inc.	8,417,770	dec.	16,442
1856-7.....	" Nov. 8 to Aug. 1,	inc.	18,088,411	dec.	281,299
1857.......	" Aug. 1 to Oct. 17,	dec.	23,351,224	dec.	577,981

In six of the thirteen periods cited, the movement of the currency was adversely to that of the loans; and in the other seven, though in the same direction, it is manifest that there was no governing sympathy between them. In one case, the loans were reduced fifteen millions of dollars, while the circulation diminished but eighteen thousand—they were then increased twelve millions, while the circulation continued to fall, but in four times greater ratio. In two instances, the loans increased eleven millions of dollars : in one of them, the currency was diminished seventy-eight thousand, and in the other it was augmented one thousand.

In one case, the circulation increased five hundred thou sand dollars, and in another it diminished six hundred thousand, with a coincident reduction in the loans of eight and twenty-three millions. Only once in the table is there an appearance of sympathy—when the loans fell thirteen millions, and the circulation one million six hundred thousand dollars; and in this case, the withdrawal of deposits fully accounted for the reduction of loans, leaving that of the circulation to be otherwise explained. The scarcity of exchange at points in debt to New York will, at any time, cause our city currency to be rapidly returned from all parts of the country.

The annexed diagram shows the relative fluctuation of the currency and the loans from August, 1853, to December, 1857. The extreme range of the former was about one and a half millions of dollars, while that of the latter was over forty millions.

The opinion that bank loans are governed by the currency was justified under the old laws, which allowed an issue of bills equal to twice the amount of capital, without a pledge of securities, and without personal liability for the debts; but it is groundless under our State system. The old laws would have given an issue of one hundred and twenty millions of bills to our present city capital; whereas, we have but ten millions, and but three-fourths of that in circulation.*

* The Superintendent of the Banking Department, in his report for 1857, in view of the fact that the New York City bank currency was contracted but a million and a half during the panic, says: "This would seem clearly to demonstrate, that whatever may lead to a suspension of specie payments, the currency of our banks, properly secured, is not an element in its production."

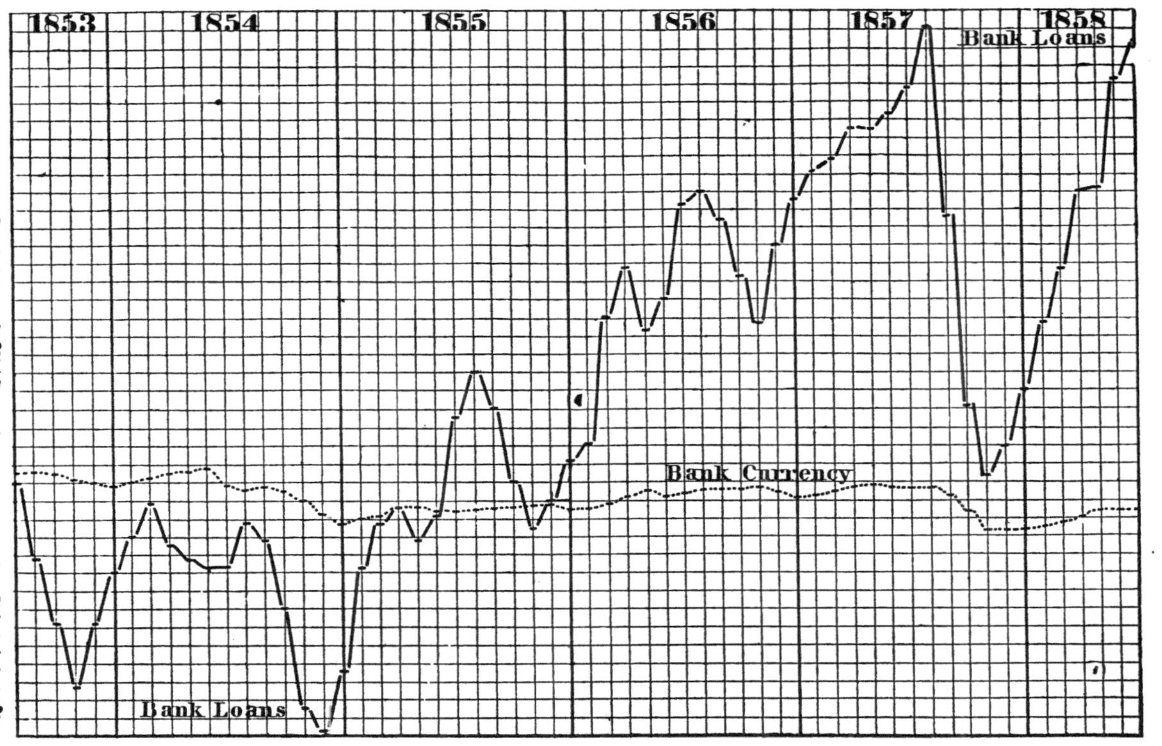

1853
1854
1855
1856
1857
1858
Bank Loans
Bank Currency
Bank Loans
120
119
118
117
116
115
114
113
112
111
110
109
108
107
106
105
104
103
102
101
100
99
98
97
96
95
94
93
92
91
90
89
88
87
86
85
84
83
82
81

A proposition, that the issue of bank bills, of a less denomination than twenty dollars, shall be prohibited by law, has met with a good deal of public commendation. It is not easy to see how this could add any security to our bank currency, nor how it would guard our financial system from the dangerous fluctuations consequent on excessive commercial credit. It might restrict loans, by making it necessary for banks to keep on hand a larger reserve of coin, and therefore lessen the profits of the business. One of two things must then follow: either banking capital will be surreptitiously employed to make up the deficiency of profit, or it will seek more productive methods of organization. Another result might be expected: credit suppressed in one form will find another, beyond the reach of legislation. The personal check, or order, would take the place of the bank bill in all remittances under twenty dollars, involving delays and expenses of collection that would fall most heavily on small dealers or laborers, who can least afford them. Men who keep no bank account, women, and minors, would be obliged to pay a broker's commission for the most trifling remittance. The amount of this small check credit would be infinitely greater than the decrease of bank currency, without its convenience or security.

In the midst of the late panic, everybody felt the necessity of doing something to prevent its recurrence; and under the weight of its consequences, various legislative restrictions have been proposed, with a view to render our banking system less unstable in future. But it may well be questioned, whether more mischief is not to be apprehended from the constant tinkering of politicians than from any other source—not excepting the errors of past legislation, which we are gradually correcting by experience, and by voluntary action, without the aid of law.

BANK-NOTE REDEMPTION.

The diversion of bank currency from its legitimate channels, and the establishment of a trade in it between the banks themselves, has had a share in the general derangement of credit, and in the misapplication of banking capital.

The only proper use of currency is, *circulation*—to pay wages, to buy commodities in store or market, and to answer the convenience of daily expenditure by the people. The privilege of issue is given by law for this purpose, and for no other. The advantage to the bank consists in the currency fulfilling this function of circulation—in its passing from hand to hand, giving life to industry, and forming the basis of the larger operations of commerce. The bank pays it out for notes discounted or for deposits, and realizes interest upon it until it is returned for redemption. The more circulation, the more profit. Itis, therefore, an object for banks to keep out their bills as long as possible. They resort to various expedients for this purpose, such as discounting notes, on condition that the bills shall be taken to a distance, and paid out for purchases of wool, for wages on a railroad, or other service. A large aggregate of currency is thus forced out upon the country, to find its way back for redemption through the usual channels of exchange. The city merchants who received this currency in remittance for debt, formerly sold it to the money-broker at a certain rate of discount, which varied more or less from one per cent. It might be resold by the broker at a smaller rate to manufacturers, who could save by this process a certain per centage on their entire disbursements, and it would then start out on a new tour of circulation through the shops. Banks could often better afford to divide with brokers the profits of a perpetual circulation than to redeem it in gold. Those banks which were least able to redeem, and whose bills were, therefore, least entitled to credit, were most persevering and ingenious in keeping the community supplied with their currency. This was a debased paper currency. Accordingly, as it supplied the market, the bills of better banks, which would not stoop to competition in such business, were kept out of circulation. The result, so far as our city banks are concerned, is, that their circulation hardly pays the cost of maintaining it.

A new source of profit was suggested to some of our city banks. If the redemption that was distributed among the money-brokers could be monopolized by one or two institutions, it would yield a rich revenue; and it could easily be attracted by reducing the rates of redemption so low as to exclude individual competition. This was the origin of the New York redemption system, copied from the Suffolk Bank of Boston. Coupled with the payment of interest on country deposits, it had grown into astonishing activity before the panic of 1857. It worked admirably as a piece of machinery, with the popular commendation that it restricted the bank currency by enforcing prompt redemption, and saved our merchants a heavy brokerage. It was a great convenience in the first days of the panic, when private capital was withdrawn from the purchase of currency, and when our merchants, but for the redeeming banks, would have been overburdened with unavailable notes.

But the Redemption System, like everything else that was susceptible of abuse, was turned aside from its legitimate purpose, and made to answer a mischievous end. The low rate at which the bills were taken in New York accelerated their return *in bulk*, as a basis of exchange, or for credit in account, and thus their distinctive character as *circulation* was in a great measure destroyed. This is plainly illustrated by the diagram on the opposite page.

The natural course of the circulation is represented by the curved lines *a*, *a*, *a*. It is paid out by the banks at Buffalo, Syracuse and Whitehall, and after performing its function in the service of trade, it reaches the common point of liquidation—New York. Here, it is assorted, charged in account to the issuing banks, and sent home by express, to be again issued, circulated, and redeemed, in the same manner. This is our bank currency in legitimate use as contemplated by law.

But the cheap redemption, so desirable in a common state of the market, became, virtually, a premium on the currency, at New York. The tendency was then to take it out of the curved lines of a health-

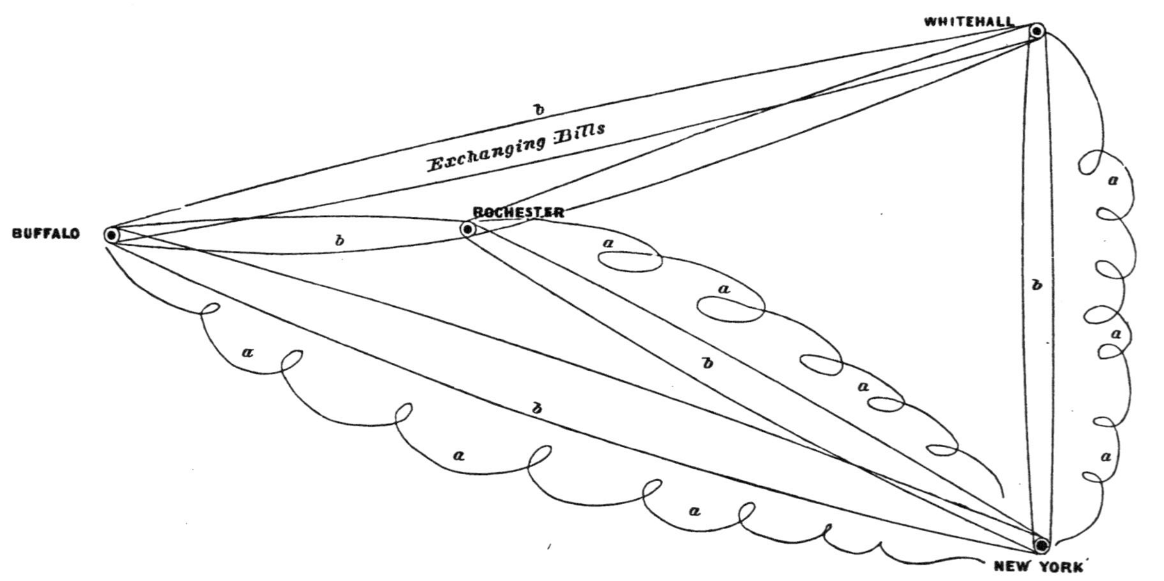
WHITEHALL
Exchanging Bills
BUFFALO
ROCHESTER
NEW YORK

ful circulation, and to throw it into the elliptical lines *b*, *b*, in which it profited nobody so much as the stockholders of the Express Companies. The country banks might keep their own bills in a perpetual circuit by exchanging them with each other, and thus creating a trade in them. The same packages were not unfrequently kept unopened in the circuit, and reissued in bulk as often as they were needed to supply balances.

When, from having been to much expanded, there arises necessity for a general contraction of credits, if then a portion of the circulation is withheld by the banks, as it should be, the redemption of the other portion would go on quietly, and no apprehension would be excited in the public mind as to the safety of bills. The proportion of capital appropriated to this special service would keep in harmony with the diminishing volume of commercial credit. But this does not commonly happen. To keep out the circulation, and to increase it, gives relief to the bank. If it cannot enforce the liquidation of its loans, it is still more urgent to keep its bills in circulation—to throw out more, and to stave off actual redemption. The redeeming banks are then likely to be required to do one of two things: either to appropriate more capital to this service, or to reject the bills. In the former case, its commercial loans must bear the brunt, and in the latter, it would spread alarm among bill holders, and aggravate the evil that it wants to ward off.

Precisely this state of things occurred in the summer of 1857. In spite of the best management by the redeeming banks, the circuit of currency credit was kept up, and relatively, if not positively, increased. Currency was made to redeem currency; that is, the bills of one bank were paid for by the bills of all others which it remitted for credit in account; and thus there was no actual redemption.

Another fact, which was claimed to be beneficial in an ordinary state of things, now proved a source of apprehension and real danger. The credit given to an unsecured currency by the indorsement of the redeeming banks had obtained for it a wide circulation, to the displacement of bills that were based on State and United States stocks. It was now seen that this credit had no other dependence than a current deposit by the issuing bank, which deposit was in very small proportion to its outstanding bills, and that the redeeming bank was prompt to the hour in repudiating those bills, if the deposit was not maintained. This was a fallacious credit, entirely independent of the separate ability of the issuing banks. The general result was, that bills were likely to fail while in transit, and they would not then be admitted as a deposit, which would involve the rejection of other bills; and so the row of bricks began to tumble in both directions.

There was no incident of the panic, that spread its terrors abroad with such sure and rapid steps, as the rejection, by the redeeming banks, of bills which they had been accustomed to receive on deposit. If it had been possible to remove all other causes of excitement, that alone would, probably, have involved the suspension of specie payments. It filled all the shops in the country with alarm. It created mobs in our savings' banks, and pushed forward the panic by exciting the fears of the multitude.

WILL SUSPENSION OCCUR AGAIN?

"Well," says a judicious bank President, "this will be a warning to our merchants! It is to be hoped that such experience will burn into them some lessons about their long and excessively-extended credits."

Yes, Mr. President; and we hope it will be a warning to you, also! It was not our long credits only, that threw us into embarrassment, but your expansion, and then your repudiation of all credits! Shall we not profit by both of these "experiences?"

Our bank officers are invested with a controlling power over the market. They can positively command the ship of commerce, and guide it through the storm, or they can dash it upon the rocks.

It is a false notion, that panic comes from mysterious and unmanageable causes. So long as we give credence to this commercial fatalism, and accept it as an excuse for the incapacity of financial managers, we shall be liable to a recurrence of panic whenever an adverse wind sweeps the ocean.

"If there had only been an able man among bank officers, in whom the others had confidence, to take the lead, the panic might have been crushed in the bud."

This was a common and freely-expressed opinion among all classes of merchants. It is a singular fact, that must occupy the foreground in any history of the suspension of 1857, whatever part different writers may assign to accessory causes. In the fright and confusion which succeeded the failure of the Ohio Life Insurance and Trust Company, our bank officers fell back, each to his separate place, to "fortify" his institution, though at the expense of every private and common interest of the market. They did not recognize, in any one of their number, that superiority of intelligence and capacity in management, which in times of anarchy and doubt never fails to be felt—never fails (where it is known to exist) to be called on *to lead.* Never, in the whole course of our commercial history, did the public distress cry louder for the ability that can unite separate interests for a common purpose; and for the want of it, no common purpose was created. Every thing went by chance, or by necessity.

As the recurrence of financial pressure is only less certain than the tides of the ocean, and as our commercial dealings are annually becoming more extended and complicated, we may look for the damage resulting from the mismanagement of banks to be more and more serious, unless measures are adopted to prevent it.

Efforts have been made, occasionally, during the last ten years, to organize something like a College of Finance, in which the general interests of the market should be kept in revision—but without success. This result, however, is now foreshadowed by the Clearing House. Its records are the theme of daily conversation in financial circles. They form the basis of our city bank administration. A nucleus is thus already created, to attract the ideas which have heretofore floated loosely in the minds of men without object.

A college composed of intelligent merchants and bankers—practical men—would combine individual experience and research. By elucidating the causes of financial fluctuation, and its bearings on the general enterprise of the country, and therefore on labor, they might aid materially to correct popular errors with respect to our banking system, whilst securing needful instruction to themselves. At present, all the statistics of finance, excepting only those of the Clearing House, are gathered up by the industry of the newspaper press. "The commercial editor" is the principal collator, analyzer, and elucidator of financial data in the city of New York; while the professional banker conceives his duty to be confined to the mere accidents of the business during five hours of each day!

With a deliberative body in existence (such as is here suggested) the suspension of specie payments could not have occurred in 1857; because the violent, separate, and destructive action of the banks, which started the panic must have been overruled by sober counsel.

There are certain anomalies in force, as applied to banks, by which they are exposed to extreme liabilities, not only in seasons of pressure, but at all times. By a strange absurdity of law, the deposits of a bank are held to be payable in specie, on demand, although the amount of specie in the whole country is not sufficient to pay the one-twentieth part of them. It is, therefore, plain, that the banks might be forced into suspension by the depositors at any moment, without regard to the state of the market.

The actual relation between the bank and the dealer gives no color of right to the latter to demand specie for his deposit. He is fully aware that the bank does not consider itself holden for the coin. He does not give coin; and why should he take it? He deposits a *form of credit*, or individual currency—*checks.* When this form of credit sinks in the general depreciation, by what rule of consistency or justice can he require the bank to fill up the deficit? The depreciation originates with the dealer, in the excess of trade, and not with the bank: it may encourage the excess by loaning too freely, but the dealer is not obliged to borrow. There is obviously no propriety in his loading the bank with the ill consequences of his own action. Yet such is the accepted rule.

This is the bull goring the ox. If the ox attempts to gore the bull, the case is changed. Debts owing by the bank are held payable in coin on the instant; but debts due to the bank, by the very same party, are held to be negotiable and renewable, consistently with commercial honor and usage. In one case, the failing debtor is declared "broken," while in the other, his credit continues unimpaired.

As a general fact, the depositors of a bank are also its borrowers; and if they demand their deposits in specie, they ought to pay their loans in specie.

But no written agreement could be made less equivocal than the understanding between the bank and the dealer, that the deposit will be held payable by check, or in bank bills; and that its demand in coin out of the usual practice, or its final withdrawal as a current account, before the payment of the loan, will be a breach of honor and good faith. No bank officer would permit an account to be opened on his books specifically subject to these contingencies.

The relation between the Savings' Banks and their depositors is an example of still greater absurdity, both in law and practice. These institutions are organized to encourage economy among the laboring classes, by paying interest on small amounts. They are conducted mostly by benevolent men, and gratuitously, excepting necessary clerk hire. The law does not leave the investment of the funds discretionary with the managers, but defines the securities that may be taken — one of the chief of which is the mortgage on real estate. The depositor is a party to this mortgage, and is cognizant of the fact, that it is not immediately convertible into money. The process of foreclosure involves a delay of three months, which cannot be shortened by law; and yet, when a panic occurs, the law sustains the depositor in his right to demand immediate payment; and because the bank does not pay immediately, it is declared "broken." This is equivalent to a legal requisition, that the bank shall keep the money of its depositors on hand in gold, and at the same time have it out on mortgage earning interest! Because this cannot be done, the whole country is to be loaded with the discredit of bankruptcy, of which the suspension of the Savings Banks is regarded as the least doubtful evidence.

Neither is this all. If the Savings' Banks had been forced to pay off their depositors in October, 1857, immeasurable wrong must have been done to the mortgagors, by selling their property at less than half its value; and the laborer also must have been involved in the common misfortune, by legal expenses and delay of payments.

Finally, this demand of the bank depositors can reach but one result. If the deposits in the Commercial and Savings' Banks of New York amount to one hundred millions of dollars, and the amount of specie on hand to twenty millions, those who apply for it first will get their money, and the eighty millions will go unpaid, or be liquidated by some form of credit.

The practice of holding *tokens of pure credit* as legally liable to immediate redemption in coin is here carried to the extremest practical absurdity; and it is so deeply imbedded in popular opinion, as to constitute a dangerous, if not an insuperable anomaly in our financial system.

The true office of gold, in commerce, is an unsettled question. It may be a question, also, whether, if once determined, it can remain so among all the changes of commerce, production, and ideas which are going on. It is hardly supposable that any commercial relations can be the same before and after such improvements as those which govern the present age. The establishment of ocean steam navigation, the construction of railroads, and of the magnetic telegraph, have practically ignored two of the principal elements in exchange—distance and time. The markets of the world have already been stimulated in an excessive degree by the opening of gold mines in California and Australia. Notwithstanding the extent to which discovery and explorations have been pushed, the scope for human energy is still enlarging. Is it likely that questions of economy alone shall not change their terms in this general growth and expansion of affairs?

The popular notions, concerning gold, are for the greater part hereditary. They are less the result of practical experience, and of reasoning on facts, than of pure theory.

The destructibility of paper money, the facility of its emission without limit, and its consequent fluctuation in market value, with the various frauds that it may serve, and especially its imposition as wages on the poor and ignorant, brought it deservedly into bad repute. The idea, that there was any *reality* about it, became almost obsolete. It was natural thence to assume, that silver or gold was the only real money in existence. It was, therefore, predicated as "the standard of value."

In the United States, politicians have made the most of this theory. The laboring masses vote; and they have flocked to the polls in support of "hard money." This is about the whole history of the case in its political bearings, which are its most influential bearings.

But paper money has been forced into narrower limits. It has been so guarded by legislative restrictions and penalties, as to have lost, in no small measure, those features in which it differed so widely from gold. It cannot be issued with the same facility as formerly, and the fluctuation of its market value is much less. In the State of New York, it has become established on such a secure basis, as to be transposable with gold in all conditions of the market, at such an insensible fluctuation, as to remove the ground of all the old objections to it. The politicians do not publicly or theoretically abandon the controversy, because it is still available in the elections. But that they no longer entertain it as a question of economy, is manifest from their participation, as legislators, in the business of making and circulating it.

It has been shown by the demonstrations of the Clearing House that the bank note currency of the city of New York is the most stable of all known forms of credit. Of an average circulation of eight millions of dollars among the people, but one million was returned for redemption in 1857, during the unexampled depreciation of every other token of credit, not excepting even the State bond, and the mortgage on real estate. And this return was made, not by individuals through alarm, but mostly by country banks to meet their bills of exchange.

It appears, therefore, as an established fact, that gold is not an indispensable pledge for the soundness of paper money, with such guarantees, and with such limitations as are established by the laws of New York.

It is not used, either, in the ordinary transactions of commerce. Debts are paid by bank notes, or by checks. But little gold passes in the channels of trade for the daily payment of fifty millions of dollars, in the city of New York. More than half of this amount is settled through the Clearing House; and here, for the first time, we meet the use of gold in any considerable sum. One million and a half of specie settles the exchanges of thirty millions of commercial currency. It is, then, in final liquidation of *balances* only, that gold is used. We find it performing the same function between Europe and America. Four hundred millions of credit pass either way— and fifty millions settle the balance.

The only other channel in which gold accumulates, or is used in large sums, is in the Postage and Revenue Departments of the Government. Here we are at the end of our facts.

Gold appears nowhere in large sums, excepting in the transactions of the Government, in any other office than as liquidator of balances. And the amount necessary to a running credit of one hundred millions of dollars in our city banks, has not heretofore exceeded an average of fifteen millions. With this sum in steady reserve, every operation of our extended commerce and labor has been satisfactorily conducted for a number of years past. It fails only when individual credit fails, from excess of trade, from speculation, and accumulated losses.

There is one fact that ought not to be overlooked: while the business of the country has steadily increased, the bank note circulation has diminished, and the difference has not been made up in coin. Other forms of credit have mostly supplied it—

especially the individual bank check. But the more active service of the circulation consequent on the telegraph, and on swifter transit by railroad, has also done much to supersede the necessity of such large bank issues as were formerly required. Why has not gold come in to fill the void? Is it not because that, too, has been quickened in its office? Has not this new element, of *activity*, practically answered for quantity? What, under the old modes of transport lay inert, because inaccessible, is now always in motion, performing its function of liquidation.

Another result has been established by the rapidity of transit. It is, comparatively, non-essential whether the gold of the market is held in one sum at New York, or whether it is distributed at various points in the country, provided it be kept within the power of the exchange. The transport of it by railway is a mere accident on the surface of things. The amount of coin in the Clearing House, at a given time, is therefore not an unerring index of the strength of the market. That it should be distributed where it is most needed to give efficiency to labor, or to develop resources, is of more consequence to the common interest.

Rapidity of communication and transit is a new feature in commerce, which economists have not yet had the opportunity to study in all its bearings. The tendency of it is, to simplify our system of trade, to cure it of local eccentricities, and to bring all its parts under the influence of one regulating principle—the *Exchange*, of which it is a vital element. In proportion as the telegraph is extended, it seems inevitable that the Exchange shall become a more perfect index of the state of commerce between different countries.

The accumulation of gold, since the panic, in the several financial centres of London, Paris, Vienna, and New York, has suggested the theory, that it is not necessary in the provincial towns in quantity beyond the current wants of the retail trade; that it is only at the liquidating points where it is ever required in large sums. The idea here is, doubtless, the true one—that gold is not the basis of credit, but the balance medium. The mass of credit settles itself by exchange; while the gold only pays up the difference between the debit and the credit column. It is precisely this office that it fills in the Clearing House.

The influx of gold into New York, after the suspension of specie payments, soon enabled the banks to resume; and it was then said, that they would not have suspended, if this gold, instead of being scattered abroad through the country, where it was not wanted, had been in the Clearing House. Therefore, to prevent panic in future, let us keep the gold in New York.

It has thus been accidentally discovered, that the true policy of finance is, to denude the country of coin, and to keep it only at points where it will be wanted if the foreign exchanges should run adversely. We ought not to be ungrateful for the knowledge of truth because it comes by blundering, however we may regret that it has not been evolved by an attentive study of facts. The error of this theory consists in assuming the results of disease in a prostrate body as indications of health in a sound body. Why not rather revert to the phenomena that existed when the body was in vigorous health, and adopt these as indications of a wholesome state of the system?

The unprecedented accumulation of gold in the banks of New York is the result of cancelling a foreign debt by insolvency, and of a general suspension of labor throughout the country. Capital has returned to its owners, and lies dead. They refuse to invest it as heretofore, in public improvements and in trade. Let labor and enterprise be resumed—let the produce of the West come into market—let our commerce with foreign nations be restored, and the coin will find its right place. The same laws of trade which have brought it here, will take it away. The amount held in reserve by the banks of New York will be adjusted by the exchanges;—it will be found expensive to maintain a reserve in opposition to them, at any point above the natural level. All uneasiness about deficiency at particular points may cease, if the exchanges are wholesome; because, as already observed, our means of communication and transit will restore every thing in a few hours.

There is a certain common property in gold, or in the liquidating medium, from which it is impossible to escape. It is not the product of individual sagacity, but of the market at large—of industry and labor generally. The moment that it is taken out of this relation, it becomes a dead and worthless weight. It must be treated as the property of the market, giving value to everything in it; and losing its value the instant that it is hoarded.

Are not these precise facts? And shall we not give weight to them, and to all other facts with respect to gold that may be developed in the progress of discovery and combination? Shall we continue to look to old theories of economy as the source of all wisdom in finance—theories which were based on a narrow range of facts, as compared with the present period; or shall we analyze, combine, and elucidate our own facts, and presuming a little on our own capacity and experience, add our knowledge to that of the past, and make the most of it!

THE

NEW AMERICAN CYCLOPÆDIA.

EDITED BY

GEORGE RIPLEY AND CHARLES A. DANA.

PUBLISHED BY

D. APPLETON & COMPANY, New York

In 16 Vols. 8vo, Double Columns, 750 Pages each.

Price, Cloth, $4.; *Sheep*, 4.75; *Half Mor.*, $5.00; *Half Russ.*, $5.5C *per Volume.*

Every one that reads, every one that mingles in society, is constantly meeting with allusions to subjects on which he needs and desires further information. In conversation, in trade, in professional life, on the farm, in the family, practical questions are continually arising, which no man, well read or not, can always satisfactorily answer. If facilities for reference are at hand, they are consulted, and not only is the curiosity gratified, and the stock of knowledge increased, but perhaps information is gained and ideas are suggested that will directly contribute to the business success of the party concerned.

With a Cyclopædia, embracing every conceivable subject, and having its topics alphabetically arranged, not a moment is lost. The matter in question is found at once, digested, condensed, stripped of all that is irrelevant and unnecessary, and verified by a comparison of the best authorities. Moreover, while only men of fortune can collect a library complete in all the departments of knowledge, a Cyclopædia, worth in itself, for purposes of reference, at least a thousand volumes, is within the reach of all—the clerk, the merchant, the professional man, the farmer, the mechanic. In a country like ours, where the humblest may be called to responsible positions requiring intelligence and general information, the value of such a work can not be over-estimated.

PLAN OF THE CYCLOPÆDIA.

The New American Cyclopædia presents a panoramic view of all human knowledge, as it exists at the present moment. It embraces and popularizes every subject that can be thought of. In its successive volumes is contained an inexhaustible fund of accurate and practical information on Art and Science in all their branches, including Mechanics, Mathematics, Astronomy, Philosophy, Chemistry, and Physiology; on Agriculture, Commerce, and Manufactures; on Law, Medicine, and Theology; on Biography and History, Geography and Ethnology; on Political Economy, the Trades, Inventions, Politics, the Things of Common Life, and General Literature.

The Industrial Arts and those branches of Practical Science which have a direct bearing on our every-day life, such as Domestic Economy, Ventilation, the Heating of Houses, Diet, &c., are treated with the thoroughness which their great importance demands.

The department of Biography is full and complete, embracing the lives of all eminent persons, ancient and modern. In American biography, particularly, great pains have been taken to present the most comprehensive and accurate record that has yet been attempted.

In History, the New American Cyclopædia gives no mere catalogue of barren dates, but a copious and spirited narrative, under their appropriate heads, of the principal events in the annals of the world. So in Geography, it not only serves as a general Gazetteer, but it gives interesting descriptions of the principal localities mentioned, derived from books of travel and other fresh and authentic sources.

As far as is consistent with thoroughness of research and exactness of statement, the popular method has been pursued. The wants of the people in a work of this kind have been carefully kept in view throughout.

It is hardly necessary to add that, throughout the whole, perfect fairness to all sections of country, local institutions, public men, political creeds, and religious denominations, has been a sacred principle and leading aim. Nothing that can be construed into an invidious or offensive allusion has been admitted.

DISTINGUISHING EXCELLENCES.

While we prefer that the work should speak for itself, and that others should herald its excellences, we cannot refrain from calling attention to the following points, in which we take an honest pride in believing that the New American Cyclopædia surpasses all others:—

I. In Accuracy and Freshness of Information.—The value of a work of this kind is exactly proportioned to its correctness. It must preclude the necessity of having other books. Its decision must be final. It must be an ultimatum of reference, or it is good for nothing.

II. In Impartiality.—Our work has undergone the examination of Argus eyes. It has stood the ordeal. It is pronounced by distinguished men and leading reviews in all parts of the Union, strictly fair and national. Eschewing all expressions of opinion on controverted points of science, philosophy, religion, and politics, it aims at an accurate representation of facts and institutions, of the results of physical research, of the prominent events in the history of the world, of the most significant productions of literature and art, and of the celebrated individuals whose names have become associated with the conspicuous phenomena of their age—doing justice to all men, all creeds, all sections.

III. In Completeness.—It treats of every subject, in a terse and condensed stylo, but fully and exhaustively. It is believed that but few omissions will be found; but whatever topics may, through any oversight, be wanting, are supplied in an Appendix.

IV. In American Character.—The New Cyclopædia is intended to meet the intellectual wants of the American people. It is not, therefore, modelled after European works of a similar design; but, while it embraces all their excellences, has added to them a peculiar and unmistakable American character. It is the production mainly of American mind.

V. In Practical Bearing.—The day of philosophical abstraction and speculation has passed away. This is an age of action. *Cui bono* is the universal touchstone. Feeling this, we have made our Cyclopædia thoroughly practical. No man of action, be his sphere humble or exalted, can afford to do without it.

VI. In Interest of Style.—The cold, formal, and repulsive style usual in works of this kind, has been replaced with a style sparkling and emphatically readable. It has been the aim to interest and please, as well as instruct. Many of our writers are men who hold the foremost rank in general literature, and their articles have been characterized by our best critics as models of elegance, force, and beauty.

VII. In Convenience of Form.—No ponderous quartos, crowded with fine type that strains the eyes and wearies the brain, are here presented. The volumes are just the right size to handle conveniently; the paper is thick and white, the type large, the binding elegant and durable.

VIII. In Cheapness.—Our Cyclopædia has been universally pronounced a miracle of cheapness. We determined, at the outset, to enlarge its sphere of usefulness, and make it emphatically a book for the people, by putting it at the lowest possible price.

Such being the character of the New American Cyclopædia, an accurate, fresh, impartial, complete, practical, interesting, convenient, cheap Dictionary of General Knowledge, we ask, who can afford to do without it? Can the merchant, the statesman, the lawyer, the physician, the clergyman, to whom it gives thorough and complete information on every point connected with their several callings? Can the teacher, who is enabled, by the outside information it affords, to make his instructions doubly interesting and profitable? Can the farmer, to whom it offers the latest results of agricultural research and experiment? Can the young man, to whom it affords the means of storing his mind with useful knowledge bearing no any vocation he may have selected? Can the intelligent mechanic, who wishes to understand what he reads in his daily paper? Can the mother of a family, whom it initiates into the mysteries of domestic economy, and teaches a thousand things which more than saves its cost in a single year? In a word, can any intelligent American, who desires to understand the institutions of his country, its past history and present condition, and his own duties as a citizen, deny himself this great American digest of all human knowledge, universally pronounced the best Cyclopædia and the most valuable work ever published?

www.ingramcontent.com/pod-product-compliance
Lightning Source LLC
LaVergne TN
LVHW020934110826
845150LV00004B/863